OHIO

Dissolution of Marriage

(No-Fault Divorce)

A Step-by-Step Guide
to Do-it-yourself

LawPak's Commitment and Goal

The goal of LawPak is to simplify legal information for consumers. Our LawPak's are designed to contain accurate, easy-to-read information and forms. However, no publication can take the place of a competent professional.

LawPak is committed to designing the highest quality forms and guides. We believe that non-lawyers should have access to legal information that has been researched and professionally prepared. Our publications can save the non-lawyer unnecessary legal expenses by providing information to better understand their legal problem.

However, we cannot guarantee that the way you complete the forms or that the information given will be totally accurate for and pertinent to your particular circumstances. Please be aware that laws, regulations and procedures are constantly changing and may be subject to differing interpretations.

We will guarantee that we have used extensive efforts to provide you with clear instructions and forms so that you may have the opportunity to learn about legal procedures and handle your own legal matters if you choose to do so. In order to constantly improve our legal forms and LawPaks, we welcome your suggestions and comments.

The LawPak Publishing Professionals

⇒ **Words for Thought**

"Censorship comes from the rulers' fears and the zealots' belief in the single truth: the only religion, the only system, the only morality."

A.M. Rosenthal

"Education is a private matter between the person and the world of knowledge and experience. It has little to do with school or college."

Lillian Smith

"The greater danger for most of us is not that our aim is too high and we miss it, but that it is too low and we reach it."

Michelangelo

This LawPak publication or software may not be copied, transmitted, transcribed, stored in a retrieval system, or translated into any human or computer language, in any for, or by any means, electronic, mechancial, magnetic, chemical, manual, or otherwise, without written permission of the publisher, except that the forms may be photocopied or reproduced by the purchaser for their own use, but not for resale. This publication or software is intended to be utilized by the purchaser for their own benefit and the use of this publication or software to benefit a second party may be considered the unauthorized practice of law.

LIMITED WARRANTY AND DISCLAIMER

LAWPAK, INC. MAKES NO REPRESENTATION OR WARRANTIES WITH RESPECT TO THE CONTENTS HEREOF AND SPECIFICALLY DISCLAIMS ANY IMPLIED WARRANTIES OR MERCHANTABILITY OR FITNESS FOR ANY PARTICULAR PURPOSE. IT IS UNDERSTOOD THAT BY USING THIS PUBLICATION OR SOFTWARE THE PURCHASER IS ACTING AS THEIR OWN ATTORNEY.

Although care has been taken to ensure the accuracy and utility of the information and forms contained in this publication or software, it is understood by all parties that LawPak, the authors, retailers nor distributors assume any liability or responsibility to anyone for loss or damage caused or alleged to be cause by the use of the information or forms contained in the publication or software. The liability of LawPak, the retailers, authors or distributors shall not exceed the purchase price of this publication or software. The use of this publication or software constitutes acceptance of the above terms. LawPak, Inc. reserves the right to revise this publication or software and to make changes from time to time in their content without the obligation to notify any person or organization of such revisions or changes.

This publication or software is designed to provide accurate and authoritative information in regard to the subject matter covered. It is sold with the understanding that the publisher is not engaged in rendering legal, accounting, or any other professional service. If legal advice or other expert assistance is required, the services of a competent professional person should be sought.

... From the Declaration of Principles jointly adopted by a Committee of the American Bar Association and a Committee of Publishers and Associations.

Over 15 Years Of Providing Quality Legal Information

Table Of Contents

Part One
All About Dissolution

Part Two
How To Do Your Own Dissolution

Part One

All About Dissolution

LawPak Software In Development

We are currently developing software which can be used to download the Ohio Dissolution of Marriage court forms and a reference manual from our web site at **www.elawpak.com**.

The forms can be downloaded onto your disk and then into your word processing system. Use the word processing system on the computer to complete the required information on the forms and print them on the computer's printer.

When using this method you **will not** have to remove the blank forms from this publication and then type the required information on the form in a typewriter.

There is a charge to download the forms from our Internet site which will require that you input valid credit card information before the download can take place.

Please check our web site to determine if we have completed the development of this option.

CHAPTER
A
Introduction

A1 About This LawPak

The intent of this LawPak guide is to assist you and your spouse in obtaining an Ohio Dissolution of Marriage. However, you may use a LawPak as one of many source materials to help you gain a better understanding of your legal needs and still decide to consult with an attorney. LawPak's are written in easy to understand language and address the most common questions and procedures about obtaining an Ohio Dissolution of Marriage.

Although, LawPak, Inc., is a publishing company and as such does not attempt to form opinions, offer solutions or give legal advice concerning any aspect of your particular situation. The opinions expressed in this book are those of the authors and should not be interpreted as representing those of the entire legal community.

Throughout this LawPak you are advised of situations when you *should* speak with a lawyer. Consult a lawyer if you have **any** doubts or questions about any matters including anything discussed in LawPak. It should be noted that certain situations require professional legal assistance.

If you and your spouse have decided that you can and should do your own Dissolution, you should first read this *entire* book before doing anything. It is written in plain language, but read it *carefully*. Do not do anything unless you fully understand what you want to accomplish.

A2 Basic Information

There are three ways that a marriage may be legally terminated in Ohio. They are divorce, dissolution, and annulment. Under previous Ohio law, only a divorce was granted to one of the parties of the marriage after a judge determined that grounds were sufficient for divorce. A witness was required to testify under oath that the alleged wrongdoing had been committed by one of the parties. Divorce is based on the concept of fault and is an adversary proceeding.

In 1974 the Ohio legislature decided that there should also be a way to end a marriage without fault. It passed the law which created the dissolution, a simple no-fault method of legally terminating a marriage. No witnesses are required and no fault needs to be established. A dissolution is granted to both parties.

However, apart from legal usage, the word "divorce" is still the word most commonly used in describing the termination of a marriage. This guide is concerned with the legal process and we will use the word "dissolution" to define a no-fault divorce.

A3 Finding The Right Attorney

LawPaks are not written to replace lawyers. They are intended to give you a basic understanding of your legal situation and offer an affordable option to those individuals who decide that they can do certain legal procedures themselves. You must decide if or when the services of a lawyer may be necessary for your circumstances

There are not any laws which require you to hire a lawyer to represent you or sign your legal documents. When you represent yourself, you are said to be acting propia persona or the shorter version is *pro per* which is Latin for *yourself*.

If you have a problem with some part of your Dissolution of Marriage or need additional information, you may decide that a conference with a lawyer would be beneficial. Instead of having the attorney do the complete Dissolution, you might seek assistance with only part of it. Most attorneys may not be willing to assist you. You may have to call several attorneys until you find one who is responsive to the idea.

The best way to find an attorney is through a trusted person who has had a satisfactory experience with one. When you call, don't be intimidated. Ask what their fees would be for a Dissolution of Marriage and how much an initial interview will cost. Attorney fees will vary considerably. Most attorneys will do the first interview for $20 to $30. Hourly rates run from $85 to $300 per hour, with a fee of $400 to $1,000 being fairly common for a Dissolution of Marriage.

Before you go to see an attorney, be sure you know exactly what you expect from their services. Have all relevant documents and information with you. As we just mentioned, most attorneys work and charge for their services based upon an hourly rate.

Many federally funded legal aid offices which were created to assist people with low incomes without charge, *will not* normally help you with a Dissolution case because a Dissolution case is "fee generating". This means that lawyers (the legal community) object to Legal Aid handling a case for free which could generate a fee to another lawyer working outside of Legal Aid.

A4 Commonly Asked Questions

How does Dissolution of Marriage differ from Divorce?

A Dissolution is totally no-fault; takes less time; divides all property and settles all issues of spousal support, assignment of a custodial parent ('residential parent'), child support and visitation by voluntary agreement of the spouses; and requires only one Court hearing.

How much will it cost to do my own Dissolution?

A court filing fee plus the cost of this LawPak if you do it yourself. Since court filings are subject to change and may vary from one county to the next, it is advised that you get this information by telephoning the Office of the Clerk of the county where you intend to file your Dissolution.
NOTE: most counties will not take a personal check unless it is certified. (A listing of Ohio counties with the Clerk's telephone numbers are contained in APPENDIX B).

How long will it normally take to obtain my Dissolution?

Approximately 35 to 45 days. **By Ohio law:** a dissolution cannot be set for hearing any sooner than 30 days after filing your Petition with the Court and cannot be set for hearing any later than 90 days after filing your Petition.

Can I get my Dissolution without a Court hearing?

NO—A hearing is necessary in every case and both spouses **must** attend.

Will I need a witness at the hearing?

No.

How soon after the Dissolution can I remarry?

You can remarry after the Decree of Dissolution is entered and recorded with the Clerk of Court. This is usually on or near the day of your hearing.

Can the wife have her name changed?

Yes—if desired, the Separation Agreement can provide for a name change.

What is a Separation Agreement?

It is a legal contract that sets forth all property matters and rights, who pays what debts, who is considered the custodial or residential parent, how much and in what manner child support and/or spousal support is to be paid, what visitation arrangements have been made or set and many other issues that are important to you, your spouse and to the Court.

What if my spouse and I enter into a Separation Agreement, file our petition and other documents with the Court and before we even get to our hearing, he/she does not live up to our agreement or fails to show the day of the hearing?

If, before or during the hearing either spouse states that the Separation Agreement is no longer acceptable; or if either spouse states he or she does not want a Dissolution of Marriage; the Court will not approve the Separation Agreement and will not grant the Dissolution. The Petition will be dismissed and you may lose all of your court costs or at least a portion of them. You will probably have to consult an attorney and file a Divorce action rather than trying a Dissolution.

Will an attorney have to sign my forms to make them legal?

No—The law says that it is your right to represent yourself.

When do I go to Court?

Ohio law requires that no **sooner than 30** days or **no later than 90** days from the filing date (that is when you pay your court costs to the Clerk) that you and your spouse make a personal appearance before the Court and acknowledge that you have voluntarily entered into a Separation Agreement and you are satisfied with its terms and that you seek a Dissolution of Marriage.

Does a dissolution have tax consequences?

Yes—Almost every aspect of a Dissolution could possibly have important tax consequences. The tax rules are numerous and change frequently, but there is a booklet that tells you most of the things you will want to know. Call your local Internal Revenue Service office and ask for IRS publication 504, "Tax Information for Divorced or Separated Individuals." It should be free.

May there be *other forms* that I may need to do my Dissolution, other than those contained in this LawPak?

Yes—Most counties have special questionnaires and other forms pertaining to income and expenses (for child support), information for the collection of census data, and social service forms. We have made our **best** efforts to make this packet as complete as possible, but **could not** include each of these different forms for all eighty-eight counties in Ohio. Be sure that you contact the Office of the Clerk of the county where you intend to file your Dissolution. The Clerk's office should provide you with blank copies of any local form required by the County. These local forms are created by public servants paid with tax revenues. You have a right to receive *blank copies* of these forms without having to go to a lawyer to obtain them.

Can my spouse and I really do our own Dissolution of Marriage?

Yes—Thousands of couples in Ohio have done their own Dissolution without an attorney.

No—If you and your spouse *cannot agree one hundred percent* on all legal issues or if one of you hires an attorney and files legal papers to oppose the dissolution. You should still read this book because it will give you practical information concerning the process.

A5 Advantages of Doing Your Own Dissolution

■ It's Much Cheaper To Do It Yourself

Probably the most obvious advantage to doing your own Dissolution is the savings in lawyer fees. Various surveys have reported fees ranging from $300 to $1500 for a lawyer doing a simple uncontested dissolution with most fees ranging between $400 and $700. Many attorneys feel few cases are uncontested. In almost every case where one spouse gets an attorney, the other spouse will get one also. This will then at least **double** the cost.

The major point is that you will save at least $300 more like $500, by doing your dissolution yourself.

■ The Satisfaction of Knowing You Did It Yourselves

We all receive a personal satisfaction in knowing that we can accomplish important tasks ourselves. Doing your own dissolution may be a temporary inconvenience, but you should understand each step, make your own decisions, and control your own life.

■ Keep It Simple

Most people can begin with a simple dissolution case with the parties in agreement on most legal issues. But, that doesn't mean the simple case will stay that way. What can complicate the process is the legal system of divorce. Our system of justice is known as "the adversary system" which usually pits one spouse against the other.

A lawyer is trained to be a combatant. Their training emphasizes aggressive and defensive strategies to gain the best possible financial advantage for their client. The systems and lawyers have a way of making almost anything more complicated. You don't need a lawyer to tell you that litigation is time consuming, expensive, and stressful. The fees for a contested divorce case can cost thousands of dollars. However, it should also be noted that a minority of couples go to divorce court to wage war. If opposing parties are after *emotional revenge* and cannot agree on a *fair* and legal settlement, then attorneys must act as arbitrators to negotiate a settlement and a judge will resolve the dispute.

The point is that if you and your spouse are willing to agree on all issues and capable of doing your own dissolution, you are increasing the probability of keeping a simple dissolution, simple.

A6 Basic Decisions Which You Must Make

You pay lawyers to give you information and assist you with making decisions about your affairs. They know standards and rules of court procedure.

If, after reading this LawPak, you can make your own decisions based on your own knowledge, then you probably don't need a lawyer. If after you have gathered enough information, you still have *questions or doubts,* then you should seek professional advice. It may be that you and your spouse are having a problem with only a certain area of your dissolution. You may seek legal advice to resolve the issue and return to completing your dissolution yourself.

BASIC DECISIONS

■ the marriage should be ended,
■ how to divide any property and debts that you have accumulated,
■ if there should be spousal support.

If you have minor children, you must also decide:

■ who will be the custodial parent;
■ how much is to be paid for child support;
■ how and when visitation is to occur;
■ who will obtain and be responsible for health insurance coverage for the minor child(ren).

The law is concerned with SETTLING THE PRACTICAL AFFAIRS OF THE COUPLE AND PROTECTING THE WELL-BEING OF THE CHILDREN. You must decide and agree to these things listed above in order to do a Dissolution. You must be able to talk to each other and come to a formal agreement which is made in writing.

A7 Why Agree

In a Dissolution, the parties settle the issues before going to the court hearing. There are obvious advantages to agreeing.

1. It is much easier, which makes the process faster and somewhat cheaper.

2. You can be more certain how the judge will rule during the court hearing. The judge is more likely to follow your agreed upon terms, unless the terms are unfair to one of the parties.

3. Your future relationship with your ex-spouse could be more positive. Sometimes people just want to fight. They are hurt and angry and want to hurt back. They want to use the law as revenge against their ex-spouse. This usually turns a dissolution into a contested divorce which can be a very unpleasant and expensive experience. No one really wins a court battle. Remember that a dissolution/divorce cannot be viewed as a final solution to the relationship, particularly if there are children.

A8 Seeking Additional Assistance

Try to discuss your relationship with your spouse in a rational, practical, and constructive manner. Usually, fighting will not prevent the dissolution or divorce, it will only make the process more unpleasant.

If you find that you and your spouse cannot communicate, you may consider involving a third professional person in your discussions. It is important that this person be a professionally trained counselor who will be objective and not take sides. Advice from well meaning friends and relatives may further aggravate the situation.

Counselors would prefer to help you with your marital problems, but they also may assist both spouses in dissolving the marriage more peacefully. Counselors guide people in giving them direction in their search for solutions. It is the people themselves who solve their problems in the final analysis.

If you feel that professional counseling would be beneficial before, during or after a dissolution, be very careful in choosing a counselor. Some counselors may not be properly trained to deal with family issues. Contact your family doctor, minister, priest, rabbi or governmental service agencies for assistance in obtaining a counselor.

> DO NOT proceed with your own Dissolution if you and your spouse are not in *complete* agreement (one hundred percent) on all issues. If there is any opposition from either party, the judge (impartial authority) will not decide the case in a Dissolution proceeding.

A9 Required Conditions for An Ohio Dissolution

In order for you to do your Own Ohio Dissolution of Marriage, you must meet **ALL** the following requirements.

1. You or your spouse must have lived in Ohio for at least *six months* before the day you file your PETITION FOR DISSOLUTION with the Court. Temporary business trips or vacations do not count against residency time.

2. Both you and your spouse must want a Dissolution of Marriage and voluntarily agree on **ALL** issues of property division, repayment of debts, spousal support, assignment of a custodial parent, child support, and visitation, where applicable.

3. Both you and your spouse must attend *one court hearing* together, no sooner than thirty (30) nor later than ninety (90) days from the date you file your Petition.

4. The wife is not pregnant.

If you do not meet all of the above conditions, you will not be able to obtain a Dissolution of your Marriage in Ohio.

A10 Required Waiting Period

Ohio law imposes a *required waiting period* in case you decide to change your mind and reconcile. As we have previously stated, Ohio law states that a dissolution cannot be set for hearing any **sooner** than 30 days after filing your Petition with the Court—and it cannot be set for hearing any **later** than 90 days after filing your Petition.

A11 Common Law Marriages

As of October 1991, common law marriages cannot be legally established in Ohio. A marriage can only occur if the marriage is accomplished by a person authorized to perform a marriage. The following persons are authorized to perform a legally binding marriage:

- Mayor of a municipality.
- Any municipal, county, or probate judge.
- A licensed minister of any religious society who has obtained a license issued by the Ohio secretary of state.
- Any religious society pursuant to the regulations of its church (This applies to certain religious societies which do not have regular clergy.).

Only those listed above may create a legally binding marriage and only after the couple has been issued a marriage license through the county probate court.

However, any common law marriage entered into prior to October 1991 remains legally valid. A common law marriage is defined as a marriage entered into without obtaining a marriage license or performing a formal marriage ceremony. Under Ohio law, no time limit needs to be established (the amount of time a couple may have lived together) to create a common law marriage. A common law marriage is established when the following criteria occurs:

- The couple are of legal age, physically and mentally competent, not related, and do not have another living spouse.

- The couple have presented themselves to the community as living together as husband and wife. This may be accomplished by creating a joint checking or savings account as husband and wife, creating a mailing address as husband and wife, wearing wedding rings, or the wife adopting the husband's name. If the couple only live together with no intention of creating a marriage, then no marriage exists.

- The couple mutually agreed to be married, but any words which state some future agreement to be married are not valid in determining a common law marriage.

- The couple are treated by the community as husband and wife.

If a common law marriage is legally established, the couple must go through the divorce or dissolution court process to terminate the marriage. The couple cannot end the marriage by a simple agreement because a common law divorce is not legally recognized.

A12 Other Agreements

a Cohabitation Agreement

Ohio courts do not recognize or award palimony. This means that if a couple lives together, this living arrangement alone does not create a right to any form of spousal support to either party upon dissolving the relationship.

Individuals who live together may consider creating a cohabitation agreement to protect each parties property if the relationship is dissolved. The agreement may state each parties expectations and rights if the relationship should end by death or separation, what each party expects from the relationship, what property belongs to each, what property will be inherited upon the death of either party, and how property acquired jointly will be distributed if the living together relationship should end.

b Antenuptial Agreement

An antenuptial agreement or pre-nuptial agreement is an agreement (written contract) created by a couple prior to marriage. The agreement should state in advance of marriage what property rights each party will assume. The agreement should describe the distribution of property (property obtained before and during the marriage) and the payment of alimony if any, upon the death of either party, or if the marriage should end in divorce, dissolution, or separation.

The antenuptial agreement must conform to the following to be legally binding:

- Must be in writing.
- Both parties must be competent and have capacity to create a contract.
- Neither party can be under any restraint or undue influence.
- Must be executed prior to marriage.
- Must be reasonable and fair.
- Must be voluntarily made.
- Both parties must know the value and extent of each other's property prior to the execution of the contract.

CHAPTER B
Dividing The Property and Debts

One of the more difficult and important aspects of doing your own dissolution is agreeing on what you both feel is a fair division of the property. TO SUCCESSFULLY COMPLETE A DISSOLUTION OF MARRIAGE, YOU BOTH MUST AGREE ON A DIVISION OF ALL PROPERTY (FOR EXAMPLE, CARS, BANK ACCOUNTS, STOCKS, ETC.) AND OBLIGATIONS, AND PERHAPS SPOUSAL SUPPORT: AND IF YOU HAVE CHILDREN, VISITATION, ASSIGNMENT OF A CUSTODIAL PARENT, AND CHILD SUPPORT. THE JUDGE WILL NOT DECIDE THESE ISSUES FOR YOU IN A DISSOLUTION.

If you *cannot* agree on a division of property, then you *cannot* do a dissolution of marriage with this LawPak or with the help of an attorney. Part of the services you receive from an attorney is their assistance in reviewing your estate with you to understand what you own, what you owe, and how it can be divided. If you and your spouse can understand your own estate, then you can decide how to divide it yourselves.

B1 Understanding What You Own

Only your marital property needs to be divided in the dissolution, since separate property already belongs to each spouse. Generally property acquired by either spouse during the marriage is marital property and belongs to both spouses (even though one spouse's name appears on the title).

Separate Property belongs to only one spouse and is not considered marital property.

Separate property includes:

- Property which a spouse received prior to your marriage while single or married to another usually belongs to that spouse.

- Property which one spouse received by **gift** or **inheritance** during or before the marriage, may belong only to that spouse.

The following is a list of types of property which must be divided and provided for in your written agreement:

Motor Vehicles, Motorcycles, Boats
Real Estate (Your Home)
Checking and Savings Accounts
Mobile Homes, Recreational Vehicles
Stocks, Bonds, Mutual Funds, and Other Securities
Credit Union Shares
Life Insurance that has a Cash Surrender Value
Trust Funds

Retirement/Pension Benefits With Your Employer
Royalty Interests
Profit-Sharing Interests
Business Interests
Debts Owed to You
Leases
Pending Lawsuits for Personal Injury
Appliances
Household Furniture and Furnishings
Income Tax Refunds
Clothing and Personal Effects
IRA'S

This list is intended to serve only as a *guide* and may not be a complete list of your property.

If you and your spouse disagree over whether property belongs to both spouses or one particular spouse, you may want to talk with an attorney on a simple consultation. Some situations when you *should* talk with an attorney are:

■ You or your spouse own a lot of property.

■ You are not sure whether property you own belongs to both spouses or is separate property of one spouse.

■ You or your spouse own all or a large share of your own business.

■ You or your spouse have earned considerable retirement benefits.

■ You or your spouse receive money from royalties or a trust fund.

■ You or your spouse are concerned about the tax results of transfers, exemptions or alimony.

a Pension, IRA and Retirement Plans

The division of a pension fund can be a difficult part in writing your agreement. If both you and your spouse have worked during your entire married life, and at the same job during that time, chances are you each have a pension fund. If only one of you has worked during your marriage, or one of you has changed jobs frequently during your married life, one of you probably has a greater cash value in pension than the other. Each spouse is generally entitled to *one-half* of the *present cash value* of the pension earned by the other spouse during the marriage.

If your spouse has a pension fund with his or her company or union, you are generally entitled to *one-half the present vested interest in that plan*. Even though your spouse would not be entitled to his or her pension fund until a certain age, you are entitled to your one-half share at the time of the Dissolution unless the two of you otherwise agree.

With the many different pension plans, they can be very difficult to value before payments are actually due. Most of the time, the employee has paid in some amount which is payable at any time upon termination, and this amount will be easy to determine. The employer's contributions are generally payable in the form of pension payments which are due only if and when the employee works to retirement age. At the time of your Dissolution, the retirement fund may be unvested, thus making it extremely complex to value.

Correct valuation of the present value of a future pension fund is best accomplished by a professional actuary who specializes in pensions. If you and your spouse have been married for a long time, you may wish to hire an actuary (see the yellow pages for actuary), because this may be a major marital asset.

Another option is to contact the responsible person within your company that manages the pension plan and ask for pension information such as: how the plan works, dates of the employee's participation, amount of employer contribution, amounts due to the employee in the event of immediate termination, and their estimate of the current worth of the plan.

Social Security is NOT marital property and not subject to division by a Court. It is a federal program. Contact the Social Security Administration concerning your rights after divorce.

Military retirement is governed by both federal and state law. If you are married to someone in the military, and you are seeking a division of the pension, *consult* an attorney.

Other Options Concerning Pension Funds

1. Trade a marital asset of a value equal to a fifty percent share of the pension fund that was given up.

2. Make a promissory note due on a certain date, or when benefits become payable.

3. A spouse could waive (give up) all their interest in exchange for nothing.

4. If both spouses have worked during their entire marriage, then each spouse may want to keep their own pension fund without determining a value.

If you feel that you have a right in a pension plan that might be worth protecting beyond the methods we have described here, then you should *consult* an attorney.

IRA's should also be divided, but only if acquired during the marriage. These should be divided equally; however, you must take into consideration the fact that one party may have a pension at his or her place of employment. Since tax laws are ever-changing, we would suggest that you talk with an accountant to determine that the transfer of IRA's does not cause penalties.

b Stocks, Bonds and Securities

Stocks, bonds, and securities should be divided in half unless you and your spouse otherwise agree.

If any of the above was a gift or inheritance that belongs to one of you, you should receive this amount back before the balance is divided in half.

If you or your spouse owned any of the above prior to marriage, and the asset is still remaining but now in a joint account, it should be returned to the person who originally owned the stocks, bonds or securities.

If the accounts were acquired during the marriage, you and your spouse may decide to divide the accounts in an unequal fashion if the other party is receiving property instead of taking any of the above. For example, one spouse may keep the IRA's and all the savings accounts and the other spouse will keep all the stocks and bonds.

Some employers also have stock plans, and you may have acquired stock during the marriage. This is also considered a marital asset and should also be divided; or the other party should receive an asset of equal value.

If the above are not in the name of the spouse who is to receive them, an attorney or stockbroker can make the transfer.

If you have United States saving bonds and do not wish to cash them to divide the proceeds, and they are not in the name of the spouse who is to receive them, you can get the proper form from the bank to transfer ownership.

c Saving And Checking Accounts

Accounts should be divided in half unless you and your spouse otherwise agree.

If the money was a gift or inheritance that belongs to one of you, you should receive this amount back before the accounts are divided in half.

If you or your spouse had a savings account prior to marriage, and there is still money remaining in a joint account that would cover this amount, it should be returned to the person who originally had the account.

You and your spouse may also decide to divide the accounts in an unequal method if the other party is receiving a larger asset, such as one spouse is getting a car that is paid off; the other spouse still has to make payments on the car he/she is receiving.

The key factor to remember is that each party should be made financially equal if possible. If the money belonged to one spouse prior to marriage or was from a sale of a premarital asset, that money should be returned to that spouse.

You can also divide your savings accounts in the way you think is most fair. It does not always have to be fifty-fifty to be approved by the Court.

The checking account, if joint, should be closed, and new individual accounts should be opened. Make sure that all checks written have cleared the bank before you close the account.

Funds in this account should also be divided equally unless otherwise agreed upon.

d Motor Vehicles And Mobile Homes

In your Separation Agreement you must decide the following:

■ Which spouse will keep which motor vehicle(s).

■ Who will pay the balance owed on any vehicle(s) you and your spouse own.

■ You must also make arrangements for the payment of the auto insurance on the vehicles.

■ You must also make arrangements for the transfer of the title if necessary.

If your vehicle is a mobile home you should refer to the real estate section and make the same decisions as are needed for real estate.

If title to a vehicle or mobile home is already in the spouse's name who will be receiving it, nothing needs to be done regarding transfer of title. If title is not in your name, your spouse should sign the title over to you. However, you will not be able to sign over the title unless the vehicle is paid-off.

The spouse who will be keeping a vehicle must take responsibility for paying the insurance on it. REMEMBER IN OHIO, INSURANCE IS REQUIRED BEFORE PLATES WILL BE ISSUED.

This section also applies to boats, campers, motorcycles, or any other vehicles that you and your spouse may own. Even if the title to the vehicle you will be keeping is in your name, you *must* still list who is to receive it in the Separation Agreement. It is advisable for the spouse who takes a particular vehicle to pay the debt on that item. Otherwise, if your spouse agrees to make the payments and fails to do so, the auto that you are driving may be repossessed without notice to you.

If you have a mobile home, you should also copy part of the real estate provision as to who shall occupy the home, pay the utilities and be responsible for the payments.

e Life Insurance

If you have a life insurance policy with a cash surrender value, it is subject to division with other property of the marriage. If you choose you can cash the policy and divide the proceeds; or one party can pay the other party for his or her interest. You should also speak with the insurance company to determine what other steps may be taken to conclude the matter.

In addition, remember to change the beneficiary on the policy if your spouse is the named beneficiary after the dissolution hearing is completed. Even if you are divorced or you have a Last Will and Testament which provides otherwise, the life insurance will still be paid to the named beneficiary on the policy.

f IRS Liabilities And Refunds

This section is especially important if you owe taxes to the IRS or other taxing authority; or if you will be filing a joint income tax return prior to the time your Dissolution will be granted or if you have filed a joint return and are awaiting a refund. If you have any concerns about taxes you should contact a **tax accountant or lawyer** to advise you.

If you own taxes you must tell the Court on the Separation Agreement which party will be paying the debt. If you are expecting a tax refund you must tell the Court on the Separation Agreement how you will be dividing the refund. If the debt is for taxes owed prior to the marriage, the spouse who owed the debt prior to the marriage should be responsible for payment. If the debt is for taxes owed during your marriage, it will depend on the circumstances, your earning abilities and by agreement of the parties to determine which spouse will pay the tax debt.

Even when you file a separate income tax return after the marriage is dissolved, the IRS may still attach future years refunds from both parties for taxes previously due during the marriage until the IRS debt has been paid in full. This could happen because the tax debt is perceived by the IRS as being owed by both parties as joint debtors.

An income tax refund can be divided anyway the parties may choose. If receiving a refund it may be divided fifty-fifty or the refund can be used to pay debts and any remaining proceeds divided. You must tell the Court on the Separation Agreement how any tax refunds will be divided between the parties.

The following are additional points to keep in mind concerning taxes:

☐ You cannot file a joint tax return with your spouse unless you are married on the last day of the year. If your Dissolution Decree was filed with the court and signed by the Judge prior to the end of the year, you are considered a single taxpayer for that year by the IRS.

☐ Alimony payments paid by a former spouse are generally considered as earned income to the spouse receiving them and they are tax-deductible for the spouse making them.

☐ Child support payments received by a spouse are **not** considered earn income and therefore are not taxed, but child support payments **are not** tax-deductible to the spouse making them. If there are minor child/ren of the marriage, only one spouse may claim the child/ren as an exemption.

g Real Estate (Real Property)

When you consider what to do with your home or other real property, you will want to know how much of it you actually own. Your equity in any property is the difference between what you can get for it on the current market less the amount(s) due on it and less the cost of selling it. You can find out the current market value of your property by consulting a professional real estate appraiser.

Assuming the house was held by both spouses jointly, and acquired during the marriage, the entire amount is marital property, and each spouse is entitled to half.

IN DIVIDING REAL ESTATE YOU MUST PROVIDE FOR THE FOLLOWING:

■ the payment of any mortgages on the real estate

■ the payment of insurance and taxes on the real estate

■ the determination as to which of you will live in the house and for how long

■ the payment of all utilities, including water, electricity, gas, heat, sewage, trash pick-up and any improvements or assessments

■ if it is sold, the division of the net proceeds from the sale of the real estate

■ if one party is keeping the real estate, the transfer of the property from you to your spouse (or vice-versa)

Note: LawPak prints a publication "Real Estate Contracts" which includes the contracts and guides the consumer through the process of selling residential real estate. (see the LawPak title listing and order form in the back of this publication).

There are many ways you can dispose of your real estate. Some common arrangements are:

■ The property is deeded to one spouse (money may or may not be paid to the spouse transferring for his/her equity interest, if any depending on your agreement.

■ You and your spouse agree that after the Dissolution, both of you will continue to own the property. If it is a house, one of you may continue to live in it and be responsible for all the utilities, payments, maintenance, etc.. You may or may not provide for a sale at a later date and provide for a division of the sale proceeds.

■ You and your spouse agree that the house will be sold prior to the Dissolution and the proceeds will be divided according to the terms of your agreement.

EXAMPLES: REAL ESTATE CLAUSE

(1) Husband/Wife shall execute a quitclaim deed to the husband/wife for the real estate located at _____ .
Husband/Wife shall be responsible for the mortgage payments on said property and shall hold husband/wife harmless therefrom. Husband/Wife shall occupy said premises and shall be responsible for the telephone, the utilities, and any other miscellaneous minor expenses concerning the maintenance of said real estate. If there shall be a major repair, husband/wife shall be responsible for said repairs. In consideration of the foregoing husband/wife shall execute a second mortgage and promissory note to husband/wife in the amount of $ _____ , said amount shall be paid pursuant to the terms set forth in the second mortgage and promissory note, releasing husband/wife of any further obligation to the husband/wife.

(2) The real estate located at _____
shall be listed for sale immediately and both parties shall, with best efforts, aid in the sale of said real estate. Until said real estate is sold, husband/wife shall be responsible for the mortgage payments on said property and shall hold husband/wife harmless therefrom. Husband/Wife shall occupy said premises and shall be responsible for the telephone, the utilities, and any other miscellaneous minor expenses concerning the maintenance of said real estate. If, prior to the sale of the real estate, there shall be a major repair, husband/wife shall be responsible for said repairs. After the real property is sold, the profits from the sale of said real estate shall be divided as follows: the following debts and amounts shall be paid directly from the proceeds: (list debts & amounts):

Creditor: _____ Amount: _____

Creditor: _____ Amount: _____

Creditor: _____ Amount: _____

Creditor: _____ Amount: _____

Creditor: _____ Amount: _____

Creditor: _____ Amount: _____

After the aforementioned debts and any outstanding mortgages have been paid, the net proceeds shall be divided equally.

(3) Husband/Wife shall execute a quitclaim deed to the husband/wife for the real estate located at _____ .
Husband/Wife shall be responsible for the mortgage payments on said property and shall hold husband/wife harmless therefrom. Husband/Wife shall occupy said premises and shall be responsible for the telephone, the utilities, and any other miscellaneous minor expenses concerning the maintenance of said real estate. If there shall be a major repair, husband/wife shall be responsible for said repairs. In consideration of the foregoing husband/wife shall receive no moneys from the husband/wife for the reason that _____
_____ .

Husband/Wife shall have no claim on any moneys from the sale of the real estate now or at any future time.

(4) The real estate located at _____
shall be listed for sale immediately and both parties shall, with best efforts, aid in the sale of said real estate. Until said real estate is sold, husband/wife shall be responsible for the mortgage payments on said property and shall hold husband/wife harmless therefrom. Husband/Wife shall occupy said premises and shall be responsible for the telephone, the utilities, and any other miscellaneous minor expenses concerning the maintenance of said real estate. If, prior to the sale of the real estate, there shall be a major repair, husband/wife shall be responsible for said repairs. After the real property is sold, the profits from the sale of said real estate shall be divided as follows: equally between the parties after the outstanding mortgage, taxes, and any debt owing on said real estate have been paid.

(5) The real estate located at _____
shall be listed for sale immediately and both parties shall, with best efforts, aid in the sale of said real estate. Until said real estate is sold, husband/wife shall be responsible for the mortgage payments on said property and shall hold husband/wife harmless therefrom. Husband/Wife shall occupy said premises and shall be responsible for the telephone, the utilities, and any other miscellaneous minor expenses concerning the maintenance of said real estate. If, prior to the sale of the real estate, there shall be a major repair, husband/wife shall be responsible for said repairs. After the real property is sold, the profits from the sale of said real estate shall be divided as follows: after the outstanding mortgage, taxes, or any debt owing on said real estate is paid husband/wife shall receive a lump sum payment of $ _____ and the balance of the net proceeds shall go to the husband/wife.

(6) The real estate located at _____
shall be listed for sale immediately and both parties shall, with best efforts, aid in the sale of said real estate. Until said real estate is sold, husband/wife shall be responsible for the mortgage payments on said property and shall hold husband/wife harmless therefrom. Husband/Wife shall occupy said premises and shall be responsible for the telephone, the utilities, and any other miscellaneous minor expenses concerning the maintenance of said real estate. If, prior to the sale of the real estate, there shall be a major repair, husband/wife shall be responsible for said repairs. After the real property is sold, the profits from the sale of said real estate shall be divided as follows: when the sale of the subject real estate is completed, husband/wife shall receive credit for all principal s/he has paid on the mortgages presently secured by said real estate from the date of the filing of the decree until the actual closing date on the sale of the subject real estate. Husband/Wife shall also be given credit for one-half of any real estate taxes and/or property insurance they paid for the period of time from the date of the filing of the decree until the actual closing date on the sale of the subject real estate. After the husband/wife has been given credit for the aforementioned, the profit shall be divided as follows: husband shall receive: $ _____ and the wife shall receive: $ _____ .

If you are going to have the property transferred to only one of you in your Dissolution, proceed as follows:

1. Be sure you have listed it in your Separation Agreement under the spouse's name who is to receive it.

2. When you describe the property be sure to use the full street address including the number, city, state, and zip code.

3. Go to an attorney to have a new deed drawn up. After the deed is completed and signed, be sure to have it recorded in the offices of the County Auditor and Recorder in the county where the property is located. This recording process must be completed **after** you receive your final decree of Dissolution. **Do not fail to do this.** If you or the attorney does not record the Deed at the Courthouse, it will not be put in your name and when you try to sell your real estate you may not be able to do so.

4. If you decide not to complete your Dissolution and have already signed and filed your deed at the Courthouse, you should have an attorney change the deed back to the way it was.

If you still have trouble dealing with your real property after reading this—how to value it, divide it, or transfer it—it may be best if you *consult* an attorney, at least on this one point.

h Household Goods

Dividing your household goods can be an easy task if both parties agree. Any household goods which you owned prior to your marriage should be returned to you. Any household item that was a gift from a family member should also stay with that spouse. The same rules apply for wedding presents.

Example: *Wife's mother gave a microwave as a Christmas present, this should be the property of the wife.*

You can divide your household goods in any manner that you and your spouse agree upon. If you cannot agree on a division, the two of you should place a value on each of the items and then take turns selecting items until all goods are divided.

The household goods should actually be in the possession of the person who will be keeping them at the time your Petition, Waiver and Separation Agreement are filed.

Example:

Husband
bedroom suite
kitchen chairs
washer

Wife
stereo
living room suite
microwave

⚏ Personal Property

Personal property includes clothes, shoes, books, jewelry, cosmetics, hairdryers, exercise equipment, pictures, photo albums, guns, tools, sporting goods equipment and all items that are for your personal use.

If you gave your spouse a gift during or before your marriage, he or she should be allowed to keep that gift.

▣ B2 Understanding What You Owe

If you and your spouse have accumulated debts, you must decide who is going to pay which debts. When you are dividing your debts, remember to take into consideration the division of the property.

It is a good idea for the spouse who takes a particular item to take the debt owed on that item. For example, if you bought a couch on a charge card and the husband takes the couch, he should also take the debt. Otherwise if the wife does not make the payment, the couch can be repossessed.

Remember that creditors are not affected by your Dissolution/Separation Agreement. If you and your spouse both sign on a debt and the spouse who agreed to pay the debt in your Separation Agreement fails to pay it, the creditor can still come after you for the money or merchandise.

If only one of you has signed on a debt, the creditor may have difficulty enforcing the obligation against the spouse who did not sign. However, if you are sued on a debt that you think your spouse owes, you should *consult* an attorney because your wages can be garnished and your property attached if you ignore the lawsuit.

If you and your spouse incurred debts prior to the marriage, in most cases only the person who signed for it is liable and that person should continue to pay it.

The following is a list of possible debts that must be divided in your separation agreement:

Credit Cards
House Mortgage Payments
Real Estate and Other Types of Taxes
Gas, Electric and Utility Bills for the Time Period You were Living Together
Auto, Boat, Motorcycle or Mobile Home Payments
Credit Union Loans
Signature Loans
Promissory Notes
Finance Companies
Bank Loans
Broken Leases
Lawsuits Against You and Your Spouse
Medical, Dental, Drug and Optical Bills
Student Loans

You may divide a debt any way you wish. One spouse can pay one entire bill or both spouses can pay part of each bill. You must be sure to list all your debts. If one spouse used a credit card entirely for his/her own use, that party usually pays the debt. If you are going to live in the real estate or mobile home, or keep a certain car, you should probably pay that debt, unless you and your spouse have made other arrangements due to your personal financial condition.

B3 Wills

A Finalized Dissolution *changes* the validity of a Will already in existence. You should write a *new* Will after a Dissolution. LawPak also provides a guide on drafting a Last Will and Testament.

CHAPTER
C
Providing For Your Children

C1 General Information

If you and your spouse have child(ren) together either natural or adopted who are under the age of eighteen (18) or still in high school, you both must agree on who will be the custodial parent (residential parent), child visitation, child support, medical insurance for the child(ren), payment of medical expenses not covered by insurance, and who will claim the child(ren) for income tax purposes.

Only one true test exists for making decisions concerning the care of your child(ren): "What is in the child's best interest?" This is the *primary question* that concerns the Court in respect to the care of your children. A Dissolution of Marriage does not dissolve a parent's responsibilities and obligations to their children. Both parents have to work *together* for what is in the best interest of their children.

As of April 1991, the Ohio Legislature enacted additional laws and made changes concerning *child custody, child support,* and *visitation.* These laws were passed to improve the collection of child support, create the best possible parental environment for the child, and create the best equitable agreements concerning the child(ren) for the parents.

In changing and/or adding to the Ohio laws concerning children in a dissolution of marriage, the legislature made substantial changes in the legal terminology used on the forms which you are required to file with the court.

The following are examples of revisions in the legal terminology contained in the new forms:

- the custodial parent (the parent who is primarily allocated the parental rights and responsibilities for the care of the child(ren) is now designated as the "residential parent", and the non-custodial parent is now designated as the parent who is *not* the residential parent or the "nonresidential parent".

- joint custody is now called "shared parenting".

- in addition to the Bureau of Support there also is a "Child Support Enforcement Agency".

C2 The Residential Parent And Legal Custodian

The residential parent (the parent who assumes custody), assumes the primary responsibility for raising the children. The residential parent becomes the principle decision maker for almost every aspect of the child's upbringing. Careful thought should be exercised therefore in deciding which parent is to assume the position of residential parent.

In virtually every case, the Court will grant your wishes in determining who will assume the position of residential parent as named in the Separation Agreement. The Court is relying on you and your spouse to make a decision which is in the best interest of the children, since you will only be in court a few minutes.

NOTE: *At the discretion of the judge, a child of* **any age** *may be interviewed by the court to determine the child's wishes regarding the allocation of parental rights (custody and visitation) and for the purpose of resolving any issues related to the court making a decision concerning their care.*

The court will first determine the **reasoning ability** *of the child and if the judge concludes that the child* **does not** *have sufficient reasoning ability to express their wishes concerning parental rights, then the court* **will not** *consider the child's expressions in determining the allocation of parental rights.*

But, if the court finds that the child **has** *sufficient reasoning ability to express their wishes, then the court* **may consider** *the child's wishes and proceed to make a determination in the granting of parental rights.*

The interview with the child has to be conducted in chambers, and no person other than the child, the child's attorney, the judge, any necessary court personnel, and in the judges; discretion the attorney of each parent, shall be permitted to be present in the chambers during the interview.

If you use a LawPak to assist you in obtaining a Dissolution of Marriage, you *must agree* on which spouse will be the residential parent and legal custodian for the children. If you can agree to all issues concerning the child(ren), the judge will not usually interview your children to determine their care. This procedure is only utilized when there appears to be major disagreements between the parents concerning the care of the children.

Ohio law recognizes three different methods in determining the allocation of parental rights and responsibilities (you must choose only *one method* for *all* your children):

1 **Sole Parental Rights And Responsibilities**

This allocation procedure is used when one parent called the "sole residential parent" is allocated all rights and responsibilities for raising *all* the child(ren) of the marriage. The other parent is then known as the "non-residential" parent.

2 **Split Parental Rights And Responsibilities**

This allocation procedure is used when one parent assumes responsibility for one or more child(ren) and the other parent assumes responsibility for one or more child(ren). Example: The mother is allocated the parental rights and responsibilities for raising the girl(s) and the father is allocated the parental rights and responsibilities for raising the boy(s).

3 **Shared Parenting (previously known as joint custody)**

A shared parenting plan addresses the allocation of parental rights and responsibilities for the care of the minor children by including in the Separation Agreement a plan under which both parents will have shared rights and responsibilities for the care of the minor children. The Shared Parenting Plan is filed with the Petition For Dissolution of Marriage. The court may approve shared parenting only if it determines that it is in the best interest of the children.

Either parent or both parents of the children may file a motion with the court requesting the court to grant *both* parents shared parental rights and responsibilities for the care of their children. In determining the best interest of the children and allocating parental rights, the court will consider all revelant factors including the following:

- The wishes of the child's parents regarding his care;
- If the court has interviewed the child in chambers, the child's wishes and concerns as to the allocation of parental rights;
- The child's interaction and interrelationship with his parents, siblings, and any other person who may significantly affect the child's best interest;
- The child's adjustment to his home, school, and community;
- The mental and physical health of all persons involved;
- The parent more likely to honor and facilitate visitation rights approved by the court;
- Whether either parent has failed to make all child support payments;
- Whether either parent has been convicted of any criminal offense involving any act that resulted in a child being abused or neglected;
- Whether the residential parent or one of the parents subject to a shared parenting decree has continuously and willfully denied the other parent visitation rights;
- Whether either parent has established a residence, or is planning to establish a residence outside the state of Ohio.

In determining whether shared parenting is in the best interest of the child/ren, the court will consider these additional factors:

- The ability of the parents to cooperate and make decisions jointly, with respect to the children;
- The ability of each parent to encourage the sharing of love, affection, and contact between the child and the other parent;
- Any history of, or potential for, child abuse, spouse abuse, other domestic violence, or parental kidnapping by either parent;
- The geographic proximity of the parents to each other, as the proximity relates to the practical considerations of shared parenting;

NOTE: *When allocating parental rights and responsibilities for the care of the children, the court will* **not** *give preference to a parent because of that parent's financial status or condition.*

Since the Shared Parenting Agreement is dependent on each families individual needs and may become very complex. We have included a Shared Parenting Plan and Shared Parenting Decree in this edition, but be aware that the court may modify your agreement in any manner that the court determines is in the best interest of your children. We suggest that if you and your spouse desire Shared Parenting that you *seek the advice* of an attorney in preparing the Shared Parenting Agreement which will be acceptable to the Court.

If you or your spouse decide that shared parenting is a better method for allocating parental responisbility than one parent being primarily responsible (sole residential/parent), then you will have to develop a *written* "Shared Parenting Agreement" which is submitted to the court for approval. A plan for shared parenting should include provisions covering all factors that are relevant to the care of the child/ren (but not limited to) the following provisions:

■ physical living arrangements;
■ child support obligations;
■ children's medical and dental care;
■ school placement;
■ visitation.

The court may *modify* your Shared Parenting Agreement in any manner that the court determines is in the best interest of the child/ren.

The procedures necessary to obtain a final decree for shared parenting from the court are as follows:

■ You will have to make a motion to the court that you and your spouse are requesting approval for a shared parenting arrangement for the children.
■ You and/or your spouse will have to draft a Shared Parenting Agreement which includes all provisions for the care of the children.
■ The court will either modify your agreement and ask you to submit it again after incorporating the court requested changes, or the court will accept your agreement and issue a shared parenting final decree.

C3 Visitation

In most dissolution cases, the nonresidential parent will have to have "reasonable visitation" with the children. Generally, this means that the nonresidential parent will have visitation on every other weekend and one day during the opposite week. Visitation should also include every other holiday and a minimum of two weeks in the summer. In addition, both parties may agree on an extended summer vacation schedule.

NOTE: *The Court can find the residential parent in contempt of court and modify child support obligations if the residential parent withholds visitation of the children to the nonresidential parent.*

By law each Ohio County Court of Common Pleas, Division of Domestic Relations, has to adopt *standard visitation guidelines.* The Court does have discretion in deviating from the county standard visitation guidelines if it is in the best interest of the children.

NOTE: *Obtain a copy of these standard visitation guidelines from your county clerk of of domestic relations to ensure that your Separation Agreement meets the county standards for visitation (see example County guidelines in Appendix).*

You must present a schedule that is *reasonable* and *fair* to the Court. If you and your spouse cannot agree on visitation, you cannot dissolve the marriage. A divorce action must be filed and the Court will determine the times and hours of visitation.

During visitation, the child support should continue, unless the visitation is extended for more than a month. If you intend that the nonresidential parent have visitation for extended period of time, your Separation Agreement can state that child support will not be paid during that time or it will be reduced by a certain percentage, for example fifty percent.

As the residential parent you *cannot* tell your former spouse who you want around the children. If you and your spouse are dissolved, neither one of you can restrict the company the other chooses to keep. The only way visitation should be restricted would be if you could prove that someone was undesireable, that is, a drug user, alcohol abuser, child abuser or molester. If you can prove any one of the above, you might be able to restrict visitation.

In addition, if the "residential parent" (parent who has custody) intends to move to a residence other than the residence specified in the visitation order granted by the court, the residential parent will have to give notice of their intent to relocate to the court.

The Court will then send a copy of the notice of relocation to the other parent. And the court or "the parent *not* considered the residential parent" *may* file a motion to schedule a hearing to determine whether it is in the best interest of the child to revise the visitation schedule because of the relocation.

Also, when the court grants visitation rights to a parent the court has to determine if the parent "has ever been convicted of or pleaded guilty to any crime involving a victim who at the time of the commission of the offense was a member of the family or household that is the subject of the proceeding and caused physical harm to the victim in the commission of the offense or has been determined to be the perpetrator of the abusive act that is the basis of an adjudication that a child is an abused child."

NOTE: *If you have been convicted of a crime involving family abuse or neglect toward your spouse or child/ren, you are going to have to prove to the court's satisfaction that these problems have been resolved before the court grants visitation.*

The parent who is considered "not to be the residential parent" (nonresidential parent) is entitled to access, under the same terms and conditions under which is provided to the residential parent, and to any record or school activity that is related to the child, unless it is determined by the court that it would not be in the best interest of the child.

The fact that your former spouse is *not paying child support* as agreed does not mean you can deny visitation. In Ohio, the court has determined that child support and visitation are not related but two separate issues. You must allow your former spouse visitation, even if they are not paying child support. If you deny visitation for any reason, other than your former spouse being an unfit parent, you may be charged with Contempt of Court.

C4 Life Insurance

Most Courts like to see a provision in your Separation Agreement reciting that there is a life insurance policy in effect for the benefit of your children until they reach the age of eighteen. The beneficiary should be the children and not your former spouse. If you are employed full time, most employers provide some type of life insurance in the event of your death.

You can also purchase a separate policy on your life, making the children beneficiaries. After the children reach the age of eighteen and are graduated from high school, you can cancel the policy, or make someone else the beneficiary.

C5 Medical Insurance For Minor Children

In Ohio, to obtain a Dissolution of Marriage with children, it is now a requirement that the minor children must be covered by some form of health care coverage. The Court will issue a court order to make sure that coverage is current and/or obtained and remains effective. Either the obligor (individual paying child support) or the obligee (individual receiving child support), will have to obtain a heath care policy for the children no later that thirty days after a child support order is granted by the court. In addition, on an ongoing bases, written proof must be furnished to the Child Support Enforcement Agency that the required health insurance coverage has been obtained and remains effective and current.

If you are employed full or part time, your employer in many cases will provide you with medical insurance at no cost or with some additional cost for dependents. If your employer does not have medical insurance then one party must cover the children under a private policy. The cost of the policy can be divided between the parties or one party can pay for it. In determining who should pay for the health coverage, you should consider the amount of child support being paid and the earnings of each party. The Court *may not* approve a Separation Agreement that does not provide for medical insurance for the children.

If neither the father nor the mother can obtain health insurance coverage for the health care of the minor children, then the court will issue a court order stating that the cost of the medical and health needs of the child(ren) will be a shared liability according to a predetermined formula set out in the court order, normally fifty-fifty between the parent after the residential pays the first $200 per child per calendar year.

Other medical expenses (medical, dental, drug, optical) not covered by a health care policy are usually divided fifty-fifty after the residential parent pays the first $200 per child per calendar year. You must make these provisions within your Separation Agreement because the court will not decide these issues for you and may not grant a Dissolution of Marriage without the proper provisions for health care coverage for the children.

C6 Helping Your Children Cope With Separation

The way you cope with your dissolution will greatly influence how your children will deal with the situation. Your responsibilities as a parent will not end because of the dissolution. You must continue to play a vital role in their lives and give them the love, affection, and concern of a loving parent. Do not let bitterness create hateful actions to force your children to take sides. Children should understand that each parent will continue to love and care for them although the parents could not live happily together.

■ Do not change the child's normal routine too abruptly.

■ Allow the child time for readjustment after the dissolution.

■ Do not force a child to take sides.

■ Try to be direct in telling the child what is happening. Keep it simple so that the child will understand. The explanation should be brief, timely, direct, and honest.

■ Control any bitter feelings toward your spouse and refrain from voicing criticism of the other parent when the child is present.

■ Make sure that the child understands that they are not the cause for the termination of the marriage.

■ The child will still need control, direction, and discipline. Do not attempt to buy your child's love by special treatment, making promises, or accepting improper behavior from the child.

It is important that the spouse who has left the original home environment maintain contact with the child. This will reduce the child's feelings of rejection and concern about not seeing the other parent again.

■ Visits should be pleasant for both the child and parents. There should be no displays of hostility.

■ Visits should take place away from the child's home.

■ The child should be available at the time and place agreed upon for visitation.

■ Visits should be as frequent as possible.

■ Visits should not be used to check on the other parent.

C7 Sample Visitation Guidelines

The following is a sample of the type of Visitation Guidelines that some Ohio counties are adopting. Be sure to check with your local county Clerk of Courts to determine if your county has adopted visitation guidelines for the non-residential parent.

■ The non-residential parent shall have visitation on *alternate* weekends from Friday at 6:00 p.m. to Sunday evening at 6:00 p.m.

■ The non-residential parent shall have visitation from 5:30 p.m. to 8:30 p.m. on a week night *preceding* the weekends during which there is visitation.

■ During *even* numbered years, the non-residential parent shall have visitation on New Year's Day, President's Day, Memorial Day, Veteran's Day and Thanksgiving. Each of these visitations shall begin at 10:00 a.m. and continue until 8:30 p.m.

■ During *odd* numbered years, the non-residential parent shall have visitation on Martin Luther King Day, Easter, Fourth of July, and Labor Day. Each of these visitations shall begin at 10:00 a.m. and continue until 8:30 p.m.

■ During the *even* numbered years, the non-residential parent shall have the children from 1:00 p.m. until 8:30 p.m. on Christmas Eve, and during *odd* numbered years, Christmas Day from 10:00 a.m. and continue until 8:30 p.m.

■ On Mother's Day, the children shall be with the mother and on Father's Day, the children shall be with the father, no matter whose turn for visitation it is. Visitation shall begin at 10:00 a.m. and continue until 8:30 p.m.

■ During *even* numbered years, the non-residential parent shall have visitation on the child's birthday. If the child's birthday falls on a non-school day, the visitation shall take place from 10:00 a.m. and continue until 8:30 p.m. If the child's birthday falls on a school day, visitation shall take place from 5:30 p.m. to 8:30 p.m.

■ The non-residential parent *shall not* exercise visitation on holidays other than those which the non-residential parent is entitled as described in the above paragraphs, except as otherwise agreed by the parties.
Note: The holiday schedule may be modified to accommodate the parties religious preference.

■ The non-residential parent shall be entitled to four weeks of additional visitation each year. This visitation may be exercised during the child's school break at Christmas time, the child's break from school and summer visitation, or at any other appropriate time during the year.

■ Extended visitations are to be arranged within seven days from the time the parent's vacation schedules are posted by their employers. The non-residential parent shall notify the residential parent in writing of the time desired for extended visitation no later than 30 days prior to the requested extended visitation.

■ The children and/or the residential parent do not have to wait for the non-residential parent to arrive for visitation for more than thirty minutes. The non-residential parent who is more than thirty minutes late for a particular visitation, shall forfeit that visitation.

■ The non-residential parent who is more than thirty minutes late in returning the children without calling to make arrangements for just cause shall be subject to contempt.

■ The residential parent may not remove the children from the State of Ohio and establish residence for them in another state without a Court order or an agreement signed by the parties.

■ Make-up days shall be given if due to an emergency, the child or non-residential parent cannot visit at the scheduled time or if the residential parent denies visitation without just cause. All make-up days shall be rescheduled and exercised within thirty days.

■ In the event that the parties are unable to reach an agreement regarding transportation for visitation, _____ shall provide transportation at commencement of the visitation period and _____ shall provide transportation at termination of the visitation period.

■ The residential parent shall arrange for the appropriate school officials to release to the non-residential parent any and all information concerning the children.

■ The residential parent shall authorize the release of any and all medical information and records concerning the child to the non-residential parent. In the event the child's illness requires medical attention, by a physician, the residential parent shall promptly notify the non-residential parent. Elective surgery shall only be performed after consultation with the non-residential parent.

■ Any child who is *twelve years of age or older* may set and determine visitation with the non-residential parent.

Note: Willful non-compliance with the visitation order of the Court may result in a Finding of Contempt with up to thirty days incarceration, a $250.00 fine, and an award of attorney's fees.

CHAPTER
D
Support

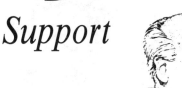

 Child Support

The duty of the parent to support his or her children is most important to the Court in the approval of your Dissolution of Marriage. The obligation lasts until the child dies, marries, becomes emancipated (self-supporting), or until the child's 18th birthday.

The amount of child support to be paid is determined by the following:

1. The financial resources of the child;
2. The financial resources and needs of the residential parent and of the non-residential parent as well as future earning abilities;
3. The standard of living the child would have enjoyed had the marriage continued;
4. The physical and emotional condition of the child;
5. The educational needs of the child and the educational opportunities that would have been available to she/he had the circumstances requiring a court order for support not arisen;
6. Responsibility for the support of others;
7. Ages of the parties and the children.

The Court will balance the needs of the children against the ability of the non-residential parent to pay for the support.

Many counties in Ohio have prepared guidelines for the payment of child support, but these guidelines will *vary widely* from county to county. You *will need to contact your* County Clerk of Courts to determine what guidelines and additional forms the county has established for the payment of child support.

One particular model which all Ohio Counties will have to adopt by Ohio law is the "Income Shares Model". This Model is based on the concept that the child *should* receive the same proportion of parental income that he/she would have received if the parents had stayed together. The economic study that developed the "Income Shares Model" found that the proportion of household spending devoted to children is systematically related to the level of household income and to the number and ages of the children.

Based on this economic evidence, the county guidelines were developed which calculate child support as the share of *each* parent's income. If one parent has custody the amount calculated for that parent is presumed to be spent on the child. The amount calculated for the non-residential parent establishes the amount of child support to be paid to the residential parent (See Exhibit A).

NOTE: *Exhibit A contains a schedule which combines the gross income from both parents (total family income) in the first column. Across the top is listed the number of child/ren within the household. To determine the total annual dollars spent on your child/ren, find your total family income with the number of child/ren in your household.*

For obligors (non-residential parent) with income of less than $500. per month, a case-by-case determination and income review is made by the Court.

a Determining The Dollar Amount of Child Support

As previously stated, many Ohio Counties have prepared guidelines for the payment of child support, but these guidelines will *vary* considerably from county to county. You will have to contact your County Clerk of Courts to receive the guidelines and required forms. The County Clerk will usually have prepared packets which contain blank forms and guidelines. You will have to fill-in the necessary information and file these forms with your Petition for Dissolution.

We have included child support forms from several Ohio counties within this LawPak to serve as examples. **CAUTION:** these forms are only *examples. They may not* be correct for your county, so be sure to check with your County Clerk.

1. Family Income and Expense Worksheet (Exhibit B)

This worksheet is intended to compute total family income and each spouse's shared percentage of total family income. With the worksheet, you can compute what each spouse is currently contributing financially toward the care of the child/ren to determine what the non-residential parent should pay in child support.

Gross income is the total income before taxes from all sources during a one year period.

Gross income includes salaries, wages, overtime, commissions, royalties, tips, bonuses, rents, dividends, severance pay, pensions, interest, trust income, annuities, reoccurring capital gains, social security benefits, workers' compensation benefits, unemployment, disability insurance benefits, spousal support actually received from another who is not a party to this case, and all other sources of income including income from property, reoccurring capital gains, or potential cash flow from any source. For income from self-employment, proprietorship of a business, or joint ownership of a partnership or closely held corporation, or rents, gross income is defined as gross receipts minus ordinary and necessary expenses incurred in generating such income.

Exclude from gross income, Aid for Dependent Children (ADC), General Relief, Supplemental Social Security Income, Foodstamps, and child support payments received for child/ren not of this present marriage.

NOTE: *To Calculate annual gross payroll income:*

- if paid weekly, multiply gross weekly pay by 52;
- if paid every other week, multiply gross pay by 26;
- if paid twice each month, multiply gross pay by 24;
- if paid monthly, multiply gross pay by 12.

2. Pre-existing Child Support Obligations

The amount(s) of any pre-existing court order for child support shall be deducted from gross income to the extent payment can be verified with supporting documentation.

3. Health Insurance Coverage

If either parent pays for health insurance for the child/ren due support, the cost of coverage should be deducted from gross income. If coverage is provided through an employer, only the employee contribution should be deducted.

4. Computation of Child Support for Sole Custody

The obligation of child support utilizing the worksheet is computed by multiplying each parent's percentage share of family income from the worksheet *Exhibit B - Line 14,* by the total child support obligation from the schedule contained in *Exhibit A.*

5. Income Documentation

All Ohio counties require a Financial Worksheet such as Exhibit B, be prepared and submit proof (income verification) to the Court. Acceptable proof includes:

Documentation of current earnings and income (at least six full months) includes paystubs, employer statements, or receipts and expenses if self-employed. Documentation of current earnings and income should be supplemented with copies of the most recent tax returns. Each party will be responsible for providing his or her own *complete* information to the Court.

Some guidelines mandate the submission of the above documentation even where the amount of support is agreed. The Court will permit you to waive (give up) that requirement provided that **both parties** sign a waiver (Exhibit C).

Commencing August, 1987, *some* Ohio counties *will not* approve a Dissolution in which there are minor children unless the following requirements are met:

1. Either a waiver (attached to the proposed Decree) or the requisite income documentation must be presented at the time of the hearing (Exhibit C).

2. A support formula worksheet must be filed with the Separation Agreement and must be attached to the proposed Final Decree of Dissolution and made available to the Court at the hearing (Exhibit B).

3. If the amount of support agreed upon differs from the formula amount from the worksheet and schedule, the decree should state with specificity the reason for the difference. If there is no difference, you should also state this in the Decree. (this will be explained in Part II - the forms section)

EXAMINE THE ANNUAL CHILD SUPPORT
OBLIGATION SCHEDULE
(Exhibit A)

Combined Gross Family Income *$49,200.00*

Annual Dollars to Support One Child .... *$ 6,576.00*

Father's share equals .... $6,576.00   X 75.2% = $4945.15

Father is paid weekly .... $\dfrac{\$4{,}945.15}{52 \text{ weeks}}$ = $95.10 per week in child support

Mother's share equals .... $6,576.00   X 24.8% = $1,630.00

Mother is paid weekly .... $\dfrac{\$1{,}630.00}{52 \text{ weeks}}$ = $31.36 per week in child support

---

SOLE RESIDENTIAL PARENT WORKSHEET

(Exhibit B)

EXAMPLE: There is *one* minor child within the family and the mother will be the *sole residential parent*. The father's total annual gross income is $37,000.00 and the mother's total annual gross income is $12,200.00.

Worksheet Line 13 .... Combined Family Income = *$49,200.00*

Worksheet Line 14 .... Percentage of Parent's Income
Towards Total Family Income

  A. Father .... Line 12 total income = *$37,000.00*

Line 14 Percentage = $\dfrac{\$37{,}000.}{\$49{,}200.}$ = 75.2% of Family Income

---

  B. Mother .... Line 12 total income = *$12,200.00*

Line 14 Percentage = $\dfrac{\$12{,}200.}{\$49{,}200.}$ = 24.8% of Family Income

Although a monetary obligation is computed for each parent, the residential parent (in this example the mother), is presumed to spend their share of support directly on the child/ren. The non-residential parent (in this example the father), is obligated to pay $95.10 a week in child support plus $1.90 to the court as an account administration fee (poundage - which is normally about 2% of support payment, but will *vary* from county to county), for a total of $97.00 a week in child support.

b Split Parental Rights And Responsibilities

There is a *separate* child support computation worksheet for a split custody arrangement (the split Parental Rights Worksheet is located in the blank forms section of the appendix). Split Custody refers to a situation where there is more than one child and in which each parent has custody of at least one of the children. The support payment is determined for each parent for the child/ren in the custody of the other. The obligations are then offset, with the parent owing the larger amount paying the net amount in child support.

c Shared Parenting
(previously known as Joint Custody)

To figure child support in a shared parenting arrangement, use the same worksheet and calculations as utilized for a sole residential parent as found in Exhibit B.

d Method of Payments for Child Support

In Ohio, in December 1986, a new child support law (House Bill 509) went into effect, which made some important changes in the way child support is paid. This law was passed to improve and eliminate the substantial amounts of unpaid child support obligations through enforcement of support Court orders. You must *comply* with this new Ohio law.

The new Ohio law states the following:

1. All child support **must** be paid through the Bureau of support within your county. Any support not paid through the Bureau is considered a *gift* and not child support.

2. If you are paying child support, and are employed and are receiving a pay check, the child support payment **must** be deducted from your check. You have **NO** choice (see Exhibit D).

3. If you are receiving workers' compensation benefits or employment benefits, the child support payments **must** be deducted from those benefits.

4. If you are self-employed, or are not receiving any benefits, the child support payments **must** be automatically deducted from a bank account.

5. If you do not have a bank account, you **must** post a bond of at least $1000.00 to the Bureau of Support.

6. If you have no income, and do not have enough money to post a bond, the Court can order you to get a job.

7. Both parents **must** keep the Court and Bureau of Support advised of their current mailing and street addresses, and their current employer and employer's address.

8. Both parents **must** keep the Court and Bureau of Support advised of any changes in the custody of the children—such as custody changing from one parent to another, the children marrying, enlisting in the military, graduating from high school, reaching the age of 18, or leaving home for any reason, etc.

9. Any parent who *does not pay* child support or does not comply with the child support law, as stated above, may be held in contempt of court. If you are found in contempt, the maximum penalty for the first offense is 30 days in jail and a $250.00 fine; the maximum penalty for the second offense is 60 days in jail and a fine of $500.00; and the maximum penalty for the third offense is 90 days in jail and a fine of $1000.00.

10. The Bureau of Support **must** report anyone who is more than $1000.00 behind in their child support payments to the credit bureau.

11. An employer who is ordered to withhold child support payments from an employee's paycheck **must** comply with that order. If the employer does not comply with the order, the employer can be found in contempt of court. Additionally, an employer *may not* fire an employee because the employer has to withhold child support payments from the employee's paycheck.

You need to check with the Clerk of Court's office or the Bureau of Support within your county to get the proper Child Suppport Deduction Order form which must be completed and filed with the court at the time you file your Petition for Dissolution. We have included a Child Support Deduction form as an example for persons employed and receiving a paycheck (Support Deduction Order/Employer - Exhibit D). This form is usually a multi-copy form which produces several copies, and is mailed to all parties.

NOTE: *When typing your LawPak Decree, you* **must** *choose* **one** *of the following types of support orders:*

- Support Deduction Order (Employer)
- Unemployment and Notice Only
- Workers' Compensation
- Public Systems Benefits
- Miscellaneous Notice
- Financial Institution
- Bond Order

e Child Support Payment Enforcement

The fact that you have a support order does not always mean that you will get the money. The new Ohio law, House Bill 509 was passed to eliminate this situation as much as possible.

If your spouse doesn't pay what is ordered, you will probably need *professional* help to collect it. He/she can be brought in for Contempt of Court. All Ohio counties now have a Child Support Enforcement Agency to assist you in maintaining and receiving child/spousal support.

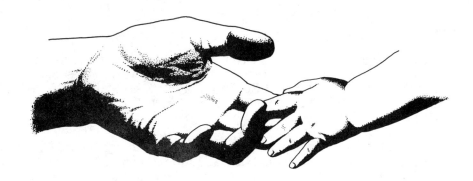

f Tuition And School Clothes

The law does not require your spouse to pay for tuition or school clothes. Payment of tuition to a private school is strictly voluntary. If you want, you can add a provision that school tuition will be divided or split. Payment for school clothes can also be included in your separation agreement. For example, your spouse may agree to pay $100 per child per calendar year to help the child get ready for school. This is strictly voluntary and would probably not be ordered by the court in a divorce.

D2 Spousal Support (Alimony)

Spousal support is second in priority to child support, but should be discussed in all cases. When considering payment of spousal support, it is very important to consider the *length* of the marriage and *earning ability* of each spouse.

It can be payable from the husband to the wife or from the wife to the husband. Spousal support is not the same as child support. The main difference is that child support continues until a child no longer must be legally supported by his or her parents, and spousal support generally stops at the happening of some event: remarriage by the person receiving it, living with a member of the opposite sex, death, or sometimes when the family home is sold, or after a certain number of installments and/or amount of money has been paid.

Spousal support can be temporary or permanent. It can last for a few weeks, months or years. It depends on the agreement that you and your spouse have reached. Spousal support, however, need not be paid in all cases. It is usually paid when one of the parties is working and the other party is not working, provided the marriage has been *long enough*.

Ohio law considers certain factors in determining spousal support. These factors include:

- The relative earning abilities of the parties.
- The ages and the physical and emotional conditions of the parties.
- The retirement benefits of the parties.
- The expectancies and inheritances of the parties.
- The duration of the marriage.
- The extent to which it would be inappropriate for a party, because he or she will be custodian of a minor child of the marriage, to seek employment outside the home.
- The standard of living of the parties established during the marriage.
- The relative extent of education of the parties.
- The relative assets and liabilities of the parties.
- The property brought to the marriage by either party.
- The contributions of a spouse as homemaker.

We strongly recommend that *you not* write your own spousal support provision. It can cause you problems for the rest of your life. Therefore, spousal support is not a subject to be taken lightly. IF YOU OR YOUR SPOUSE FEEL THAT SPOUSAL SUPPORT SHOULD BE PAID, CONSULT AN ATTORNEY. YOU SHOULD NOT ATTEMPT TO DO THIS WITHOUT HELP.

Remember, if considering spousal support, you must also consider the tax consequences; set a time period when the spousal support should start and stop; set contingencies and/or recite the number of installments to be paid and arrange to have it paid through the Court.

Spousal support is not favored in marriages of short duration where there are no children and each spouse can take care of himself or herself. Again, however, it is impossible to make suggestions as to whether spousal support should be paid and if so, the amount. In some cases spousal support for a limited period of time may be proper.

Remember, in a Dissolution you both must agree on ALL Issues, including spousal support.

NOTE: *As a general rule, you will forever* **waive your claim** *to spousal support if you fail to provide for it in your Separation Agreement.*

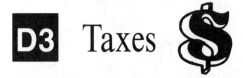

D3 Taxes

There are tax and other implications which you may want to consider in deciding whether payments should be in the form of child support or spousal support, or a combination of both.

Child support is not taxable, but spousal support is. Sometimes, the person paying spousal support can deduct such payments, and the recipient must report it as taxable income. In some cases the spouses may be able to save money by juggling these categories. Income tax exemptions are allowed for children, but when the parents are divorced, they cannot both claim the same child as a dependent. Currently, a tax exemption for the children is considered a property issue. Once you decide who will receive the exemption, it cannot be changed (unless it is subject to the continuous jurisdiction of the court). The rules for who can claim the child as an exemption are, as you might guess, subject to change. The Separation Agreement can specify who may claim the children as a dependent. Be sure to get the IRS tax information pamphlet described in Common Questions Section - Chapter A.

D4 Wife's Name Change

The wife may request that her name be changed to her maiden name or a former name. If the wife decides to change her name she must change her drivers' license, social security card, and all other credit cards or identification to the name which she has chosen. This should be accomplished after the court hearing and the final approval by the court of the Decree of Dissolution.

Child Support Exhibits

The payment of child support and health care insurance for the minor child/ren of the marriage is mandatory and in most cases will not be waived by the court. In addition, the court will not normally deviate from the child support payment amount as figured on the child support worksheet and required by the child support payment schedule. The court will determine what is in the best financial interest of the minor child/ren in maintaining their current standard of living.

All of the following required child support court forms will have to be submitted to the court for approval. In some cases the court may require supporting documentation such as payroll receipts and account numbers. Any deviation from the required child support payment amount, (even when agreed upon by the parties) will have to receive final approval from the court.

In addition, many counties now require that **both** the father and mother of the minor children take parential education classes before a dissolution of marriage will be granted to parties with minor child/ren. Ask the clerk of courts for domestic relations if these parential classes are required in the county in which you are filing your paperwork. If required both parties **must** attend to obtain a dissolution. Ask for a class schedule and to whom you contact to attend.

EXHIBIT	FORM TITLE
A	Child Support Schedule
B	Worksheet - Child Support Computation (Sole Residential Parent or Shared Parenting)
C	Financial Disclosure
D	Child Support Deduction Order (Employer)
E	Dependent Health Care Order

EXHIBIT A

Combined Gross Income	One Child	Two Children	Three Children	Four Children	Five Children	Six Children
6600*	600	600	600	600	600	600
7200*	600	600	600	600	600	600
7800*	600	600	600	600	600	600
8400*	600	600	600	600	600	600
9000*	849	859	868	878	887	896
9600*	1259	1273	1287	1301	1315	1329
10200*	1669	1687	1706	1724	1743	1761
10800*	2076	2099	2122	2145	2168	2192
11400*	2331	2505	2533	2560	2588	2616
12000*	2439	2911	2943	2975	3007	3039
12600*	2546	3318	3354	3390	3427	3463
13200*	2654	3724	3765	3806	3846	3887
13800*	2761	4029	4175	4221	4266	4311
14400*	2869	4186	4586	4636	4685	4735
15000*	2976	4342	4996	5051	5105	5159
15600*	3079	4491	5321	5466	5524	5583
16200*	3179	4635	5490	5877	5940	6003
16800*	3278	4780	5660	6254	6355	6423
17400*	3378	4924	5830	6442	6771	6843
18000*	3478	5069	5999	6629	7186	7262
18600*	3578	5213	6169	6816	7389	7682
19200*	3678	5358	6339	7004	7592	8102
19800*	3778	5502	6508	7191	7796	8341
20400*	3878	5647	6678	7378	7999	8558
21000*	3977	5790	6847	7565	8201	8774
21600*	4076	5933	7015	7750	8402	8989
22200	4176	6075	7182	7936	8602	9204
22800	4275	6216	7345	8116	8798	9413
23400	4373	6357	7509	8297	8994	9623
24000	4471	6498	7672	8478	9190	9832
24600	4570	6639	7836	8658	9386	10042
25200	4668	6780	8000	8839	9582	10251
25800	4767	6920	8163	9020	9778	10461
26400	4865	7061	8327	9200	9974	10670
27000	4963	7202	8490	9381	10170	10880
27600	5054	7332	8642	9548	10351	11074
28200	5135	7448	8776	9697	10512	11246
28800	5216	7564	8911	9845	10673	11418
29400	5297	7678	9045	9995	10833	11592
30000	5377	7792	9179	10143	10994	11764
30600	5456	7907	9313	10291	11154	11936
31200	5535	8022	9447	10439	11315	12107
31800	5615	8136	9581	10587	11476	12279
32400	5694	8251	9715	10736	11636	12451
33000	5774	8366	9849	10884	11797	12623
33600	5853	8480	9983	11032	11957	12794
34200	5933	8595	10117	11180	12118	12966
34800	6012	8709	10251	11328	12279	13138
35400	6091	8824	10385	11476	12439	13310
36000	6171	8939	10519	11624	12600	13482
36600	6250	9053	10653	11772	12761	13653
37200	6330	9168	10787	11920	12921	13825
37800	6406	9275	10913	12058	13071	13988
38400	6447	9335	10984	12137	13156	14079
39000	6489	9395	11055	12215	13242	14170
39600	6530	9455	11126	12294	13328	14261
40200	6571	9515	11197	12373	13413	14353
40800	6613	9575	11268	12451	13499	14444
41400	6653	9634	11338	12529	13583	14534
42000	6694	9693	11409	12607	13667	14624
42600	6735	9752	11479	12684	13752	14714
43200	6776	9811	11549	12762	13836	14804
43800	6817	9871	11619	12840	13921	14894
44400	6857	9930	11690	12917	14005	14985
45000	6898	9989	11760	12995	14090	15075
45600	6939	10049	11830	13073	14174	15165

Combined Gross Income	One Child	Two Children	Three Children	Four Children	Five Children	Six Children
46200	6978	10103	11879	13146	14251	15250
46800	7013	10150	11949	13203	14313	15316
47400	7048	10197	12000	13260	14375	15382
48000	7083	10245	12052	13317	14437	15448
48600	7117	10292	12103	13374	14498	15514
49200	7152	10339	12155	13432	14560	15580
49800	7187	10386	12206	13489	14622	15646
50400	7222	10433	12258	13546	14684	15712
51000	7257	10481	12309	13603	14745	15778
51600	7291	10528	12360	13660	14807	15844
52200	7326	10575	12412	13717	14869	15910
52800	7361	10622	12463	13774	14931	15976
53400	7396	10669	12515	13832	14992	16042
54000	7431	10717	12566	13889	15054	16108
54600	7468	10765	12622	13946	15120	16178
55200	7524	10845	12716	14050	15232	16298
55800	7582	10929	12814	14159	15350	16425
56400	7643	11016	12918	14273	15474	16558
57000	7704	11104	13021	14388	15598	16691
57600	7765	11192	13125	14502	15722	16824
58200	7825	11277	13225	14613	15842	16953
58800	7883	11361	13324	14723	15961	17079
59400	7941	11445	13423	14832	16079	17206
60000	8000	11529	13522	14941	16197	17333
60600	8058	11612	13620	15050	16315	17460
61200	8116	11696	13719	15160	16433	17587
61800	8175	11780	13818	15269	16552	17714
62400	8233	11864	13917	15378	16670	17840
63000	8288	11945	14011	15481	16783	17958
63600	8344	12024	14102	15582	16893	18075
64200	8399	12103	14194	15683	17002	18193
64800	8454	12183	14285	15784	17111	18310
65400	8510	12262	14376	15885	17220	18427
66000	8565	12341	14468	15986	17330	18544
66600	8620	12421	14559	16087	17439	18661
67200	8676	12500	14650	16188	17548	18778
67800	8731	12579	14741	16289	17657	18895
68400	8786	12659	14833	16390	17767	19012
69000	8842	12738	14924	16491	17876	19129
69600	8897	12817	15015	16592	17985	19246
70200	8953	12897	15107	16693	18094	19363
70800	9008	12974	15196	16791	18201	19476
71400	9060	13047	15281	16885	18302	19585
72000	9111	13120	15366	16979	18804	19694
72600	9163	13194	15451	17073	18506	19803
73200	9214	13267	15356	17167	18608	19912
73800	9266	13340	15621	17261	18709	20021
74400	9318	13413	15706	17355	18811	20130
75000	9369	13487	15791	17449	18913	20239
75600	9421	13560	15876	17543	19015	20347
76200	9473	13633	15961	17636	19116	20456
76800	9524	13707	16046	17730	19218	20565
77400	9576	13780	16131	17824	19320	20674
78000	9627	13583	16216	17918	19422	20783
78600	9679	13927	16300	18012	19523	20892
79200	9731	14000	16385	18106	19625	21001
79800	9782	14073	16470	18200	19727	21109
80400	9834	14147	16555	18294	19829	21218
81000	9885	14220	16640	18387	19930	21326
81600	9936	14292	16723	18480	20030	21434
82200	9987	14364	16807	18573	20131	21541
82800	10038	14439	16891	18665	20235	21651
83400	10090	14514	16979	18762	20340	21763
84000	10142	14589	17066	18859	20444	21875
84600	10194	14663	17154	18956	20549	21987
85200	10246	14738	17241	19052	20653	22099

Combined Gross Income	One Child	Two Children	Three Children	Four Children	Five Children	Six Children
85800	10298	14813	17329	19149	20758	22211
86400	10350	14887	17417	19246	20863	22323
87000	10403	14962	17504	19343	20967	22435
87600	10455	15037	17592	19440	21072	22547
88200	10507	15111	17679	19537	21176	22659
88800	10559	15186	17767	19633	21281	22771
89400	10611	15261	17855	19730	21386	22883
90000	10663	15335	17942	19827	21490	22995
90600	10715	15410	18030	19924	21595	23107
91200	10767	15458	18118	20021	21700	23219
91800	10819	15559	18205	20118	21804	23331
92400	10872	15634	18293	20215	21909	23443
93000	10924	15709	18380	20311	22013	23555
93600	10976	15783	18468	20408	22118	23667
94200	11028	15858	18556	20505	22223	23779
94800	11080	15933	18643	20602	22327	23891
95400	11132	16007	18731	20699	22432	24003
96000	11184	16082	18818	20796	22536	24115
96600	11236	16157	18906	20892	22641	24227
97200	11289	16231	18994	20989	22746	24339
97800	11341	16306	19081	21086	22850	24451
98400	11393	16381	19169	21183	22955	24563
99000	11446	16450	19255	21279	23062	24676
99600	11491	16516	19334	21366	23156	24777
100200	11536	16583	19413	21453	23250	24878
100800	11581	16649	19491	21539	23345	24978
101400	11625	16714	19569	21625	23437	25077
102000	11670	16779	19646	21710	23530	25177
102600	11714	16844	19724	21796	23623	25276
103200	11759	16909	19801	21881	23715	25375
103800	11803	16974	19879	21967	23808	25475
104400	11847	17039	19956	22052	23901	25574
105000	11892	17104	20034	22138	23994	25673
105600	11934	17167	20108	22220	24083	25769
106200	11979	17232	20186	22305	24176	25868
106800	12023	17297	20263	22391	24269	25968
107400	12068	17362	20341	22476	24361	26067
108000	12110	17425	20415	22559	24451	26162
108600	12155	17490	20493	22644	24543	26262
109200	12199	17555	20570	22730	24636	26361
109800	12243	17620	20648	22815	24729	26460
110400	12286	17683	20722	22897	24818	26556
111000	12331	17748	20800	22983	24911	26655
111600	12375	17813	20877	23068	25004	26755
112200	12419	17878	20955	23154	25096	26854
112800	12462	17941	21029	23236	25186	26949
113400	12506	18006	21107	23322	25278	27049
114000	12551	18071	21184	23407	25371	27148
114600	12595	18136	21262	23493	25464	27247
115200	12640	18202	21339	23578	25557	27347
115800	12682	18264	21414	23660	25646	27442
116400	12727	18329	21491	23746	25739	27542
117000	12771	18394	21569	23831	25832	27641
117600	12815	18460	21646	23917	25924	27740
118200	12858	18522	21721	23999	26013	27836
118800	12902	18587	21798	24084	26106	27935
119400	12947	18652	21876	24170	26199	28034
120000	12991	18718	21953	24256	26292	28134
120600	13034	18780	22028	24338	26381	28229
121200	13078	18845	22105	24423	26474	28329
121800	13123	18910	22183	24509	26567	28428
122400	13167	18976	22260	24594	26659	28527
123000	13210	19038	22335	24676	26749	28623
123600	13254	19103	22412	24762	26841	28722
124200	13299	19168	22490	24847	26934	28821
124800	13343	19234	22567	24933	27027	28921

Combined Gross Income	One Child	Two Children	Three Children	Four Children	Five Children	Six Children
125400	13386	19296	22642	25015	27116	29106
126000	13430	19361	22719	25101	27209	29115
126600	13474	19426	22797	25186	27302	29215
127200	13519	19492	22874	25272	27395	29314
127800	13561	19554	22949	25354	27484	29410
128400	13606	19619	23026	25439	27576	29509
129000	13650	19684	23104	25525	27669	29608
129600	13695	19750	23181	25610	27762	29708
130200	13739	19815	23259	25696	27855	29807
130800	13783	19879	23335	25780	27946	29905
131400	13828	19945	23414	25868	28041	30007
132000	13874	20012	23494	25955	28136	30108
132600	13919	20079	23573	26043	28231	30210
133200	13963	20143	23649	26127	28323	30308
133800	14008	20210	23729	26215	28418	30410
134400	14054	20276	23808	26302	28513	30511
135000	14099	20343	23887	26390	28608	30613
135600	14143	20407	23964	26474	28699	30711
136200	14188	20474	24043	26561	28794	30813
136800	14234	20541	24123	26649	28889	30914
137400	14279	20607	24202	26737	28984	31016
138000	14323	20671	24278	26821	29075	31114
138600	14368	20738	24358	26908	29170	31215
139200	14414	20805	24437	26996	29265	31317
139800	14459	20872	24516	27083	29361	31419
140400	14503	20936	24593	27168	29452	31517
141000	14549	21002	24672	27255	29547	31618
141600	14594	21069	24751	27343	29642	31720
142200	14639	21136	24831	27430	29737	31822
142800	14683	21200	24907	27515	29828	31920
143400	14729	21267	24986	27602	29232	32021
144000	14774	21333	25066	27690	30018	32123
144600	14820	21400	25145	27777	31113	32225
145200	14865	21467	25225	27865	30208	32327
145800	14909	21531	25301	27949	30300	32424
146400	14963	21596	25377	28041	30396	32526
147000	15006	21659	25452	28124	30486	32622
147600	15049	21722	25527	28207	30576	32718
148200	15090	21782	25599	28286	30662	32810
148800	15133	21845	25674	28369	30752	32907
149400	15176	21908	25749	28452	30842	33003
150000	15218	21971	25823	28534	30931	33099

* Use below chart until July 1, 1994, or a later date as specified by statute:

Combined Gross Income	One Child	Two Children	Three Children	Four Children	Five Children	Six Children
6000	240	372	468	528	576	612
7200	1068	1308	1428	1608	1656	1692
8400	1884	2244	2388	2688	2736	2784
9600	2052	3180	3348	3768	3816	3876
10800	2208	3432	4308	4848	4896	4968
12000	2439	3684	4620	5208	5676	6060
13200	2654	3924	4920	5556	6048	6456
14400	2869	4186	5208	5880	6408	6840
15600	3079	4491	5508	6204	6756	7224
16800	3278	4780	5796	6528	7116	7608
18000	3478	5069	6072	6840	7464	7980
19200	3678	5358	6339	7140	7788	8352
20400	3878	5647	6678	7440	8112	8688
21600	4078	5935	7018	7755	8448	9036

EXHIBIT B

WORKSHEET
_____**YOUR**_____ COUNTY DOMESTIC RELATIONS COURT
CHILD SUPPORT COMPUTATION
SOLE RESIDENTIAL PARENT OR SHARED PARENTING ORDER

Name of Parties _____**John and Mary Doe**_____ Case No. A _____

Number of minor children _____**1**_____ . The following parent was designated as the residential parent and legal custodian (disregard if shared parenting order): ____**X**____ Mother _____ Father. Father has ___**52**___ pay periods annually; mother has ___**26**___ pay periods annually.

		Column I Father	Column II Mother	Column III Combined
1a.	Annual gross income from employment OR, when determined appropriate by the court or agency, average annual gross income from employment over a resonable period of years (exclude overtime and bonuses)	$ **35,000.**	$ **12,200.**	**$47,200.**

1b. Amount of overtime and bonuses:

FATHER:		MOTHER:	
YR. 3 $ **2,000**		YR. 3 $ **0**	
YR. 2 $ **2,000**		YR. 2 $ **0**	
YR. 1 $ **2,000**		YR. 1 $ **0**	
AVERAGE $ **2,000**		AVERAGE $ **0**	

(Include in Column I and/or Column II the average of the three years or the year 1 amount, whichever is less, IF THERE EXISTS A RESONABLE EXPECTATION THAT THE TOTAL EARNINGS FROM OVERTIME AND/OR BONUSES DURING THE CURRENT CALENDAR YEAR WILL MEET OR EXCEED THE AMOUNT THAT IS THE LOWER OF THE AVERAGE OF THE THREE YEARS OR THE YEAR 1 AMOUNT. IF, HOWEVER, THERE EXISTS A REASONABLE EXPECTATION THAT THE TOTAL EARNINGS FROM OVERTIME/BONUSES DURING THE CURRENT CALENDAR YEAR WILL BE LESS THAN THE LOWER OF THE AVERAGE OF THE THREE YEARS OR THE YEAR 1 AMOUNT, INCLUDE ONLY THE AMOUNT REASONABLY EXPECTED TO BE EARNED THIS YEAR.) ....

		Father	Mother	Combined
	(1b continued)	**2,000**	**0**	
2.	Annual income from interest and dividends (whether or not taxable)	**0**	**0**	
3.	Annual income from unemployment compensation	**0**	**0**	
4.	Annual income from workers' compensation or disability insurance benefits	**0**	**0**	
5.	Other annual income (identify)	**0**	**0**	
6.	Total annual gross income (add lines 1-5)	**37,000.**	**12,200.**	**$49,200.**
7.	Annual court-ordered support paid for other children	**0**	**0**	
8.	Adjustment for minor children born to either parent and another parent, which children are living with this parent (number of children times federal income tax exemption less child support received for the year, not to exceed the federal tax exemption)	**0**	**0**	
9.	Annual court-ordered spousal support paid to a former spouse	**0**	**0**	
10.	Amount of local income taxes actually paid or estimated to be paid	**0**	**0**	
11.	For self-employed individuals, deduct 5.6% of adjusted gross income or the actual marginal difference between the actual rate paid by the self-employed individual and the F.I.C.A. rate	**0**	**0**	
12.	For self-employed individuals, deduct ordinary and necessary business expenses	**0**	**0**	
13.	Total gross income adjustments (add lines 7-12)	**0**	**0**	
14.	Adjusted annual gross income (subtract line 13 from 6)	**37,000.**	**12,200.**	
15.	Combined annual income that is basis for child support order (add line 14, Col. I and Col. II)			$ **49,200.**
16.	Percentage of parent's income to total income:			
	a. Father (divide line 14, Col. I by line 15, Col. III)	**75** %		
	b. Mother (divide line 14, Col. II by line 15, Col. III)		**25** % = 100%	

- 1 -

47   Child Support Payment Worksheet

PAGE 2/Worksheet-Sole Residential Parent or Shared Parenting Order	Column I Father	Column II Mother	Column III Combined
17. Basic combined child support obligation (Refer to basic child support schedule in division (D) of section 3113.215 of the Revised Code; in the first column of the schedule, locate the sum that is nearest to the combined annual income listed in line 15, Col. III of this worksheet, then refer to the column of the schedule that corresponds to the number of children in this family. If the income of the parents is more than one sum and less than another sum in the first column of the schedule, you may calculate the basic combined child support obligation based upon the obligation for those two sums.)			$7,152.
18. Annual child care expenses that are work, employment training, or education related, as approved by the court or agency (deduct the tax credit from annual cost, whether or not claimed)	0	3,000.	
19. Marginal, out-of-pocket costs, necessary to provide for health insurance for the children who are the subject of this order	2,400.	0	
20. Total child care and medical expenses (Add lines 18 and 19, Col. I and II)	2,400.	3,000.	
21. Combined annual child support obligation for this family (Add lines 17 and 20, Col. I and II)			$12,552.
22. Annual support obligation/parent: a. Father (multiply line 21, Col. III, by line 16a) .... b. Mother (multiply line 21, Col. III, by line 16b)	9,414.	3,138.	
23. Adjustment for actual expenses paid for annual child care expenses and marginal, out-of-pocket costs, necessary to provide for health insurance (enter number from line 18 or 19 if applicable)	2,400.	3,000.	
24. Actual annual obligation (Subtract line 23 from Line 22a or 22b)	7,014.	138.	
25. Gross household income per party after exchange of child support (add lines 14 and 24, Col. I or II for residential parent or, in the case of shared parenting order, the parent to whom child support will be paid; subtract line 24 Col. I or II from line 14 for parent who is not the residential parent or, in the case of shared parenting order, the parent who will pay child support)	29,986.	19,214.	
26. Comments, rebuttal, or adjustments to correct figures in lines 24, Col. I and 24, Col. II if they would be unjust or inappropriate and would not be in best interest of the child or children (specific facts to support adjustments must be included	7,014.		

NONE

27. Final figure (this amount reflects final annual child support obligation)	7,014.	FATHER/MOTHER/OBLIGOR	
28. For Decree: child support per month (divide obligor's annual shares, line 27, by 12 and by number of children)	584.50	per child, per month	
29. For deduction order: child support per pay period (calculate support per pay period from figure on line 28) plus appropriate poundage	134.88	per week (1 child)	

Calculations have been reviewed.

Signatures: _____ **Father's Signature** _____

Father - (I do/do not consent)

Sworn to before me and subscribed in my presence this _____ day of _____ , 19 _____

_____ **Notary Signature** _____

Notary Public

_____ **Mother's Signature** _____

Mother - (I do/do not consent)

Sworn to before me and subscribed in my presence this _____ day of _____ , 19 _____

_____ **Notary Signature** _____

Notary Public

Exhibit C   Financial Disclosure   SAMPLE

COURT OF COMMON PLEAS
DIVISION OF DOMESTIC RELATIONS
____Hamilton_____COUNTY, OHIO

IN RE THE MARRIAGE OF:

	DATE: _____
Name: ___John Lee Doe_____ :	CASE NO. A: _____
SS #: _123-45-6789_____ 10/09/50____ :	FILE NO. E: _____
Petitioner, DOB :	
-and- :	JUDGE _____
Name: ___Mary Ann Doe_____ :	
SS #: _987-65-4321_____ 11/17/54____ :	**FINANCIAL DISCLOSURE**
Petitioner, DOB :	**O.R.C. 3113.21 (C)**

Now comes _____John Lee Doe_____ and, after being duly cautioned and sworn, says:
Obligor

1. I ☒ am employed.
   ☐ am not employed.   My employer is ____**Acme Corporation**_____

   __6244 Oak Lane_____ **Columbus**_____ **OH**_____ **43202**____
     Employer's Payroll Address   City   State   Zip Code

   I receive ☐ 12 ☐ 24 ☐ 26 ☒ 52 paychecks per year.

2. I ☐ am ☒ am not receiving Workers' Compensation under Claim No. _____.

   ☐ am ☒ am not receiving Unemployment Compensation under Claim No. _____.

3. I ☒ do

   ☐ do not have funds on deposit in Financial Institutions. (List all funds in all accounts in any Bank, Savings & Loan, Credit Union, Regulated Investment Company, Mutual or Other Financial Institutions. Account may include one or more of the following: checking, certificate of deposit ("CD"), investment, savings, individual retirement ("IRA"), stock options, etc. USE ADDITIONAL PAGES IF NEEDED).

Name of Financial Institution	Address of Financial Institution	Account No.	Name(s) on Account	Balance as of Date of the Affidavit
_First National Bank__	_446 Main St._____ _Columbus, Oh 43201_	_6721-8724__	_John Lee Doe_	_956.00 Savings
_First National Bank__	_446 Main St._____ _Columbus, Oh 43201_	_86193-421____	_John Lee Doe__	22,000. 00 IRA_
_____	_____	_____	_____	_____

4. I have the following additional sources of income. (List sources, address and amount including but not limited to pension (public and private) annuities, allowance, sick pay, disability pay or other benefit, commissions, trusts, bonuses, profit sharing payments or distributions, lottery winnings, lump sum payments, and private Workers' Compensation payments).
   _Acme Corporation vested pension plan worth $46,000.00 in the name of John Lee Doe_____.

5. I ☐ do
   ☒ do not have other assets from which child support/spousal support can be paid or secured. (If affirmative, list all such assets on a separate sheet of paper).

____Husband's Signature_____
Affiant - Obligor

STATE OF OHIO   )
) SS:
COUNTY OF __Hamilton_____)

Sworn to and subscribed in my presence this _____ day of _____, 20____.

Notary Public ____**Notary's Signature**_____

I hereby acknowledge receipt of a copy of this affidavit _____ **Wife's Signature**_____
Obligee

SAMPLE Support Deduction Order — Exhibit D

COURT OF COMMON PLEAS
DIVISION OF DOMESTIC RELATIONS
___FRANKLIN_____COUNTY, OHIO

_ John Lee Doe_____

Plaintiff / Petitioner   **X** Obligor ☐ Obligee

Enter ____**Court Assigned**_____

___123-45-6789_____10/09/50____

SS#   DOB

Date _____

-vs / and-

Case No. A _____**Court Assigned**_____

__Mary Ann Doe_____

File No. E _____

Defendant / Petitioner   ☐ Obligor **X** Obligee

___987-65-4321_____11/17/54___

SS#   DOB

Judge _____

TO:

X Employer (D)(1)/Employer Paying Workers' Compensation (D)(2)

☐ Bureau of Workers' Compensation (D)(2)

☐ Financial Institution (D)(5)

☐ Public Pension System (D)(3)

☐ Other (D)(4) _____

X SUPPORT DEDUCTION ORDER
☐ ORDER FOR MODIFICATION OF
SUPPORT DEDUCTION ORDER
O.R.C. 3113.21 (D)

X You are hereby ordered to comply in the following manner:

☐ You are hereby ordered to MODIFY the prior Order of this Court in the following manner:

PURSUANT to Civil Rule 75(B)(3), as the employer/income withholder of _____**John Lee Doe**_____, (hereinafter referred to as the Obligor) Account/Claim No. ____**647-89-41__(Court Assigned)**_____ you are hereby joined as a party to this action and are ordered to withhold from the personal earnings, benefits or funds of the Obligor in the sume of $___**91.80**_____ which includes poundage every **week**___ for support until further order. To defray expenses in complying with this order, an employer, including an employer paying Workers' Compensation benefits, may deduct an additional sum not to exceed 1% of the amount withheld from personal earnings of the Obligor or $2.00 whichever is greater. A Financial Institution my deduct a fee of $5.00 or a fee not to exceed the lowest rate, if any, charged for a similar debit transaction, whichever is less. Any Deducting Organization under O.R.C. 3113.21 D (3) and (4) may deduct a fee of $2.00 or 1% of the deduction, whichever is less.

THE DEDUCTING ORGANIZATION IS ORDERED to begin withholding NO LATER THAN ONE WEEK FROM RECEIPT OF THIS ORDER or on _____ but you do not have to alter your pay cycle.

THE DEDUCTING ORGANIZATION IS ORDERED to forward the payment IMMEDIATELY UPON WITHHOLDING to the __**Franklin**_____ COUNTY Child Support Enforcement Agency (BUREAU OF SUPPORT), ____**Franklin**_____ COUNTY COURTHOUSE, ___**Columbus**_____ OHIO __**43201**_____. The employee's name and file number shall accompany the check.

To the extent possible, the Deducting Organization shall deduct the above amount notwithstanding the limitations of Sections 2329.66, 2329.70, 2716.02, 2716.05, 2716.13 and 4123.67 of the Ohio Revised Code. However, in no case shall the amount withheld including fees, exceed the maximum amount permitted under Section 303(b) of the "Consumer Credit Protection Act", 15 U.S.C. 1673(b).

IT IS ORDERED that the Obligor is personally responsible to make payments as indicated above by cash, certified check or money order to the Child Support Enforcement Agency (Bureau of Support) until such time is as said amount is withheld from Obligor's funds.

IT IS FURTHER ORDERED that said Deducting Organization shall notify the Child Support Enforcement Agency in writing within ten (10) days of the occurrence of any of the events listed on the reverse side of said Deduction Organization's copy of this order;

THE DEDUCTING ORGANIZATION IS FURTHER ORDERED to notify the Child Support Enforcement Agency immediately of any lump sum payments of $500.00 or more to be paid to the Obligor, hold the lump sum payment for thirty (30) days after the date that it is due before making payment, and upon Order of the Court pay any specified amount of the lump sum payment to the __**Franklin**_____ COUNTY CHILD SUPPORT ENFORCEMENT AGENCY (BUREAU OF SUPPORT). Notice shall be given to the Child Support Enforcement Agency no later than 45 days before payment is due unless the determination is made in less than 45 days, then immediately.

Failure to send any notification required by the Court is a Contempt of Court. In addition to all powers this Court has to punish contempt the employer/Other deducting organization may also be subject to a fine of not more than $200.00.

A Deducting Organization's failure to withhold in compliance with this order could subject the employer to liability for the amount that was not witheld pursuant to O.R.C. 3113.213.

The law provides penalties for an employer who discharges, refuses to hire or disciplines any employee based upon an order to withhold personal earnings. THIS ORDER APPLIES TO ALL SUBSEQUENT EMPLOYERS AND/OR OTHER SOURCES OF INCOME OF THE OBLIGOR, as determined by the Child Support Enforcement Agency. Upon the commencement of employment the Court may cancel any prior 3113.21 order and issue a Deduction Order to Obligor's employer.

IT IS FURTHER ORDERED that each party to this action shall notify the Child Support Enforcement Agency, in writing, of their respective current mailing address and current residence address, and each party shall notify the court IMMEDIATELY IN WRITING of any change in either of these addresses. This duty to notify the Court of any change in address shall continue until further notice from this Court. You are notified that service of future notices shall be deemed complete upon the posting of ordinary mail to your last known address on record with the CHILD SUPPORT ENFORCEMENT AGENCY.

IT IS FURTHER ORDERED that the obligor and obligee shall immediately notify the Child Support Enforcement Agency in writing of any of the events on the reverse side of their copy of this order.

INSTRUCTIONS TO THE CLERK

YOU ARE DIRECTED TO MAIL A COPY OF THIS ORDER TO THE DEDUCTING ORGANIZATION AND TO THE OBLIGOR AND OBLIGEE BY ORDINARY MAIL, WITH PROOF OF MAILING, UNLESS THEY HAVE ACKNOWLEDGED RECEIPT BY SIGNATURE BELOW.

☐ Deducting Organization

____**ACME Corporation**_____

_____**6422 West Weber Ave.**_____

_____**Columbus, OH 43236**_____

☐ Obligor

_____**John Lee Doe**_____

_____**100 West Broad St.**_____

_____**Columbus, OH 43026**_____

☐ Obligee

_____**Mary Ann Doe**_____

_____**200 South High St.**_____

_____**Columbus, OH 43021**_____

Current order of support is $ ___**91.80**____ **wk**/mo. plus $ _____**-0-**____ wk/mo. past due support.

EXHIBIT E

John Doe
_____
Plaintiff/Petitioner   ☒Obligor ☐Obligee

123-45-6789   10/09/50
_____
SS#   DOB

-vs- / -and-

Mary Doe
_____
Defendant/Petitioner   ☐Obligor ☒Obligee

234-56-7890   11/17/54
_____
SS#   DOB

Enter _____

Date _____

Case No. A _____

File No. E. _____

Judge _____

DEPENDENT HEALTH CARE ORDER
(Obligor)
O.R.C. 3113.217

SAMPLE

DESIGNATED INSURER _____ John Doe _____

WHEREAS, the Court finds that health insurance coverage for the named child(ren) is available to the Obligor at a reasonable cost and that the Obligor has been ordered to secure/maintain health insurance coverage for the child(ren),

IT IS THEREFORE ORDERED THAT:

1. The following group health insurance and health care policies, contracts and plans are available at a reasonable cost to the Obligor or Obligee (Include name of insurer that issues each policy, contract or plan):

National Health Insurance Company   Policy Number 910385-23-674

2. Obligor shall designate (list full names and birth dates of children) _____
John Doe Jr.   3/15/76

_____ as dependents eligible for health insurance coverage in the group health insurance policy offered (i) by Obligor's Employer or (ii) through a group health care policy, contract, or plan available to Obligor and as indicated above within thirty (30) days from the date of this order.

3. Obligor shall provide the insurance company with a copy of this order. Obligor shall within thirty (30) days of the issuance of this order furnish written proof to the Child Support Enforcement Agency that the coverage has been obtained, that the insurer has been provided with a copy of this order, and that Obligee has been provided with all documents/information as set forth in paragraph 4 below.

4. Obligor shall supply Obligee with (i) insurance forms necessary to receive payment, reimbursement or other benefits, (ii) necessary insurance cards, and (iii) information regarding the benefits, limitations, and exclusions of the health insurance coverage.

5. (a) Obligee shall be responsible for the first $200.00 per calendar year per child to a maximum amount of $600.00 per calendar year (for three or more children) for all uninsured medical, dental, hospital, prescription, optical, psychological, psychiatric and orthodontic expenses including co-payments and deductibles (designated "ordinary"), or (other agreement or order)

_____

(b) Costs of remaining uninsured (designated "extraordinary") expenses, including additional co-payments and/or deductibles under the health insurance plan for the child(ren), shall be shared by Obligor and Obligee in the following amounts: Obligor 50% and Obligee 50% or (other agreement or order)

_____

6. Obligor shall be entitled to secure a second opinion at his/her own expense for all psychological, psychiatric and orthodontic treatment of a non-emergency nature.

7. The insurer of Obligor shall reimburse directly to ☐Obligor ☒Obligee the amount of out of pocket medical, optical, hospital, dental, prescription or other reimbursable expenses covered under the policy and paid for by the named person on behalf of the insured child(ren) upon filing of the necessary insurance claims forms. The insurer may continue to make payment for medical, optical, hospital, dental or prescription services directly to any health care provider in accordance with the applicable health insurance or health care policy, contract or plan.

8. Pursuant to O.R.C. 3113.217 (E), this order is binding upon the Obligor and Obligee, their employers, and any insurer that provides health insurance for them or their child(ren).

9. If the Obligor fails to provide health insurance coverage for the child(ren) within 30 days as ordered or to comply within 30 days with any of the foregoing orders, the Child Support Enforcement Agency shall notify the Court in writing of the failure to comply. Upon receipt of the notice from the agency, the Court shall issue an order to the employer. The employer, upon written order of the Court, is required to take whatever action is necessary to make application to enroll the Obligor in any available group health insurance policy or health care policy with coverage for the child(ren) who are the subject of the child support order, to submit a copy of this order for health insurance coverage to the insurer at the time that the employer makes application to enroll the child(ren) in the health insurance or health care policy contract or plan, and, if the Obligor's application is accepted, to deduct any additional amount from the Obligor's earnings necessary to pay the additional cost for that health insurance coverage.

10. During the time that this order is in effect, and after the employer has received a copy of this order, the employer of the Obligor who is the subject of the order shall comply with the order and, upon written request from the Obligee or agency, shall release to the Obligee and the Child Support Enforcement Agency all information about the Obligor's health insurance coverage that is necessary to ensure compliance with this section or any order issued under this section, including, but not limited to, the name and address of the insurer and any policy, plan, or contract number. Any information provided by an employer pursuant to this division shall be used only for the purpose of the enforcement of an order issued pursuant to O.R.C. 3113.217.

11. Any employer who receives a copy of an order issued under O.R.C. 3113.217 shall notify the Child Support Enforcement Agency of any change in or the termination of the Obligor's health insurance coverage that is maintained pursuant to an order issued under this section.

12. Any insurer who receives a copy of an order issued under O.R.C. 3113.217 shall comply with that section, and any order issued under that section, regardless of the residence of the child(ren).

INSTRUCTIONS TO THE CLERK

YOU ARE DIRECTED TO MAIL A COPY OF THIS ORDER TO THE EMPLOYER AND TO THE OBLIGOR AND OBLIGEE BY ORDINARY MAIL, WITH PROOF OF MAILING, UNLESS THEY HAVE ACKNOWLEDGED RECEIPT BY SIGNATURE BELOW.

☐Employer of Obligor	☐Obligor	☐Obligee
Acme Corporation	John Doe	Mary Doe
6422 Oak Avenue	100 Main Street	200 West Avenue
Yourtown, Ohio 40021	His City, Ohio 40012	Her City, Ohio 40(
	Telephone No. 123-4567	Telephone No. 765-4300

51   Child Health Care Order

Part Two

How To Do Your Dissolution

1

How To Use The Forms

This LawPak publication contains one original of each of the forms you will need to file with the court to obtain a dissolution of marriage. In addition you will need to contact the Domestic Relations Clerk of Courts within your county to determine whether there may be additional local county forms which are required for a dissolution such as a multiple copy child support deduction order or health care order, social questionnaire, or a county form for reporting income and expenses. You must request these local county forms from the clerk of courts and their telephone numbers by county are listed in the appendix. The local forms are usually self explanatory and simple to complete.

In the following pages you will find SAMPLES of completed forms. These samples are to serve only as a guide or reference to assist you when completing your own dissolution forms. You and your spouse must first decide which items to be answered are appropriate for you and fill in the appropriate information carefully. If certain information within a blank or clause does not apply to you simple type N/A in the blank space for "non-applicable"..

BEFORE YOU BEGIN **TYPING** THE BLANK COURT FORMS WE STRONGLY SUGGEST THAT YOU MAKE COPIES OF ALL THE BLANK COURT FORMS **BEFORE** YOU ATTEMPT COMPLETING THE INFORMATION ON THE COURT FORM. THIS WAY IF YOU MAKE MISTAKES ON THE BLANK COURT FORMS BY ACCIDENT OR YOU LATER CHANGE YOUR MIND CONCERNING INFORMATION CONTAINED ON THE FORM, YOU CAN USE THE ORIGINAL BLANK FORMS TO MAKE NEW ADDITIONAL COPIES.

General rules when completing the blank court forms:

1. PHOTOCOPY all the blank forms **before** you attempt to complete any information on the form. Keep the original blank forms as reference TO MAKE A NEW COPY should you make mistakes.

2. TYPE your final draft and **carefully** proofread each form to be sure all information is correct.

3. USE FULL NAMES on all court papers. Be consistent and names should appear exactly the same on each form including signatures. Use names in their normal order, first name first, then middle name, then last name. Use the wife's full married name unless a form requests her maiden name.

4. The court will always keep the original of each form. You will need a copy for yourself and one copy for your spouse. Several counties require the original and two copies. Type each form neatly, check for errors and then have the desired number of copies made. You should make at least five additional copies.

5. BE THOROUGH and give the requested information on the court form. If information is not complete or left off a form the court may view your motives with suspicion.

6. BE HONEST and accurate as possible when completing the court forms. At certain places on the court forms you will write your signature on a signature line. Signing these court forms has the same effect as an oath or sworn statement.

2
Local County Forms And Guidelines

Local dissolution forms have not been standardized from county to county in Ohio. Each county can require certain local forms that only the clerk of courts for domestic relations in your county can supply to you. We do not attempt to maintain all these local forms for the eighty-eight Ohio counties since these local forms are in constant change.

 We suggest you telephone your clerk of court for domestic relations in your county (county listing with telephone numbers in the appendix) and ask what local forms are required to file with a dissolution proceeding; whether the court can mail them to you or must you personally pick them up and if so, where, and whether there is a court fee charged in order to receive these blank forms. Also ask when the form must be filed and with whom since most of these local forms are filed at the same time you file the Petition and Separation Agreement.

In addition ask the following:
- the current filing fee for the Court to process the paperwork for a dissolution of marriage.
- the required number of copies of your court papers (Petition, Separation Agreement and Decree and whether the forms are required to be in a specific order when filing.
- does the court require your court forms be signed in the presence of a notary public who will witness you signatures on the court forms.

- if you have minor children of the marriage ask the clerk of courts if both parties must attend parental education classes before a dissolution will be granted. If the classes are required by the court ask when and where you and your spouse may attend.

Addition guidelines for court forms:
- If the amount of space allocated on the printed form is not sufficient to list all the necessary information such as your debts and property, use a blank sheet of paper and label it "Continuation Page #1, put your full name on the page and list the remaining information and attach it to the printed form.

> EXAMPLE: Continuation Page #1
> In re: John and Mary Doe, Petitioners
> Separation Agreement, List of Debts continued
> List the remaining debts which would not fit on the printed forms

- Do not leave blank spaces on a printed form. If the question or information does not apply to you type "not applicable" in the space on the form. If the question requires a dollar amount type -0- .

The Clerks in the Domestic Relations Court **will not** be willing to give you legal advice or any information on how to complete the blank forms because they are not lawyers. It would be illegal for them to give you legal advice. They will probably tell you to go "hire a lawyer" if you begin to ask them specific legal questions. Although, they still can be very helpful in giving you information concerning the procedures in their court, filing the dissolution paperwork, and giving you copies of any required **blank** forms. Always be polite when asking questions about the court's procedures and the required forms. Although, you may get frustrated with a few court personnel because a few county courts still are not very helpful to self-helpers, but the court system is still suppose to be operated by public servants for the public good.

3

How To File Your Dissolution Forms And Receive Your Hearing Date

1. This is a very simple process. After you have completed filling out and **typing** the forms and made the necessary number of copies, fasten the pages of each set of forms together by stapling them in the upper left hand corner.

2. You and your spouse will then sign the original and the copies of the Petition, Separation Agreement and Decree in black ink where indicated on the forms. If a notary's signature is required in your county **do not** sign the court forms until you **both** are in the presence of a notary.

3. Take the originals and the necessary copies of the forms with your filing fee in cash (no personal checks) to the office of the Clerk of Courts Division of Domestic Relations in the county where you reside. As previously stated you have already called the clerks office to determine the number of copies needed and the exact filing fee.

4. Tell the clerk that you wish to file your dissolution paperwork and give the clerk the originals and copies along with your filing fee. The clerk will keep the original Petition, Separation Agreement and your other required forms. The clerk will then stamp your case number and the date filed on all the paperwork and return copies of them to you with a receipt for your filing fee. You will take the original of your Decree with you when you appear for the court hearing.

5. Ask the clerk the name of the judge or referee who has been assigned to your dissolution case and then write the name down so you will not forget it. If a judge assignment is made at a later date ask the clerk from whom this information may later be obtained.

6. Ask the clerk what steps are *required to set a hearing date*. Procedures will differ in each county. In some counties you will not have to set the hearing date; the court will set the hearing date later and notify you by mail. In other counties you may have to go to another section or department of the courthouse to receive a hearing date. Whatever the procedure within your county the clerk will be able to tell you what the procedure is for setting the hearing date for a dissolution of marriage.

Remember that the hearing date you are given cannot be less than 30 days or more than 90 days from the day you file your Petition and Separation Agreement or your case will be dismissed.

4

The Court Forms And Their Purpose

• (a) The Petition And Waiver Of Service

The Petition and Waiver of Service is the first form that you will need to complete, sign and file with the court. It includes the following information: your name, complete address, social security number, date of birth, date and place of your marriage, the six month residency requirement, a statement that you have voluntarily agreed to a dissolution of marriage, and that you are at least eighteen years of age and under no mental disability. Both you and your spouse must sign and date all forms in blank ink. You must also sign the forms in the presence of a notary if a notary's signature is a requirement in your county.

The Waiver of Service section stipulates to the court that you and your spouse consent to the court granting you a dissolution of marriage and waive the requirement of a summons process or notice sent to you by the court.

• (b) The Separation Agreement

The Separation Agreement is the most important form in your dissolution because this agreement is a legal contract between you and your wife providing for the division of all your property, debts, spousal support and makes all the necessary provisions for any minor children of the marriage. Both you and your spouse must sign and date this form in black ink. You must also sign this form in the presence of a notary if a notary's signature is a requirement in your county.

The Separation Agreement is filed with the Petition form when you file your documents with the county clerk of courts.

• (c) The Decree Of Dissolution

This is the final document that you and your spouse will present to the court at the time of your hearing. The decree is the only legal document that you present to the court that the judge or referee will sign to certify that the marriage is legally dissolved. The decree is also signed by you and your spouse in black ink.

The decree of dissolution is not presented to the court *until* your dissolution hearing. It is the document that approves your separation agreement and finalizes the dissolution of marriage. The decree is the final step in ending the marriage.

SAMPLE Petition

COURT OF COMMON PLEAS
DIVISION OF DOMESTIC RELATIONS
____FRANKLIN_____COUNTY, OHIO

IN RE THE MARRIAGE OF:

Name: _John Lee Doe_____ :
Address: _100 West Broad St._____ :
              _Columbus, Oh 43026_____ :   Case No. **_Clerk of Courts Will Assign__**
SS #:   _123-45-6789_____ :
DOB: _10/09/50_____ :
Telephone #: _(614) 123-4567_____ :
              Petitioner,   :
                            :   **PETITION FOR DISSOLUTION OF**
           -and-   :   **OF MARRIAGE AND WAIVER OF**
                            :   **SERVICE OF SUMMONS**

Name: _Mary Ann Doe_____._____ :
Address: _200 South High St._____ :
              _Columbus, Oh 43021_____ :
SS #:   _987-65-4321_____ :
DOB: _11/17/54_____ :
Telephone #: _(614) 765-4321_____ :
              Petitioner,

1. At least one of the Petitioners has been a resident of the State of Ohio for at least six (6) months or more immediately prior to filing this Petition.

2. Petitioners were married on the __29th_ day of ___December_____ __1984____, in _____**Cincinnati**_____, _____**Ohio**_____.

3. The names and dates of birth of all living minor child/ren, natural or adopted to the Petitioners are:

     Name ___**John, Jr**._____   Date of Birth _____**03/16/86**_____
     Name _____   Date of Birth _____
     Name _____   Date of Birth _____

4. A Separation Agreement, agreed to and signed by both Petitioners, which provides for a division of all property and spousal support, child support, visitation rights, and provides for a residential parent and legal custodian of the minor child/ren, where applicable, is attached hereto and incorporated herein.

5. Both Petitioners acknowledge that they have voluntarily entered into the attached Separation Agreement appended to the Petition herein; that they are satisfied with its terms; and that they seek a Dissolution of the Marriage.

6. The wife is not pregnant.

     WHEREFORE, both Petitioners request the Court to grant a Dissolution of Marriage, incorporating the attached Separation Agreement.

___**Wife's Signature**_____   ___**Husband's Signature**_____
Signature of Petitioner/Wife   Date   Signature of Petitioner/Husband   Date

WAIVER OF SERVICE OF SUMMONS

     Petitioners state that they are at least eighteen (18) years of age and not under disability, and waive service of summons herein, and consent to the Court herein granting a Decree of Dissolution of Marriage, incorporating the Separation Agreement herein.

___**Wife's Signature**_____   ___**Husband's Signature**_____
Signature of Petitioner/Wife   Date   Signature of Petitioner/Husband   Date

STATE OF OHIO   )
) SS:
COUNTY OF __**FRANKLIN**_____)
Sworn to and subscribed in my presence this _____ day of _____, 20_____.
Petition Page One   Notary Public _____**Notary's Signature**_____

SAMPLE Separation Agreement

Separation Agreement

This Separation Agreement voluntarily made and entered into by Petitioner/Wife _____**Mary**_____ __**Ann Doe**_____ hereinafter referred to as "wife", and Petitioner/Husband _____**John**_____ _____**Lee Doe**_____ hereinafter referred to as "husband", represents that:

1. The date and place of the marriage of the Petitioners are:
Date Of Marriage: _**December 29, 1984**_____ Place of Marriage: _**Cincinnati**_____, _**Ohio**_

2. The names and date of birth of all living minor children, natural or adopted, common to the Petitioners are:

Name	Date of Birth
_____John, Jr._____	____March 16, 1986_____

3. Differences have a risen between the Petitioners and we are now living separate and apart from each other.

4. The parties hereto desire to, and by this Agreement do, settle and determine and hereby provide for a division of all property belonging to the parties, spousal support, child support, visitation rights and provide for a residential parent and legal custodian of the minor children, where applicable.

NOWTHEREFORE, in consideration of the foregoing and the mutual promises and agreements hereinafter set forth, the parties agree as follows:

ARTICLE ONE: SEPARATION
Each party shall hereinafter continue to live separate and apart from the other, and neither shall annoy, molest, interfere with or harass the other in any manner, either directly or indirectly.

ARTICLE TWO: DIVISION OF PROPERTY
All property, real and personal, and whatever situated which the parties own jointly or individually, or in common with each other, shall be divided as follows:

A. REAL PROPERTY
- ☐ We have no real property.
- ☐ The husband has real property which he owned prior to marriage and the wife is waiving her claims on his real property, now and in the future.
- ☐ The wife has real property which she owned prior to marriage and the husband is waiving all his claims on her real property, now and in the future.
- ☒ The parties jointly own real property and agree that it shall be divided as follows:

__ **The real estate located at 100 West Broad Street Columbus, Ohio 43026 shall be listed for sale immediately and both parties shall , with best efforts, aid in the sale. Until said real estate is sold, husband shall be responsible for the mortgage payments on said property and shall hold wife harmless therefrom notwithstanding the filing of bankruptcy. Husband shall occupy said premises and shall be responsible for the telephone, the utilities, and any other miscellaneous expenses concerning said real estate. After the real property is sold, the profits from the sale of said real estate shall be divided as follows: the following debts and amounts shall be paid directly from the proceeds: First National Bank $40,000.00, Master Card $990.00. After the aforementioned debts and any outstanding mortgage have been paid, the net proceeds shall be divided equally between the parties.**

Separation Agreement Page One

SAMPLE Separation Agreement

B. SPOUSAL SUPPORT

☒ Neither the wife or the husband shall pay spousal support to the other party and state that all future rights to spousal support are being waived.

☐ _____ shall pay spousal support to the _____ in the amount of _____ per week, plus _____ % poundage, payable through the _____ County Bureau of Support/Support Enforcement Agency effective _____, 20 _____. Said spousal support shall terminate on _____ 20 ____ or upon the happening of the earliest of the following events: death of the spouse receiving or paying the spousal support, cohabitation with another person, or _____.

C. MOTOR VEHICLES

☐ There are no motor vehicles.

☐ Husband shall receive no motor vehicle.

☒ Husband shall receive, free and clear of any claims of the wife, all right, title and interest in the ___**1997 Ford Mustang**_____ automobile/truck. Husband shall hold wife harmless from any debts owing thereon.

☒ Husband shall also receive the following vehicles: ____**1994 Honda Motorcycle**_____.

☐ Wife shall receive no motor vehicle.

☒ Wife shall receive, free and clear of any claims of the husband, all right, title and interest in the ___**1996 Oldsmobile Cutlass**_____ automobile/truck. Wife shall hold husband harmless from any debts owing thereon.

☐ Wife shall also receive the following vehicles: _____.

D. HOUSEHOLD GOODS

☐ We agree that our household goods and possessions are already divided and we are satisfied with the division there.

☒ Husband shall receive the following household goods: ____**Color television, dining room furniture, oak bedroom furniture, and kitchen dishes** _____.

☒ Wife shall receive the following household goods: _____**Black and White television, microwave, maple bedroom furniture, and china dishes**_____.

☐ See the attached list for the division of household goods.

E. PERSONAL PROPERTY

☒ We agree that our personal property is already divided.

☐ We agree that each party may have his/her own personal property.

☐ See the attached list for the division of personal property.

F. SAVINGS ACCOUNTS

☐ We agree that our savings accounts are already divided and we are satisfied with the division,

☒ Husband shall receive the following savings account(s): _**First National Bank Acct.# 6721-8724.**

☐ Wife shall receive the following savings account(s): _____.

☐ We have no savings account.

G. CHECKING ACCOUNTS

☒ We agree that our checking accounts are already divided.

☐ Husband shall have the following checking account(s): _____.

☐ Wife shall have the following checking account(s): _____.

☐ We have no checking accounts.

SAMPLE Separation Agreement

H. CREDIT UNION ACCOUNTS AND/OR STOCKS AND/OR BONDS
- ☐ We agree that the above listed assets are already divided and we are satisfied with the division.
- ☒ Husband shall receive the following credit union accounts/stocks/bonds: _____
  __XYZ Corporation 25 Shares worth $750.00_____.
- ☐ Wife shall receive the following credit union accounts/stocks/bonds: _____
  _____.
- ☐ We do not have any credit union accounts and/or stocks and/or bonds.

I. PENSION/PROFIT SHARING AND/OR IRA'S
- ☐ We agree that the above listed assets are already divided and we are satisfied with the division.
- ☒ Husband shall receive the following pension/profit sharing and/or IRA account(s)_**vested pension Acct. with Acme Corporation worth $46,000.00 IRA with First National Bank @$22,000.**
- ☒ Wife shall receive the following pension/profit sharing and/or IRA account(s): _**vested pension__ Acct. with ABC Trucking Co. worth $18,000.00 IRA with First National Bank @ $13,000.00.**
- ☐ We do not have any pension/profit sharing and/or IRA accounts.

J. LIFE INSURANCE
- ☐ We agree that the cash value of our life insurance policies has already been divided.
- ☒ Husband shall receive the following life insurance policy, free and clear of any claims of the wife:_**Whole Life Policy with Mass Mutual Life cash value is $12,000.00**_____.
- ☐ Wife shall receive the following life insurance policy, free and clear of any claim of the husband: _____.

The parties have no life insurance policies with a cash surrender value.

K. INCOME TAX REFUNDS AND/OR LIABILITIES
- ☐ We agree that our income tax refund(s) for the last year has been divided to our satisfaction.
- ☐ Husband shall receive the following amount from our joint refund: $ _____.
- ☒ Husband shall pay the following amount $ _**440.00**___ to __**IRS**_____ for taxes.
- ☐ Wife shall receive the following amount from our joint refund: $ _____.
- ☐ Wife shall pay the following amount $ _____ to _____ for taxes.

L. DEBTS
- ☒ Husband shall pay any debts incurred by him personally from this day forward, including any debts or expenses incurred after the separation and prior to the granting of divorce or dissolution. Wife shall pay any debts incurred by her personally from this day forward, including any debts or expenses incurred after the separation and prior to the granting of divorce or dissolution.
- ☐ We have no debts.
- ☒ We agree to the payment of all debts we owe as follows:

Husband shall pay:

OBLIGATION	CREDITOR	BALANCE
1. **Washer & Dryer**	Sears	$ 550.00
2. **Mortgage**	First National Bank	$40,000.00
3. **Credit Card**	Visa acct. 4216-4456-9818-0044	$ 256.00
4. **Federal Income Taxes**	IRS due for 1999	$ 440.00
5.		

Wife shall pay:

1. **Medical Services**	Dr. CJ Anonymous	$ 698.00
2.		
3.		
4.		
5.		

Separation Agreement Page Three

SAMPLE Separation Agreement

ARTICLE THREE: NON-USE OF OTHER'S CREDIT

The parties agree that neither shall hereinafter incur any debts or obligations upon the credit of the other, and each shall indemnify the other from any debts and obligation so charged or incurred.

ARTICLE FOUR: NAME CHANGE
- ☐ The wife's name is not changed.
- ☒ The wife's name is changed to: ____**Mary Ann Johnson**_____.

ARTICLE FIVE: RESIDENTIAL PARENT AND LEGAL CUSTODIAN
- ☒ The mother shall be the sole residential parent and legal custodian of the following child/ren: _____**John Jr.**_____.
- ☒ The father shall be the sole residential parent and legal custodian of the following child/ren: _____**None**_____.
- ☐ The parties shall have shared parenting of the minor child/ren, pursuant to the Shared Parenting Plan attached hereto and incorporated herein.

A. VISITATION TIMES
- ☐ The nonresidential parent is granted reasonable visitation with the minor children, including every other weekend, every other holiday, and at least two weeks during the summer. All other visitation is subject to agreement by the parties.
- ☒ The nonresidential parent is granted the following visitation: ____**Every Tuesday from 4:00 P.M. to 9:00 A.M. every other Sunday, three weeks during the summer, and Fathers Day**_____.
  _____
  _____
  _____.
- ☐ The parties shall have visitation of the minor child/ren, pursuant to the Shared Parenting Plan attached hereto and incorporated herein.

B. CHILD(REN) SUPPORT
- ☒ The nonresidential parent shall pay to the residential parent as child support the amount of $ __**138.88**_____ per child per week. Said payments shall begin the date of the final hearing on a divorce or dissolution, and shall be payable every week thereafter, through _____ ___**Franklin**_____ County Bureau of Support (CSEA), with appropriate poundage, which payments, with current poundage of __**2**____ %, total $ __**137.58**__, or $ __**584.50**_____ per child per month, with ___**2**_____ % poundage, for a total monthly payment of $ __**596.19**__. Said child support shall continue until each said minor child has reached the age of majority (18) eighteen and attends on a full time basis any recognized and accredited high school, or otherwise is emancipated. All payments is satisfaction of said obligation which are not made through the _____**Franklin**_____ County Bureau of Support (CSEA) shall be deemed gifts.
- ☐ The _____ shall pay child support for the minor children, prusuant to the Shared Parenting Plan attached hereto and incorporated herein.

C. LIFE INSURANCE FOR THE MINOR CHILD/REN
- ☐ The parties will not maintain life insurance policies for the benefit of the minor child/ren.
- ☒ The father shall maintain the minor children of the parties as beneficiaries on his life insurance policy in the amount of $ __**100,000.00**_____ until said child/ren are emancipated.
- ☐ The mother shall maintain the minor children of the parties as beneficiaries on her life insurance policy in the amount of $ _____ until said child/ren are emancipated.
- ☐ Life insurance shall be maintained for the benefit of the minor child/ren, pursuant to the Shared Parenting Plan attached hereto and incorporated herein.

Separation Agreement Page Four

SAMPLE Separation Agreement

D. MEDICAL INSURANCE

Each parent shall have access to all the child/ren's health records.

☒ The father shall provide and maintain health insurance coverage for the benefit of the minor child/ren through his employer as specified in the attached Health Care Order for the minor child/ren of the parties. A copy of the health care insurance policy enforce for the minor children shall be continuously submitted as due to the _____**Franklin**_____ County Child Support Enforcement Agency. The designated health insurance carrier is _____**Acme**_____ _____**Corporation**_____ , whose address is _____**6244 Oak Lane**_____ _____**Columbus, Ohio 43202**_____.

☐ The mother shall provide and maintain health insurance coverage for the benefit of the minor child/ren through her employer as specified in the attached Health Care Order for the minor child/ren of the parties. A copy of the health care insurance policy enforce for the minor children shall be continuously submitted as due to the _____ County Child Support Enforcement Agency. The designated health insurance carrier is _____ ___Corporation_____ , whose address is _____.

☐ Both the mother and father shall provide and maintain dual health insurance coverage for the benefit of the minor child/ren through their employers as specified in the attached Health Care Order for the minor child/ren of the parties. A copy of the health care insurance policy enforce for the minor children shall be continuously submitted as due to the _____ County Child Support Enforcement Agency. The designated health insurance carrier of the father is_____,whose address is _____ _____.

The designated health insurance carrier of the mother is _____, whose address is _____ _____.

☐ Neither the father nor the mother have health insurance coverage available to them at a reasonable cost through a group health insurance plan offered by an employer or through any other health insurance care policy, contract, or plan for the benefit of the minor children. The father and mother will share liability for the cost of the medical and health care needs of the child/ren as specified in the attached Health Care Order.

☐ The _____ shall provide health insurance coverage for the benefit of the minor child/ren, pursuant to the Shared Parenting Plan attached hereto and incorporated herein.

E. UNCOVERED MEDICAL, DENTAL, DRUG, OPTICAL, ORTHODONTAL, PSYCHIATRIC, AND PSYCHOLOGICAL CARE

☒ Any medical, dential, drug, optical, orthodontal, psychiatric and psychological expenses not covered by health insurance for the benefit of the minor child/ren will be divided equally between the parties as specified in the attached Health Care Order.

☐ Any medical, dential, drug, optical, orthodontal, psychiatric and psychological expenses not covered by health insurance for the benefit of the minor child/ren will be covered one-hundred (100%) by the father.

☐ Any medical, dential, drug, optical, orthodontal, psychiatric and psychological expenses not covered by health insurance for the benefit of the minor child/ren will be covered one-hundred (100%) by the mother.

☐ Any medical, dential, drug, optical, orthodontal, psychiatric and psychological expenses not covered by health insurance for the benefit of the minor child/ren will be covered pursuant to the Shared parenting Plan attached hereto and incorporated herein.

Separation Agreement Page Five

SAMPLE Separation Agreement

ARTICLE SIX: TAX EXEMPTIONS

☒ The mother shall have the tax exemption for the following child/ren of the parties:
_____**John Jr.**_____.

□ The father shall have the tax exemption for the following child/ren of the parties:
_____.

□ The parties shall alternate the tax exemption for the minor child/ren of the parties. The mother shall have the tax exemption for the year _____ and the father shall have the tax exemption for the year following; the parties shall alternate the tax exemption for the child/ren from that date forward.

□ The parties shall allocate tax exemption(s) for the minor child/ren, pursuant to the Shared Parenting plan attached hereto and incorporated herein.

ARTICLE SEVEN: RECORDS

The parties agree that it is in the best interest of the minor child/ren that the nonresidential parent shall be entitled to access to all records pertaining to the child/ren as provided in R.C. 3109.05 (H), (I) and (N). The parties further agree that it is in the best interest of the minor child/ren that the nonresidential parent have equal access to any student activity of the minor child/ren as provided in R.C. 3109.051 (J).

ARTICLE EIGHT: RELOCATION

In the event that the residential parent intends to relocate their residence outside ___**Franklin**_____ County, Ohio the residential parent agrees to notify the nonresidential parent of their intent to do so in accordance with R.C. 3109.05 (G).

ARTICLE NINE: COMPLETE DISCLOSURE

The parties agree that each has made a full and complete disclosure of his or her property, and that neither has knowledge of any personal property of any kind which the parties so agreeing have any beneficial interest. If it is later discovered that either party has possession or control of, or has disposed of by gift or conveyance, any undisclosed beneficial interest in any property, such party on demand, shall transfer and assign to the other party one-half interest therein, or shall pay to the other party a sum equal to one-half of the fair market value of said beneficial interest.

ARTICLE TEN: INCORPORATION INTO DECREE

This Agreement or any amendment thereto, shall be submitted to any court in which a Petition for Dissolution of Marriage or action between the parties for a divorce may be pending, and if found by the Court to be fair and equitable, and approved or validated by the Court, shall be incorporated in the Final Decree of said Court as the order of said Court. It is understood that the parties contemplate the possibility of filing a divorce or dissolution within four (4) months after the execution of this separation agreement.

ARTICLE ELEVEN: COMPLETE AGREEMENT

This Agreement shall inure to the benefits of and be binding upon the parties and their respective heirs, executors, administrators, successors and assigns, and may not be modified or changed other than by further agreement of the parties in writing.

ARTICLE TWELVE: PERFORMANCE OF NECESSARY ACTS

Each party shall execute any and all deeds, bills of sale, or other documents, and perform any acts which may be required or necessary to carry out and effectuate any and all of the purposes and provisions herein set forth:

ARTICLE THIRTEEN: ADDITIONAL MATTERS

□ There are no additional matters that we have agreed to or need to agree to.

☒ We agree to the following additional matters: _____**The Wife shall maintain ownership of the family dog Ruff**_____
_____
_____.

SAMPLE Separation Agreement

ARTICLE FOURTEEN: EQUAL DIVISION
The parties acknowledge that each is entitled to an equal division of marital property in accordance with R.C. 3105.171, and further acknowledge that the division of marital property provided for in the Agreement is not precisely equal. Accordingly, both parties waive any right to an equal division of marital property.

ARTICLE FIFTEEN: SEVERABILITY
If any provision or clause in this Agreement is held invalid, such invalidity shall not affect any other provision of this Agreement.

ARTICLE SIXTEEN: APPLICABLE LAW
All provisions of this Agreement shall be construed and enforced in accordance with the laws of the State of Ohio.

ARTICLE SEVENTEEN: ATTORNEY WAIVER
The Petitioners are aware of their rights to have an attorney represent them in this matter, hereby with full knowledge of all assets and liabilities of the marriage and of both parties own wish; the Petitioners are waiving their right to an attorney herein and specifically request the Court to proceed with full knowledge of such waiver.

ARTICLE EIGHTEEN: EFFECTIVE DATE
This Agreement shall be effective upon the date last signed by a party to the Agreement.

_____**Wife's Signature**_____   _____**Husband's Signature**_____
Signature of Petitioner/Wife   Date   Signature of Petitioner/Husband   Date

STATE OF OHIO   )
) SS:
COUNTY OF __**FRANKLIN**_____   )

Sworn to and subscribed in my presence this _____ day of _____, 20_____.

Notary Public _____**Notary's Signature**_____

Separation Agreement Page Seven

SAMPLE Decree

COURT OF COMMON PLEAS
DIVISION OF DOMESTIC RELATIONS
__FRANKLIN_____COUNTY, OHIO

IN RE THE MATTER OF:

Name: _John Lee Doe_____   :
Address: _100 West Broad St._____   :
          _Columbus, Oh 43026_____   :   Case No. **Clerk of Courts Will Assign**
SS #:   _123-45-6789_____   :
DOB: _10/09/50_____   :   Judge _____
          Petitioner,   :
                                            :
                    -and-   :
                                            :
                                            :
Name: _Mary Ann Doe_____   :   **DECREE OF DISSOLUTION**
Address: _200 South High St._____   :   **OF MARRIAGE**
          _Columbus, Oh 43021_____   :
SS #:   _987-65-4321_____   :
DOB: _11/17/54_____   :
          Petitioner,   :

1.   This matter came on for hearing on the _____ day of _**Court Assigned Hearing Date**_, 20_____ on the Petition for Dissolution Of Marriage, filed by both Petitioners. Both parties appeared before the Court at the hearing.

2.   The Court finds that both petitioners had been notified of the hearing, in accordance with the Rules of the Court and the Ohio Rules of Civil Procedure. The Court finds that both spouses were duly served as required by law and said service is hereby approved, and the Court finds that the Court has jurisdiction of the claim for relief of the parties herein.

3.   The Court finds that at least one of the Petitioners had been a resident of the State of Ohio for at least six (6) months prior to the filing the Petition herein.

4.   The Court finds that the Petitioners were married on _**29th**_ day of _**December**_____, _**1984**, in _____**Cincinnati**_____ , _____**Ohio**_____.

5.   The Court finds that there were ___**one**_____ child(ren) born the issue of the parties, namely:

____**John Jr.**_____ born _**16th** day of ___**March**_____, __**1986**__;

_____ born _____ day of _____, _____;

_____ born _____ day of _____, _____;

_____ born _____ day of _____, _____.

6.   The Court further finds that both spouses appeared before the Court and both spouses acknowledge under oath that they voluntarily entered into the Separation Agreement appended to the Petition, that they are satisfied with its terms, and that they seek dissolution of marriage.

Decree Page One

SAMPLE Decree

UPON REVIEW OF TESTIMONY OF BOTH PETITIONERS, THE COURT HEREBY ORDERS THAT:

7.

☒ The mother shall be the sole residential parent and legal custodian of the following child (ren): ___**John Jr.**_____.

❒ The father shall be the sole residential parent and legal custodian of the following child(ren): _____.

❒ The parties shall have shared parenting of the minor child(ren). The Shared Parenting Plan is attached hereto and incorporated herein.

8. The Payor, ___**John Lee Doe**_____ shall pay as and for support of the minor children of the parties the sum of $ __**134.88**_____ per child per week, plus ___**2**__ % process fee for a total weekly payment of $ __**137.58**_____, until each minor child(ren) has reached the age of majority (18) and attends on a full time basis any recognized and accredited high school, or otherwise is emancipated.

For administrative purposes only, the order shall be administered in the amount of $ __**584.50**_____ per month per child, plus ___**2**__ % process fee, for a total monthly payment of $ __**596.19**_____. Said order shall be effective on the aforementioned hearing date. All payment shall be made through the _____ _____**Franklin**_____ County Bureau of Support / Child Support Enforcement Agency, with the requisite process fee. All payments in satisfaction of said obligation which are not made through the Bureau of Support / Child Support Enforcement Agency shall be deemed as gifts. The arrearage in the Bureau of Support Account shall be reduced to zero as of the commencement date.

9. It is further ordered that a Support Deduction Order and Additional Orders shall issue:

☒ The Court finds that the Payor is **employed** at ____**Acme Corporation**_____, whose address is ___**6244 Oak Lane Columbus, Oh 43202**_____, the Payor's social security number is _**123**___ - __**45**_ - _**6789**__, and the Payor's date of birth is _____**October 9**_____, __**1950**__. Said order is attached hereto and incorporated herein for all purposes.

❒ The Court finds that the Payor is receiving **Workers' Compensation** and the child support shall be deducted from Workers' Compensation. Said order is attached hereto and incorporated herein for all purposes.

❒ The Court finds that the Payor is receiving **Public Systems Benefits** from _____ _____, whose address is _____ _____ and the child support shall be deducted from these benefits. Said order is attached hereto and incorporated herein for all purposes.

❒ The Court finds that the Payor has an account at _____ **Financial Institution**, whose address is _____, and the account number is _____. The account is under the name _____, and the child support shall be deducted from this account. Said order is attached hereto and incorporated herein for all purposes.

❒ The Court finds that the Payot has posted a **bond** in the Clerk's Office in the amount of $ _____, for the payment of child support.

❒ The Court finds that the payor is **not employed,** not receiving Workers' Compensation, does not have funds on deposit in accounts, and does not have any assets from which child support can be paid or secured.

Decree Page Two

SAMPLE Decree

10. It is further ordered that:

☒ Neither the wife nor the husband shall pay spousal support to the other party and that all future rights to spousal support are being waived.

☐ The Payor, _____ , shall pay as spousal support for the _____ the sum of $ _____ per week, plus _____ % poundage, payable through the _____ County Bureau of Support/Support Enforcement Agency effective on the aforementioned hearing date. For administrative purposes only, the order shall be administered in the amount of $ _____ per month, plus _____ % poundage, for a total monthly payment of $ _____. Said spousal support shall terminate on _____ 20 _____, or upon the death of the spouse receiving or paying spousal support, cohabitation with another person or _____.
All payments in satisfaction of said obligation which are not made through the Bureau of Support/Support Enforcement Agency account shall be deemed as gifts. The arrearage in the Bureau of Support Account shall be reduced to zero as of the commencement date.

11. Regardles of the frequency or amount of child support payment to be made under this order, the Child Support Enforcement Agency that is required to administer the order shall administer it on a monthly basis. Payments under the order are to be made in the manner ordered by the Court and, if the payments are to be made other than on a monthly basis, the required monthly administration by the agency does not affect the frequency or the amount of the support payments to be made under the order.

12. All child support and spousal support ordered by this order shall be withheld or deducted from the wages or assets of the obligor under the order in accordance with ORC 3113.21 and shall be forwarded to the obligee under the order in accordance with ORC 3113.21 to 3113.24. The specific withholding or deduction requirements or other appropriate requirements to be used to collect the support shall be set forth in and determined by reference to the notices that are mailed by the Court or Child Support Enforcement Agency in accordance with ORC 3113.21 (A) (2) and (D) and 2301.371 or the court orders that are issued and mailed in accordance with ORC 3113.21 (D) (6), (D) (7), or (H), and shall be determined without the need for any amendment to the support order. Those notices and court orders, plus the notices provided by the court or agency that require the person who is required to pay the support to notify the Child Support Enforcement Agency of any change in his/her employment status or of any other change in the status of his/her assets, are final and are enforceable by the court.

13. EACH PARTY TO THIS SUPPORT ORDER MUST NOTIFY THE CHILD SUPPORT ENFORCEMENT AGENCY IN WRITING OF HIS OR HER CURRENT MAILING ADDRESS, CURRENT RESIDENCE ADDRESS, CURRENT RESIDENCE TELEPHONE NUMBER, CURRENT DRIVER'S LICENSE NUMBER, AND OF ANY CHANGES IN THAT INFORMATION. EACH PARTY MUST NOTIFY THE AGENCY OF ALL CHANGES UNTIL FURTHER NOTICE FROM THE COURT. IF YOU ARE THE OBLIGOR UNDER A CHILD SUPPORT ORDER AND YOU FAIL TO MAKE THE REQUIRED NOTIFICATION, YOU MAY BE FINED UP TP $50. FOR A FIRST OFFENSE, $100. FOR A SECOND OFFENSE, AND $500. FOR EACH SUBSEQUENT OFFENSE. IF YOU ARE AN OBLIGOR OR OBLIGEE UNDER ANY SUPPORT ORDER AND YOU WILLFULLY FAIL TO MAKE THE REQUIRED NOTIFICATIONS, YOU MAY BE FOUND IN CONTEMPT OF COURT AND BE SUBJECTED TO FINES UP TO $1,000. AND IMPRISONMENT FOR NOT MORE THAN 90 DAYS.

Decree Page Three

14. IF YOU ARE AN OBLIGOR AND YOU FAIL TO MAKE THE REQUIRED NOTIFICATIONS, YOU MAY NOT RECEIVE NOTICE OF THE FOLLOWING ENFORCEMENT ACTIONS AGAINST YOU: IMPOSITION OF LIENS AGAINST YOUR PROPERTY; LOSS OF YOUR PROFESSIONAL OR OCCUPATIONAL LICENSE, DRIVER'S LICENSE, OR RECREATIONAL LICENSE; WITHHOLDING FROM YOUR INCOME; ACCESS RESTRICTION AND DEDUCTION FROM YOUR ACCOUNTS IN FINANCIAL INSTITUTIONS; AND ANY OTHER ACTION PERMITTED BY LAW TO OBTAIN MONEY FROM YOU TO SATISFY YOUR SUPPORT OBLIGATION.

15. Any notices required by the above provisions should be sent to ____**Franklin**_____, County Child Support Enforcement Agency. The following Notices are hereby incorporated into this Decree by agreement of the parties, and made an ORDER of the Court:

A. RECORDS ACCESS NOTICE: Pursuant to ORC 3109.05 (H) and 3319.321 (b) (5) (a), the parties are notified as follows: Except as specifically modified or otherwise limited by court order, and subject to ORC 2301.35 (G) (2) and 3319.321 (F) both parties are entitled to equal access to any record that is related to the child/ren, including school and medical records. Any keeper of a record, public or private, who knowingly fails to comply with this order, is in contempt of Court.

B. SCHOOL ACTIVITIES NOTICE: Pursuant to ORC 3109.051 (J) the parties are notified as follows: Except as specifically modified or otherwise limited by the court, and subject to ORC 3119.321, both parties are entitled to equal access to any student activity that is related to the child/ren.

C. DAY CARE CENTER ACCESS NOTICE: Pursuant to ORC 3109.051 (I), the parties hereto are hereby notified as follows: Except as specifically modified or otherwise limited by court order, and in accordance with ORC 5104.011, both parties are entitled to equal access to any day care center that is or will be attended by the child/ren with whom visitation or parenting is granted.

D. RELOCATION NOTICE: Pursuant to ORC 3109.051 (G), the parties are notified as follows: If either parent intends to move with the child/ren to a residence other than the last residence of court record, s/he shall file a notice of intent to relocate with this Court. Except as provided in ORC 3109.051 (G) (2), (3) and (4), a copy of such notice shall be mailed by the Court to the other parent. On receipt of the notice, the Court, on its own motion or on the motion of the other parent, may schedule a hearing with notice to both parties to determine whether it is in the best interest of the child/ren to revise the visitation or parenting schedule for the child/ren.

16. It is further ordered that:
- ☐ the wife's name is not changed.
- ☒ the wife's name is changed to _____**Mary Ann Johnson**_____.

Decree Page Four

SAMPLE Decree

17. It is further ordered that the Petitioners shall pay the costs of these proceedings, and all further orders of the Court.

18. Upon review of the testimony of both spouses, the Court hereby approves the Separation Agreement and the Court grants a Decree of Dissolution of Marriage to the Petitioners, incorporating the Separation Agreement, and all Orders herein.

19. IT IS THEREFORE ORDERED, ADJUDGED AND DECREED THAT the marriage relationship, heretofore existing between the parties be, and the same is hereby terminated and held for naught, and both parties are hereby released and discharged from all obligations thereof.

Referee	Judge
Court of Common Pleas	Court of Common Pleas
__**Franklin**_____County, Ohio	___**Franklin**_____ County, Ohio

____**Wife's Signature**_____   _____**Husband's Signature**_____
Petitioner/ Wife's Signature   Petitioner/Husband's Signature

WAIVER

Now comes ____**John Lee Doe**_____ , payor, and says that s/<u>he</u> is eighteen (18) or more years of age and under no disability, that s/<u>he</u> has received a copy of the <u>child</u> / spousal <u>support order</u> and O.R.C. 3113.21 order and instructions and that s/<u>he</u> waives service of same.

_____   ____**Husband's Signature**_____
Date   Payor

Decree Page Five

SAMPLE Waiver Financial Disclosure

COURT OF COMMON PLEAS
DIVISION OF DOMESTIC RELATIONS
_____Franklin_____COUNTY, OHIO

IN RE THE MARRIAGE OF:

Name: _John Lee Doe_____   :   Date _____

SS #:   _123-45-6789_____   :

DOB: _10/09/50_____   :

           Petitioner,   :   Case No. __**Court Assigned**_____

                                          :

                  -and-   :   Judge _____

                                          :

                                          :   **WAIVER OF**

Name: _Mary Ann Doe_____   :   **FINANCIAL DISCLOSURE AFFIDAVIT**

SS #:   _987-65-4321_____   :   **NO CHILDREN OR SPOUSAL SUPPORT**

DOB: _11/17/54_____   :   **O.R.C. 3113.21(C)**

           Petitioner,

Now comes ___**John Lee Doe**_____ and _____**Mary Ann Doe**_____

                           Party   Party

and after being duly cautioned and sworn, says:

There is no issue of spousal support and no children involved in this matter and the Separation

Agreement being filed with the Court, and which the Court is asked to approved, contains no orders to the

same.

It is therefore represented to the Court that there is no need to file a Financial Disclosure Affidavit

in the above captioned matter and that same is hereby waived.

_____**Wife's Signature**_____   _____**Husband's Signature**_____

Affiant / Petitioner / Wife   Affiant / Petitioner / Husband

STATE OF OHIO   )

)   SS:

COUNTY OF ___**FRANKLIN**_____)

Sworn to and subscribed in my presence this _____ day of _____, 20_____.

Notary Public _____**Notary's Signature**_____

71 Waiver of Financial Disclosure

- ## (d) Waiver Of Financial Disclosure Affidavit

This form must be completed in most counties in Ohio when there are no minor children of the marriage and no spousal support will be paid by either party. It stipulates to the court that both spouses are waiving disclosure of financial information to the court because no type of support will be paid by either spouse.

However, the count in some Ohio counties (Franklin for example) **will not approve** a dissolution of marriage without filing a Financial Disclosure, Income and Expenses form even when there *are no* issues of child or spousal support. In these Ohio counties the parties **cannot waive** financial disclosure and must file the form titled "Financial Disclosure, Income and Expenses" with the court. This form outlines for the court their assets, liabilities, income and expenses of the marriage as of the filing date of the dissolution.

If there are minor children of the marriage or spousal support will be paid by either spouse then a Financial Disclosure form is **mandatory** for all Ohio counties.

Ask the clerk of courts if your county requires the form title "Financial Disclosure" when there are no issues of child or spousal support or can a waiver of financial disclosure be submitted to the court.

- ## (e) Waiver Of Representation

This form stipulates to the court that you and your spouse have agreed to the separation agreement and understand all issues of property, debts, support, etc. to legally end the marriage and you both are waiving your right to representation by a lawyer.

- ## (f) Other Local County Forms

Most Ohio counties will require a *cover sheet* (top form) which classifies the type of case being filed(dissolution, divorce, annulment, etc.) the Petitioner's names, addresses, telephone numbers, social security numbers, date of birth etc. The information required on the cover sheet is self explanatory and simple to complete.

In addition many counties may require some form of *social questionnaire* which is used to collect social data about you and your spouse such as education, occupation, number of children, prior marriages, etc. The information required on the social questionnaire is also self explanatory and simple to complete.

- ## (g) Waiver Of Venue

If for whatever reason you and your spouse may desire to have your dissolution case filed and heard by another county court near you *but not your county court of residence*, then a "Waiver Of Venue" form should be completed and you may file your dissolution paperwork in that county.

SAMPLE Custody Affidavit

COURT OF COMMON PLEAS
DIVISION OF DOMESTIC RELATIONS
_____Franklin_____COUNTY, OHIO

IN RE THE MATTER OF:

Name:	_John Lee Doe_____ :
SS #:	_123-45-6789_____ :
DOB:	_10/09/50_____ :
	Petitioner, :
	-and- :
Name:	_Mary Ann Doe_____ :
SS #:	_987-65-4321_____ :
DOB:	_11/17/54_____ :
	Petitioner,

Date _____

File No. _____
Case No. _____
Judge _____

**AFFIDAVIT IN COMPLIANCE WITH
3109.27 OF THE OHIO REVISED CODE**

STATE OF OHIO)
) SS:
COUNTY OF __Franklin_____)

Upon being duly sworn, _____**John Lee Doe**_____ does hereby state the following:
                                        (name)

1. The child/ren involved is/are _____**John Doe Jr.**_____born **03/16/86**_____
_____.

2. The child/ren's present address is/are __**200 South High St. Columbus, Oh 43021**_____
_____.

3. The places where the child/ren has/have lived the last five years are _____
_____**200 South High St. Columbus, Oh 43021**_____.

4. The names and present address of the persons with whom the child/ren has/have lived during that period is/are _____**John Lee Doe and Mary Ann Doe 200 South High St. Columbus, Oh 43021**_____
_____.

5. I have not participated as a party, witness, or in any other capacity or any other litigation concerning the allocation of parental rights and responsibilities of the same child/ren or that otherwise concerned the custody in this or any other state.

6. I have no information of any parenting proceeding concerning the child/ren pending in a court of this or any other state.

7. I know of no person not a party to the proceeding who has physical custody of the child/ren or claims to be a parent of the child/ren who is designated the residential parent and legal custodian of the child/ren or to have visitation rights with respect to the child/ren.

8. I HAVE NOT been convicted of or pleaded guilty to any criminal offense involving any act that resulted in a child being an abused or neglected child nor have I been the perpetrator of the abusive or neglectful act that was the basis of an adjudication that a child is an abused or neglected child.

    If you or your spouse have ever been a party to any civil or criminal case or investigation concerning child abuse, child neglect or domestic violence, state the name(s), case numbers, date(s) and nature of the case(s)
_____**None**_____
_____.

_____**Father's Signature**_____
Affiant / Father

STATE OF OHIO)
) SS:
COUNTY OF __Franklin_____)

Sworn to and subscribed in my presence this _____ day of _____ , 20____.
                          Notary Public _____**Notary's Signature**_____

Both you and your spouse must agree to the change of venue to another county. You will file a "Waiver of Venue" form **ONLY** if you intend to file your dissolution case in another Ohio county other than your county of residence.

In addition, if you file a "waiver of venue" form the **upper heading** on each form which appears the county name (your county of residence) will have to be changed to the new county name in which you intend to file the dissolution.

There are several reasons why parties choose to file their dissolution case in another county other than their county of residence:

- The parties choose to protect their right to privacy because some newspapers publish the names of the parties when they are granted a dissolution.

- Although it is your legal right to represent yourself in a dissolution case some counties may make the process more difficult for self-helpers. These counties may refuse to give you a local county form that only their court has produced or the clerk may reject your dissolution paperwork without explanation by not telling you what form or procedure you are missing. Most of the time when this happens the clerk will tell you to go "hire a lawyer". Keep in mind that judges are elected in Ohio and in most judicial elections the vast majority of the judge's campaign contributions may come from lawyers.

- However, also realize that a self-helper must follow the same procedures and submit the same correct dissolution paperwork in the same required manner as if a lawyer prepared them. The court will not have one set of rules for self-helpers and another set of rules for lawyers. If you lack the competence to prepare the forms and handle your case do not expect the court to be patient with you. You *should* hire a lawyer to advise you and prepare the case.

- If for whatever reason you find that your county clerk of courts is not being very helpful concerning the blank forms or the dissolution process, you should consider filling your dissolution case in another Ohio county by completing a "Waiver of Venue" form and changing the county name appearing in the heading of each form to the new county.

IF ONE OF THE SPOUSES IS PAYING SPOUSAL SUPPORT TO THE OTHER THEN THE FOLLOWING TWO FORMS ARE REQUIRED IN ADDITION TO THE PREVIOUS FORMS:

• (h) Financial Disclosure, Income And Expenses / Affidavit

The form must be filed with the court if one of the parties is paying spousal or child support to the other. The form outlines for the court you assets, liabilities, income and expenses of the marriage to date. This form will give the judge enough financial information about the marriage to determine that the amount of spousal support is fair and the amount of child support is the legal amount required by law.

SAMPLE Health Insurance Affidavit

COURT OF COMMON PLEAS
DIVISION OF DOMESTIC RELATIONS
____Franklin_____ COUNTY, OHIO

Name: _John Lee Doe_____ : Date: _____
SS #: _123-45-6789_____ : Case No. A _____
DOB: _10/09/50_____ :
  Petitioner,   :
    -and-   : File No. E _____
Name: _Mary Ann Doe_____ :
SS #: _987-65-4321_____ : **GROUP HEALTH INSURANCE**
DOB: _11/17/54_____ :   **AFFIDAVIT**
  Petitioner,   :

HUSBAND / PETITIONER		WIFE / PETITIONER
_X_ yes ____ no	Available through employment	.... ____ yes _X_ no
____ yes _X_ no	Other group plan	____ yes _X_ no

Acme Corporation/Mutual Health Ins.___ Insurer's Name _____**None**_____
_622 West Weber Ave._____ Address _____
_Columbus, Oh 43236_____   _____
_421-58669-333_____ POLICY NO. _____
$ _____0_____ Monthly premium of Individual Plan (employee share) $ _____
$ _____0_____ Monthly premium of Family Plan (employee share) $ _____
(Indicate "0" if available at no cost to party)

Coverages

Summarize health care benefits, ie., major medical only, deductible, co-payments, health maintence organization, etc. Attach separate sheet where necessary.

__80% paid after $500. deductible_____ _____
__for family - 100% Major Medical_____ _____
__50% coverage for dental_____ _____
__80% prescription coverage_____ _____

☒ yes ☐ no	Is coverage presently in effect?		☐ yes ☐ no
☒ self ☐ above named spouse	Who is cover?		☐ self ☐ above named spouse
☒ dependent children of the marriage			☐ dependent children of the marriage
☒ yes ☐ no	Is a participant card available?		☐ yes ☐ no
☒ yes ☐ no	Is a prescription card available?		☐ yes ☐ no

Mrs. Mary Smith / Personnal Dept. Employer's Ins. Coordinator's _____
_(614) 123-4567_____ Name and Telephone Number _____
$ _374.76_____ The cost to purchase COBRA coverage will be $ _____

___Husband's Signature_____ ___Wife's Signature_____
Husband / Petitioner Signature   Wife / Petitioner Signature
STATE OF OHIO   )
) SS:
COUNTY OF _Franklin_____)

Sworn to and subscribed in my presence this _____ day of _____ , 20____.

Notary Public ___**Notary's Signature**_____

SAMPLE Health Insurance Verification

PURSUANT TO YOUR HEALTH CARE ORDER YOU MUST PROVIDE VERIFICATION TO THE CHILD SUPPORT ENFORCEMENT AGENCY. FAILURE TO DO SO MAY RESULT IN A FINDING OF CONTEMPT. FAILURE TO COMPLY WITH THE HEALTH CARE ORDER MAY RESULT IN ADDITIONAL PENALTIES AS WELL. RETURN THIS FORM TO:

__FRANKLIN___**CHILD SUPPORT ENFORCEMENT AGENCY**
ADDRESS: _123 West Broad St._____
_____**Columbus, Oh 43201**_____
OR
ATTACH TO YOUR DECREE OR AGREED ENTRY

__**John Lee Doe**_____   Date _____
Plaintiff / Petitioner

123-45-6789_____ **10/09/50_**   Case No. A _____
SS#   DOB

☒ Obligor   ☐ Obligee   File No . E _____
                                              Judge _____

                  -vs / and-

                                              HEALTH CARE VERIFICATION
                                              (C.S.E.A.)

__**Mary Ann Doe**_____   ☒ Obligor   ☐ Obligee
Defendant / Petitioner

987-65-4321_____ **11/17/54__**   Insurance Policy No. _**421-58669-333**_____
SS#   DOB

☐ Obligor   ☒ Obligee   Insurer _**Acme Corp. / Mutual Health Ins.**

Whereas, ___**John Lee Doe**_____ is ordered to obtain/maintain health
                    Obligor or Obligee
coverage for the minor child(ren) and whereas O.R.C. 3163.217 imposes verification requirements upon the above named person, ___**John Lee Doe**_____ hereby swears under penality of contempt
                              Obligor or Obligee
as follows.

1. I have obtained / am maintaining health insurance coverage as ordered. Said coverage is in full force and effect.

2. I have sent, or will send contemporaneous with this affidavit, a copy of the health care order to the insurer.

3. (Obligor only) I have supplied Obligee with (a) insurance forms necessary to receive payment, reimbursement or other benefits, (b) necessary insurance cards, and (c) information regarding the benefits, limitations, and exclusions of the health insurance coverage.

                                    __**Husband's Signature**_____
                                    Affiant / Signature

STATE OF OHIO   )
) SS:
COUNTY OF _**Franklin**_____   )

Sworn to and subscribed in my presence this _____ day of _____ , 20_____.

                    Notary Public ____**Notary's Signature**_____

- ## (i) Spousal Support Deduction Order

A spousal support deduction order must be completed **if spousal support will be paid**. The party paying the spousal support must choose one of the two different types of deduction orders depending on whether the spouse paying the support (obligor) is employed or unemployed or from what type of account you desire to have the support payment be submitted to the County Bureau of Support.

- **Employer or Workers' Compensation or Financial Institution or Public Pension**

This form is a court order which is sent to the employer or financial institution of the spouse responsible for the payment of support (the obligor). The court order authorizes the employer or financial institution to withhold the necessary amount of funds from the obligor's paycheck or financial account and submit those funds to the Bureau of Support, plus an amount called poundage (administration fee).

- **Unemployment Notice Order**

If the obligor for support is unemployed at the time the dissolution is granted the court will issue an unemployment order until the obligor is again employed and at that time an employer deduction order will be issued for the payment of the support.

We have included blank copies of the support deduction order in the blank forms section of this publication but be aware that many counties require the use of a multiple copy form because of the number of copies required. You may have to transfer your support deduction information to the court required form.

IF YOU HAVE MINOR CHILDREN OF THE MARRIAGE THE FOLLOWING FORMS ARE REQUIRED IN ADDITION TO THE PREVIOUSLY OUTLINED FORMS:

Previously outlined forms:
- Petition and Waiver of Service
- Separation Agreement
- Final Decree
- Waiver of Representation
- Financial Disclosure, Income and Expenses / Affidavit
- Cover Sheet, Social Questionnaire or other local county forms

- ## (j) Affidavit In Compliance With ORC 3109.27

This affidavit (previously know as a custody affidavit), tells the court who has been responsible for the care of the minor children for the past five years and where and with whom the children have resided for the past five years. The form also tells the court where the children are currently living and that the children are not involved in any other custody proceeding in any other state.

In addition, the forms stipulates to the court whether either party of the dissolution has ever been convicted of any criminal offense involving any act that resulted in child abuse, child neglect or domestic violence.

SAMPLE Support Deduction Order

COURT OF COMMON PLEAS
DIVISION OF DOMESTIC RELATIONS
____FRANKLIN_____COUNTY, OHIO

_ John Lee Doe_____

Plaintiff / Petitioner   **X** Obligor ☐ Obligee

___123-45-6789_____ 10/09/50____

SS#   DOB

-vs / and-

__Mary Ann Doe_____

Defendant / Petitioner   ☐ Obligor **X** Obligee

___987-65-4321_____ 11/17/54___

SS#   DOB

TO:

X Employer (D)(1)/Employer Paying Workers' Compensation (D)(2)

☐ Bureau of Workers' Compensation (D)(2)

☐ Financial Institution (D)(5)

☐ Public Pension System (D)(3)

☐ Other (D)(4) _____

Enter ____**Court Assigned**_____

Date _____

Case No. A _____**Court Assigned**_____

File No. E _____

Judge _____

X SUPPORT DEDUCTION ORDER
☐ ORDER FOR MODIFICATION OF
SUPPORT DEDUCTION ORDER
O.R.C. 3113.21 (D)

X You are hereby ordered to comply in the following manner:

☐ You are hereby ordered to MODIFY the prior Order of this Court in the following manner:

PURSUANT to Civil Rule 75(B)(3), as the employer/income withholder of _____**John Lee Doe**_____, (hereinafter referred to as the Obligor) Account/Claim No. ____**647-89-41__(Court Assigned)**_____ you are hereby joined as a party to this action and are ordered to withhold from the personal earnings, benefits or funds of the Obligor in the sume of $___**91.80**_____ which includes poundage every _**week**___ for support until further order. To defray expenses in complying with this order, an employer, including an employer paying Workers' Compensation benefits, may deduct an additional sum not to exceed 1% of the amount withheld from personal earnings of the Obligor or $2.00 whichever is greater. A Financial Institution my deduct a fee of $5.00 or a fee not to exceed the lowest rate, if any, charged for a similar debit transaction, whichever is less. Any Deducting Organization under O.R.C. 3113.21 D (3) and (4) may deduct a fee of $2.00 or 1% of the deduction, whichever is less.

THE DEDUCTING ORGANIZATION IS ORDERED to begin withholding NO LATER THAN ONE WEEK FROM RECEIPT OF THIS ORDER or on _____ but you do not have to alter your pay cycle.

THE DEDUCTING ORGANIZATION IS ORDERED to forward the payment IMMEDIATELY UPON WITHHOLDING to the __**Franklin**_____ COUNTY Child Support Enforcement Agency (BUREAU OF SUPPORT), ____**Franklin**_____ COUNTY COURTHOUSE, __**Columbus**_____ OHIO __**43201**_____. The employee's name and file number shall accompany the check.

To the extent possible, the Deducting Organization shall deduct the above amount notwithstanding the limitations of Sections 2329.66, 2329.70, 2716.02, 2716.05, 2716.13 and 4123.67 of the Ohio Revised Code. However, in no case shall the amount withheld including fees, exceed the maximum amount permitted under Section 303(b) of the "Consumer Credit Protection Act", 15 U.S.C. 1673(b).

IT IS ORDERED that the Obligor is personally responsible to make payments as indicated above by cash, certified check or money order to the Child Support Enforcement Agency (Bureau of Support) until such time is as said amount is withheld from Obligor's funds.

IT IS FURTHER ORDERED that said Deducting Organization shall notify the Child Support Enforcement Agency in writing within ten (10) days of the occurrence of any of the events listed on the reverse side of said Deduction Organization's copy of this order;

THE DEDUCTING ORGANIZATION IS FURTHER ORDERED to notify the Child Support Enforcement Agency immediately of any lump sum payments of $500.00 or more to be paid to the Obligor, hold the lump sum payment for thirty (30) days after the date that it is due before making payment, and upon Order of the Court pay any specified amount of the lump sum payment to the __**Franklin**_____ COUNTY CHILD SUPPORT ENFORCEMENT AGENCY (BUREAU OF SUPPORT). Notice shall be given to the Child Support Enforcement Agency no later than 45 days before payment is due unless the determination is made in less than 45 days, then immediately.

Failure to send any notification required by the Court is a Contempt of Court. In addition to all powers this Court has to punish contempt the employer/Other deducting organization may also be subject to a fine of not more than $200.00.

A Deducting Organization's failure to withhold in compliance with this order could subject the employer to liability for the amount that was not witheld pursuant to O.R.C. 3113.213.

The law provides penalties for an employer who discharges, refuses to hire or disciplines any employee based upon an order to withhold personal earnings. THIS ORDER APPLIES TO ALL SUBSEQUENT EMPLOYERS AND/OR OTHER SOURCES OF INCOME OF THE OBLIGOR, as determined by the Child Support Enforcement Agency. Upon the commencement of employment the Court may cancel any prior 3113.21 order and issue a Deduction Order to Obligor's employer.

IT IS FURTHER ORDERED that each party to this action shall notify the Child Support Enforcement Agency, in writing, of their respective current mailing address and current residence address, and each party shall notify the court IMMEDIATELY IN WRITING of any change in either of these addresses. This duty to notify the Court of any change in address shall continue until further notice from this Court. You are notified that service of future notices shall be deemed complete upon the posting of ordinary mail to your last known address on record with the CHILD SUPPORT ENFORCEMENT AGENCY.

IT IS FURTHER ORDERED that the obligor and obligee shall immediately notify the Child Support Enforcement Agency in writing of any of the events on the reverse side of their copy of this order.

INSTRUCTIONS TO THE CLERK

YOU ARE DIRECTED TO MAIL A COPY OF THIS ORDER TO THE DEDUCTING ORGANIZATION AND TO THE OBLIGOR AND OBLIGEE BY ORDINARY MAIL, WITH PROOF OF MAILING, UNLESS THEY HAVE ACKNOWLEDGED RECEIPT BY SIGNATURE BELOW.

☐ Deducting Organization	☐ Obligor	☐ Obligee
_____ACME Corporation_____	_____John Lee Doe_____	_____Mary Ann Doe_____
_____6422 West Weber Ave._____	_____100 West Broad St._____	_____200 South High St._____
_____Columbus, OH 43236_____	_____Columbus, OH 43026_____	_____Columbus, OH 43021_____

Current order of support is $ ___**91.80**_____ **wk**/mo. plus $ _____**-0-**____ wk/mo. past due support.

• (k) Group Health Insurance Affidavit

This affidavit gives the court notice concerning whether a group health insurance policy is in effect for the **health care of the minor children**. The form also request health insurance information such as type of coverages and benefits, monthly premium, insurers' name and address, and policy number. The left side of the form is for group health insurance coverages for the father and the right side is for the mother.

• (l) Health Care Verification

This form stipulates to the court that the party (obligor) who has agreed to obtain and maintain health insurance coverage for the minor children has done so. In addition, the form stipulates that a copy of the health care order has been or will be sent to the health care insurer and that health care coverage for the benefit of the minor children will be continuously verified to the Child Support Enforcement Agency.

Also, the party responsible for the health care coverage for the minor children must supply the other party (obligee) with all necessary insurance forms, insurance cards and information regarding coverages and benefits.

• (m) Child Support Worksheet

A child support worksheet must be completed (see Exhibit B for instructions) if there are minor children of the marriage. You must choose **one** of the two different types of worksheets depending on how you and your spouse have allocated parental responsibilities:

- *Sole Residential Parent or Shared Parenting -*
  (1) This worksheet is utilized if one party is considered the sole residential parent and legal custodian of *all* the minor children. or
  (2) both parties are requesting shared parenting for the care of the minor children.

- *Split Parental Rights And Responsibilities -*
  (1) This worksheet is utilized where there is more than one minor child and each parent is considered a residential parent (has custody) of at least one of the children. The support payment is determined for each parent for the children in the custody of the other. The obligations are then offset, with the parent owing the larger amount paying the net amount in child support to the other party.

• (n) Child Support Deduction Order

A child support deduction order must be completed if there are minor children of the marriage. You must choose one of two different types of deduction orders depending on whether the parent paying child support (obligor) is employed or from what type of account you desire the child support payments be submitted to the County Bureau of Support / Child Support Enforcement Agency.

- *Employer or Workers' Compensation or Financial Institution or Public Pension*
  The form is a court order which is sent to the employer or financial institution of the parent responsible for the payment of child support (obligor). The court order authorizes the employer or financial institution to withhold the necessary child support amount from the obligor's paycheck or financial account and submit that amount to the Bureau of Support / Child Support Enforcement Agency, plus poundage (administration fee).

- *Unemployment Notice Order*
  If the obligor for child support is unemployed at the time the dissolution is granted the court will issue this type of order until the obligor is employed and a deduction order will then be issued to the employer for the child support obligation and be deducted from the obligor's paycheck.

NOTE: We have included a blank copy of the child support deduction orders in the blank forms section of this publication, but be aware that most of the county courts have developed this form in a multiple copy format because of the number of copies required. You should be prepared to transfer the required information to the multiple copy court form.

• (o) Minor Child Health Care Order

A child health care order must be completed if there are minor children of the marriage. You must choose one of four different types of health care orders depending on which parent will be responsible for obtaining and maintaining health insurance coverage for the benefit of the minor children. The health order will be sent to the insurer and the insurer or the parent responsible for coverage (obligor) will have to submit coverage verification to the Child Support Enforcement Agency.

- *Obligor* - Health insurance coverage will be maintained by the parent paying child support.
- *Obligee* - Health insurance coverage will be maintained by the parent receiving child support.
- *Obligor and Obligee* - There will be dual health insurance coverage maintained by both parents.
- *Shared Liability* - No health insurance coverage is available at a reasonable cost or group policy and the health care costs for the minor children will be a shared cost by both parents.

NOTE: We have included a blank copy of the health care orders in the blank forms section of this publication, but be aware that most of the county courts have developed this form in a multiple copy format because of the number of copies required. You should be prepared to transfer the required information to the multiple copy court form.

• (p) Shared Parenting

If you and your spouse have decided that shared parenting (previously known as joint custody) is a better method for allocating parental responsibility than one parent being primarily responsible (sole residential parent), you will have to submit to the court a *Shared Parenting Plan* and when approved the court will issue a *Shared Parenting Decree.*

SAMPLE Shared Parenting Plan

COURT OF COMMON PLEAS
DIVISION OF DOMESTIC RELATIONS
_____Franklin_____COUNTY, OHIO

IN RE THE MATTER OF:

Name: _John Lee Doe_____   :   Date _____

SS #: _123-45-6789_____   :

DOB: _10/09/50_____   :   File No. _____

        Petitioner,   :   Case No. _____

             -and-   :   Judge _____

Name: _Mary Ann Doe_____   :

SS #: _987-65-4321_____   :

DOB: _11/17/54_____   :   **SHARED PARENTING PLAN**

        Petitioner,

The following is a Shared Parenting Plan for the minor child/ren of the parties, namely:

_____**John Doe Jr.**_____   born _16_ day of _**March**_____ _1986__;

_____   born _____ day of _____ _____;

_____   born _____ day of _____ _____;

_____   born _____ day of _____ _____;

submitted by __**Mary Ann Doe**_____ , hereinafter referred to as "mother"

and _____**John Lee Doe**_____ , hereinafter referred to as "father".

The parties agree that it is in the best interest of the minor child/ren for the parties to have shared parenting. Acknowledging that each is a caring and appropriate parent with the ability to provide guidance, concern and a proper homelife for the minor child/ren, the parties agree as follows:

ARTICLE I   SHARED PARENTING TIME

The mother shall be the residential parent from ___**Saturday at 6:00 PM**_____ _____ to _**Wednesday at 12:00 PM**_____ .

The father shall be the residential parent from _____**Wednesday at 12:00 PM**_____ _____ to __**Saturday at 6:00 PM**_____ .

Each parent has separate sleeping quarters for the minor child/ren during the time he/she is the residential parent.

The nonresidential parent shall be allowed liberal phone contact with the minor child/ren. Should any major differences of opinion regarding the best interest if the child/ren arise, the matters will be resolved through mediation or counseling provided by professional therapists.

ARTICLE II   SCHOOL/DAY CARE

During the time the child/ren are of school age/day care age, the parties will mutually agree where the child/ren will attend school. Each parent is entitled to all school records and to attend all school functions.

Page One of Three

SAMPLE Shared Parenting Plan

ARTICLE III   DISCIPLINE

The child/ren will be disciplined by the parent who is the residential parent at that particular time. The parents shall consult on all discipline matters.

ARTICLE IV   TRANSPORTATION

The residential parent at the particular time said transportation is needed shall be responsible for transportation of the child/ren for school, recreation, and medical attention, inter alia.

ARTICLE V   HEALTH AND MEDICAL EXPENSES

Each parent shall have access to all health records of the minor child/ren. The parents will select a primary care physician for the minor child/ren and make decisions in collaboration with the physician. The ___**father**_____ shall provide health insurance as specified in the attached Health Care Order for the minor child/ren of the parties. The health insurance carrier is ___**ACME**_____ __**Corporation**_____ whose address is _____**6422 West Weber Street**_____ __**Columbus, Oh 43236**_____. Any medical, dental, optical, orthodontical, psychiatric or psychological expenses not paid by health insurance shall be _**divided equally between the parties**_____.

ARTICLE VI   TAX EXEMPTIONS

__**The mother shall have the tax exemption for John Jr**._____
_____.

ARTICLE VII   SUPPORT

The _____**father**_____ shall pay child support in the amount of $ _**584.50**_____ per child per month. Said payment shall begin the date of the final hearing on a divorce or dissolution, and shall be payable every month thereafter, through the _**Franklin**_____ County Bureau of Support (Child Support Enforcement Agency), with appropriate poundage, which payments with current poundage of _**2**___ %, total $ _**596.19**____, or $ _**134.88**_____ per child per week, with __**2**__ % poundage, for a total weekly payment of $ _**137. 58**____. Said child support shall continue until each minor child has reached the age of eighteen (18) and attends on a full time basis any recognized and accredited high school, or otherwise is emancipated. All payments not made through the Bureau of Support (Child Support Enforcement Agency) shall be deemed gifts.

ARTICLE VIII   RELIGIOUS TRAINING

The minor child/ren shall be raised in the __**Catholic faith**_____.

Page Two of Three

SAMPLE Shared Parenting Plan

ARTICLE IX   LIFE INSURANCE FOR THE MINOR CHILD/REN

The ___**father**_____ shall maintain the minor child/ren of the parties as beneficiaries on his/her life insurance policy in the amount of $ _**100,000.00**_____ until said child/ren are emancipated.

ARTICLE X   RECORDS

Both parties shall have access to school/medical and all other records pertaining to the minor child/ren and access to all school activities and/or child care facilities.

ARTICLE XI   RELOCATION

The mother's present address is ____**200 South High Street**_____
City _**Columbus**_____ State __**Ohio**_____ Zip Code _**43021**_____.

The father's present address is _____**100 West Broad Street**_____
City _**Columbus**_____ State __**Ohio**_____ Zip Code _**43026**_____.

If either parent intends to move to a residence other than specified above, that parent must file a notice of intent to relocate with the Court.

ARTICLE XII   MISCELLANEOUS

Neither parent has been convicted of or pleaded guilty to a violation of the Ohio Revised Code 2919.25 involving a family member, or any other offense which resulted in physical harm to a family member, or has been determined to be the perpetrator of an abusive act that is the basis of an adjudication that a child is an abused child or has acted or contributed in any manner resulting in a child being a neglected child.

Findings of fact and conclusions of law pursuant to the Ohio Revised Code 3109.04, 3109.051 and 3109.052 are hereby waived.

The plan is submitted to the Court pursuant to the Ohio Revised Code 3109.04 (D) (1) (a) (ii).

ARTICLE XIII   MODIFICATIONS

The parties agree that this Shared Parenting Plan can be modified in the future without the mutual agreement of the parties; i.e., the Plan can be modified upon the motion of one party, with either the agreement of the other party, or with Court approval.

____**Mother's Signature**_____   ____**Father's Signature**_____
Signature of the Mother   Signature of the Father

_____   _____
Date   Date

STATE OF OHIO   )
) SS:
COUNTY OF __**Franklin**_____   )

Sworn to and subscribed in my presence this _____ day of _____, 20_____.

Page Three of Three   Notary Public ___**Notary's Signature**_____

SAMPLE Shared Parenting Decree

COURT OF COMMON PLEAS
DIVISION OF DOMESTIC RELATIONS
____Franklin_____COUNTY, OHIO

IN RE THE MATTER OF:

Name: _John Lee Doe_____   :   Date _____

SS #: _123-45-6789_____   :

DOB: _10/09/50_____   :   File No. _____

          Petitioner,   :   Case No. _____

              -and-   :   Judge _____

Name: _Mary Ann Doe_____   :

SS #: _987-65-4321_____   :   **FINAL DECREE OF**

DOB: _11/17/54_____   :   **SHARED PARENTING**

          Petitioner,

This cause came before the Court on this _____ day of _**Date of Hearing**__ 20 _____, upon the joint application of the parties for an order granting them shared parental rights and responsibilities for the care of the minor child/ren, namely:

_____**John Doe Jr**._____ born _**16**__ day of __**March**_____ _1986___;

_____ born _____ day of _____ _____;

_____ born _____ day of _____ _____;

_____ born _____ day of _____ _____;

and the shared parenting plan submitted by the parties.

Wherefore, upon review of the plan, the court approves said plan and grants a Final Decree of Shared Parenting to the parties in accordance with the plan attached hereto and incorporated herein.

The court further finds that the findings of fact/conclusions of law not required, are hereby waived by the parties, or have been addressed elsewhere by the Court. This plan is submitted in accordance with the Ohio Revised Code 3109.04 (D) (1) (i) and is not modifiable absent the express agreement of the parties.

The Final Decree of Shared Parenting is effective this _____ day of _____ 20 ___.

_____   _____

Referee   Judge

Court of Common Pleas   Court of Common Pleas

_____County, Ohio   _____ County, Ohio

___**Mother's Signature**_____   _**Father's Signature**_____

Signature of the Mother   Signature of the Father

Page One of One

We have included a sample of what items may be included in these two legal documents. Your Shared Parenting Plan should incorporate everything entailed to care for your minor children.

The LawPak samples can be modified to meet your specific family needs, but be aware that the judge can modify your Shared Parenting Plan in any manner which he/she determines to be in the best interest of the children. If the court modifies your shared parenting plan the parties will again have to submit the Shared Parenting Plan to the court after the required modifications have been implemented for approval. In addition, the judge may not approve a Shared Parenting Plan if he/she perceives it as not being in the best interest of the children, such as one of the parents maintaining a residence in another state.

SAMPLE Hamilton County Financial Disclosure

COURT OF COMMON PLEAS
DIVISION OF DOMESTIC RELATIONS
____Hamilton_____COUNTY, OHIO

IN RE THE MARRIAGE OF:

Name: ___John Lee Doe_____ : DATE: _____

SS #: ___123-45-6789_____ 10/09/50_____ : CASE NO. A: _____

Petitioner,   DOB   : FILE NO. E: _____

                -and-   : JUDGE _____

Name: ___Mary Ann Doe_____ :

SS #: ___987-65-4321_____ 11/17/54____ : **FINANCIAL DISCLOSURE**

Petitioner,   DOB   : **O.R.C. 3113.21 (C)**

Now comes _____John Lee Doe_____ and, after being duly cautioned and sworn, says:

                   Obligor

1. I ☒ am employed.
    ☐ am not employed.   My employer is ____Acme Corporation_____

__6244 Oak Lane_____ Columbus_____ OH_____ 43202_____
Employer's Payroll Address   City   State   Zip Code

I receive ☐ 12 ☐ 24 ☐ 26 ☒ 52 paychecks per year.

2. I ☐ am ☒ am not receiving Workers' Compensation under Claim No. _____.

    ☐ am ☒ am not receiving Unemployment Compensation under Claim No. _____.

3. I ☒ do

    ☐ do not have funds on deposit in Financial Institutions. (List all funds in all accounts in any Bank, Savings & Loan, Credit Union, Regulated Investment Company, Mutual or Other Financial Institutions. Account may include one or more of the following: checking, certificate of deposit ("CD"), investment, savings, individual retirement ("IRA"), stock options, etc. USE ADDITIONAL PAGES IF NEEDED).

Name of Financial Institution	Address of Financial Institution	Account No.	Name(s) on Account	Balance as of Date of the Affidavit
_First National Bank__	_446 Main St._____ _Columbus, Oh 43201_	_6721-8724__	_John Lee Doe_	_956.00 Savings
_First National Bank__	_446 Main St._____ _Columbus, Oh 43201_	_86193-421____	_John Lee Doe__	22,000. 00 IRA_
_____	_____	_____	_____	_____

4. I have the following additional sources of income. (List sources, address and amount including but not limited to pension (public and private) annuities, allowance, sick pay, disability pay or other benefit, commissions, trusts, bonuses, profit sharing payments or distributions, lottery winnings, lump sum payments, and private Workers' Compensation payments).
_Acme Corporation vested pension plan worth $46,000.00 in the name of John Lee Doe_____.

5. I ☐ do

    ☒ do not have other assets from which child support/spousal support can be paid or secured. (If affirmative, list all such assets on a separate sheet of paper).

                                          _____**Husband's Signature**_____
                                           Affiant - Obligor

STATE OF OHIO   )
) SS:
COUNTY OF __Hamilton_____)
Sworn to and subscribed in my presence this _____ day of _____, 20____.

                                Notary Public _____**Notary's Signature**_____

I hereby acknowledge receipt of a copy of this affidavit _____**Wife's Signature**_____.
                                             Obligee

SAMPLE Franklin County Financial Disclosure

COURT OF COMMON PLEAS
DIVISION OF DOMESTIC RELATIONS
FRANKLIN COUNTY, OHIO

IN RE THE MARRIAGE OF:

Name:	**John Lee Doe**	:	Case No. **Court Assigned**
SS #:	123-45-6789	:	
	Petitioner,	:	**ASSETS AND LIABILITIES AS**
	-and-	:	**OF: January 25, 2000**
Name:	**Mary Ann Doe**	:	**FINANCIAL DISCLOSURE**
SS #:	987-65-4321	:	**AFFIDAVIT**
	Petitioner,	:	

INSTRUCTIONS: YOU ARE TO DISCLOSE ALL SUCH INFORMATION THAT IS REQUESTED HEREIN AND BY THE **FRANKLIN** COUNTY COURT OF COMMON PLEAS, DIVISION OF DOMESTIC RELATIONS. BE SPECIFIC, LIST ALL ASSETS, LIABILITIES, INCOME SOURCES AND RETIREMENT ACCOUNTS SEPARATELY. ALSO LIST ACCOUNT NUMBERS, NAMES, LOCATIONS AND VALUES AND WHETHER JOINTLY OR INDIVIDUALLY HELD.

ASSETS:		LIABILITIES:	
Cash	**200.00**	Notes Payable	0
Government Bonds	0	Accounts Payable	0
Checking Account	0		
Savings Account	**956.00**	Loans on Life Ins.	0
Accts/Notes Receivable	0	Taxes	**440.00**
Stocks, Bonds, Securities	**XYZ CO.750.00 (25 shares)**	Mortgages	**40,000.00**
Life Ins. Cash Value	0	Other Debts (Itemize)	
Real Estate	**30,000.00 equity**	**Sears**	**550.00**
Automobiles	**20,000.00**	**Visa**	**256.00**
Other Assets (Itemize)	**motorcycle 4,000.00**	**Medical**	**398.00**

INCOME:

From Employment	**37,000.00**	Wife	**23,000.00**
Other Income (Itemize)	0		0

CONTINGENT LIABILITY:		RETIREMENT ACCOUNTS:	
Notes / Accounts Payable	0	Husband **Acme Corp. $46,000.00**	
Guarantor	0	**IRA $22,000.00**	Vested?
Other Contingent			
Liabilities (Itemize)	0	Wife **ABC Trucking $18,000.00**	
	0	**IRA $13,000.00**	Vested?

This may be supplemented with additional information on attached sheets. If income is derived from a business attach a profit and loss statement or copy of income tax return for the past business year and any current profit and loss information statement.

           Husband's Signature_____

           Petitioner / Husband

           Wife's Signature_____

STATE OF OHIO	)	Petitioner / Wife
	) SS:	
COUNTY OF **FRANKLIN**	)	

Sworn to and subscribed in my presence this _____ day of _____, 20_____.

Notary Public _____**Notary's Signature**_____

5
Attending The Hearing

Read your Dissolution Decree again to be sure that it has been properly completed and that you understand its provisions prior to the dissolution hearing. Take your decree and photocopies to the court hearing plus the photocopies of your separation agreement and any local county required forms.

Plan to arrive at the courthouse at least fifteen minutes early and check-in with the court clerk or bailiff to let them know that you are appearing for your dissolution hearing.

Your hearing will generally be held in open court. The procedure is formal; your testimony may or may not be taken down by a court reporter. There <u>will not</u> be anyone present who will cross-examine you. Your testimony under oath probably will take no more than five minutes. In most cases you will have the opportunity to hear the testimony of others before your turn.

When your case is called by the judge or bailiff go forward and be sworn. Then hand your original Decree of Dissolution with a copy of your Separation Agreement to the judge and sit down in the witness chair or wherever directed.

Take your time when speaking. If the judge asks questions it is only to become better informed about your case and to make sure that the legal process has been followed. Don't worry just answer what is asked and don't volunteer information that is not asked for. Always call the judge "your honor".

Either you or your spouse will usually tell the judge or referee the following. This information is in your Petition and Separation Agreement for purposes of reference:

- your name and address;
- the length of residence in Ohio;
- the name and address of your spouse;
- the date and place (city and state) of your marriage;
- if any, the names and dates of birth of all living children, natural or adopted, common to you and your spouse;
- that you have voluntarily signed and agreed to the Separation Agreement; that you still agree that it is fair and acceptable; its contents are understood by you and you request the court to approve it;
- that you still want to dissolve your marriage; that you are requesting the court to grant your dissolution and;
- that all signatures on the dissolution documents are yours.

- It usually is not necessary to repeat for the judge or referee the information in your Separation Agreement regarding division of debts and property, child custody, etc. but the judge may ask you a few questions about these matters.

- If the wife requests that her former name be restore, tell the judge or referee.

- *After one spouse has stated the above the other spouse may repeat some of the same information for the judge or referee.*

You should not leave the courtroom until the judge or referee tells you that you may do so. If there is no such indication wait until they have completed stating their findings and court orders. Then step down and leave the courtroom. The judge or referee may keep the original of your Decree or they may return it to you with instructions on what to do to finalize your dissolution. If neither occurs ask the court what steps are required for you and your spouse to record and obtain a certified copy of your Decree of Dissolution. You may be told to go to the clerk's office or elsewhere to finalize all matters.

You may be instructed to fasten the pages of the Separation Agreement *(photocopies)* to the Decree in a manner similar to when you fastened the petition and separation agreement prior to the filing of your dissolution.

Your photocopies of the Decree are for you and your spouse. If you ever lose your copy of the decree you can receive a photocopy of the original on file at the courthouse by asking for a copy at the clerk of courts office.

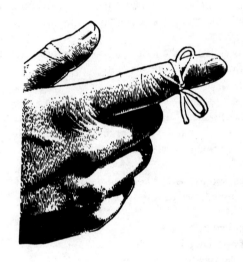

6

What Happens If Something Goes Wrong

The hearing for a dissolution of marriage generally will take five minutes without any problems occurring most of the time. If a problem should occur you should have some idea on how to respond.

Before the Hearing Begins

If a court clerk, bailiff or judge is less than helpful or polite you should stay calm, be nice and quietly but firmly pursue your goal. You have the right to be there and a right to represent yourself without a lawyer. If someone is making the process difficult for you there must be a reason. You should find the reason and attempt to correct the problem. Ask what is the problem and if necessary ask to speak with another court clerk or their supervisor. *Don't get upset.* You can always return to the clerk's office or to court another day, always be polite and don't be afraid to ask questions.

As previously discussed the court clerks are not allowed by law to give you legal advice or assist you in completing the blank forms because they are not lawyers. However, the court clerks can give you blank forms, general information and direction about how dissolution matters are handled in their court. They are required as part of their duties as public servants to give you general information about court requirements. Generally, you will find that most court personnel are very helpful and polite.

Certain local forms for an Ohio dissolution have not be standardized to be consistent in all eighty-eight Ohio counties. Some counties may require a local form that only the clerk of courts of that county can supply to you. If a county clerk refuses to give you a blank copy of local required forms and guidelines or refuses to tell you where you may obtain a copy (other than through a lawyer), request to speak with their supervisor or if necessary the domestic relations judge. Without the proper local forms the clerk of courts *will reject* your paperwork and in some cases without explanation, but usually because you have not completed a mandatory form. In addition, several counties will reject your paperwork if it is not **typed.**

Judges are elected by the people of Ohio in state and local elections. The elected judges then appoint the clerks in their court and other office and administrative personnel. The forms that you may be requesting are created and printed by personnel (public servants) who are paid with tax revenues. It is your right to have access to the legal system and these forms are part of that system. It is your legal right to represent yourself without having to hire a lawyer in order to obtain blank forms. Only you can assert your legal right to self representation whether you use a LawPak to assist you or not. If you become intimidated by the legal system then you may well be giving up a valuable civil right and freedom, the freedom to choose.

The Internal Revenue Service does not refuse to give a taxpayer the proper tax form or tell the individual that they have to seek assistance from a certified public accountant to receive a tax form in order to pay taxes. The IRS assumes that the taxpayer either has the ability to complete the form properly or seek professional assistance from an accountant or tax preparer. The point is that the taxpayer has the legal choice and access to the system.

However, as previously stated you must understand that all procedures and the completion of all forms must be done in the same manner as if a lawyer had prepared them. The court will not have one set of rules for self-helpers and another set of rules for lawyers. The legal process will be the same.

If the clerk of domestic relations court rejects your paperwork and refuses to give you any explanation or information for the rejection other than we do not honor self-help cases, you have the following options:

- Respectfully ask to speak with their supervisor, the county compliance officer or the domestic relations judge if necessary. Make it clear that you and your spouse understand your legal right to represent yourselves in a dissolution case and that you are not asking the court for legal advice, but only requesting *a blank* copy of any form required by the court and/or county guidelines for a dissolution case, or;

- Seek the services of a local lawyer to obtain the form. Their fee should be minimal since you have completed most of the paperwork yourself.

- Complete a "waiver of venue" form and file your dissolution paperwork along with the waiver of venue form in another Ohio county near you. You will have to <u>change</u> the name of the county appearing on the upper heading of all your paperwork to this <u>new</u> county. Hopefully, this different county will better accommodate self-help cases and protect your legal right to self representation.

After The Hearing Begins

This is somewhat a frightening time for something to go wrong but don't hit the panic button. You can always ask for a continuance of the case. Lawyers do it all the time.

If the judge is difficult or refuses to grant your dissolution this means that the judge feels you have left something out of your dissolution papers that is essential. Ask the judge politely to explain and ask if you might give testimony to clarify the issue. If things go very wrong and you cannot figure out what the problem is just tell the judge, "your honor, I request that this matter be reset for hearing at another time, so that I may have time to seek advice". During the next recess see if the court clerk or bailiff can assist you or if necessary ask to see the judge in chambers. Also double check your paper work.

Assuming you have figured out the problem, have your case reset for the hearing and do the hearing over again <u>within</u> the 90 days from the date of filing.

After The Hearing

If the judge grants your dissolution but refuses to sign the final decree, there must be something wrong with the decree. Ask the court clerk what is wrong with the decree or look at the clerk's docket sheet (public record). Once you have figured out what is wrong with the decree, make a new decree form as soon as possible and bring it to the court house for the judge's signature.

A Check List Of Steps To Follow For An Ohio Dissolution

ALL LEGAL FORMS MUST BE **TYPED**

☑ You and your spouse have decided that you can no longer live together as husband and wife.

☑ You and your spouse have voluntarily agreed to decide on all issues of the marriage and incorporate them into a Separation Agreement.

☑ At least one spouse has been an Ohio resident for six months or more prior to the filing of the Petition and the wife is not currently pregnant.

☑ You and your spouse agree to attend one court hearing together.

☑ You and your spouse have completed the worksheets to determine your assets, liabilities, insurance, income and expenses of the marriage. You have jointly made decisions concerning the following:

    ☑ Division of all property and debts of the marriage.

    ☑ Spousal support, if any.

    ☑ Have decided which spouse will be the residential parent and legal custodian for the minor child/ren.

    ☑ Have decided on a visitation schedule with the minor child/ren for the nonresidential parent.

    ☑ Have completed the child support worksheet to determine from the child support schedule the amount of child support the nonresidential will pay.

    ☑ Have deceided which spouse will maintain health insurance for the benefit of the minor child/ren.

☑ Or you and your spouse have agreed to shared parenting (joint custody) for the minor child/ren, you have completed the forms for the Shared Parenting Plan and the Shared Parenting Decree.

☑ You have called the Clerk of Courts for domestic relations (telephone numbers by county listed in the appendix) to determine the following:

    ☑ The fee for filing a dissolution of marriage in your county of residence.

    ☑ The number of copies the court requires of the court forms (Petition, Separation Agreement, and Decree) and whether the forms are required to be in a specific order when filing.

☑ If the court requires that you and your spouse's signatures **be notarized** on all court forms.

☑ If there are additional county forms which you are required to file with your Petition and Separation Agreement. Ask the cost of these local forms and how you may receive a blank copy of the forms to complete and file with your paperwork. (You may have to go to the courthouse, division of domestic relations to pickup a blank copy of the form).

☑ If you have minor child/ren of the marriage, ask the clerk if the court requires that both spouses attend parental education classes before the court will grant a dissolution of marriage. If the classes are required in your county, ask the clerk where and when you and your spouse may attend

☑ You have **typed the required information** on the court forms necessary to initiate your case and checked the forms for accuracy. You and your spouse have signed all court forms in **the presence** of a notary public if this is required by the court in your county.

☑ You have filed your case at the county court house and paid the filing fee to the clerk of courts for domestic relations (only cash). You have asked the clerk how to set the hearing date for your dissolution case. The clerk may set a hearing date at the time you file your court papers or the clerk may instruct you to go to another area of the court house to set the hearing date.

☑ You have received your hearing date. **Both parties** must attend the hearing or the case will be dismissed.

☑ You and your spouse have divided all property including signing titles and recording any deeds, closed checking or savings accounts etc.

☑ You and your spouse attend the hearing at the court house.

☑ The judge grants your Dissolution of Marriage and signs the Final Decree. You have recorded your Final Decree at the court house and received a copy. You have completed any additional paperwork required to transfer ownership of any other property of the marriage.

When the judgment is entered and recorded the legal process is completed. The marriage will be legally dissolved as of the date specified on the judgment and final decree.

The Following Forms
Are Worksheets
Only

These Forms Are Not
Submitted To The
Court

Assets - Liabilities

As Of Date _____

This worksheet is not required or submitted to the court but it should give you and your spouse an opportunity to organize on paper what you own (assets) and who you owe (liabilities). After you and your spouse decide how to divide the assets and who will assume the liabilities, the information can then be transferred to the Separation Agreement.

Assets

Real Estate (Home - Investment Property - Acreage)
1. Address and Description

Date Acquired _____ Cost $ _____ Current Value $ _____

Balance of Mortgage $ _____ Title Holder _____ Use _____

2. Address and Description

Date Acquired _____ Cost $ _____ Current Value $ _____

Balance of Mortgage $ _____ Title Holder _____ Use _____

Checking Accounts

Account Number	Bank Name	Date Acquired	Current Balance	Used By
1.				
2.				
3.				
4.				

Savings, C.D.'s, Money Market Funds, Mutual Funds, Treasury Bills

Account Number	Type	Date Acquired	Current Balance
1.			
2.			
3.			
4.			
5.			
6.			
7.			
8.			

Stocks and Bonds

Name And Number Of Shares	Date Acquire	Exchange	Title Holder	Cost	Value
1.					
2.					
3.					
4.					
5.					
6.					

Vehicles, Motorcycles, Boats, Motor Homes, Mobile Homes

Description	Date Acquired	Titleholder	Cost	Current Value	Loan Balance
1.					
2.					
3.					
4.					
5.					

Furnishing, Antiques, Artworks, Collections (Stamp-Coins etc.)

Description	Date Acquired	Who Acquired	Cost	Current Value	Where Located
1.					
2.					
3.					
4.					
5.					
6.					
7.					

Cash-value Life Insurance (Whole Life)

Insurance Company	Policy Number	Insured Beneficiary	Owner	Current Value	Premium
1.					
2.					

Pension and Profit Sharing

Name Of Plan	Owner / Interest	Date Entered	Vesting Date / Percent	Current Value
1.				
2.				
3.				
4.				

Closely Held Corporation

Company Name and % of Ownership	Date Acquired	Date and Amount of Last Valustion
1.		
2.		

Partnerships and/or Joint Ventures

Company Name and % of Ownership	Date Acquired	Amount of Investment	Curr Value	Income/Loss
1.				
2.				

Sole Proprietorships

Nature Of Business	Date Acquired	Market Value	Average Income / Loss
1.			
2.			

Account Receivable and Notes Due

Payable To	Name Of Debtor	Balance Due	Amt. Of Payments	Nature Of Debt
1.				
2.				

Patents, Copyrights, Royalties

Owner	Description Of Interest	Date Acquired	Benefits To Date	Current Value
1.				
2.				

Miscellaneous Assets

Describe	Date Acquired	By Whom	Cost	Current Value	Source Of Payment
1.					
2.					
3.					
4.					
5.					

Liabilities

Secured Debts And Real Estate Taxes or Assessments (Home, Car, Furniture etc.)

Creditor	Date & Loan No.	Debtor	Current Balance	Payments	Security/Co-Signer
1.					
2.					
3.					
4.					
5.					
6.					
7.					
8.					

Unsecured Debts And Income Taxes (credit Cards etc.)

Creditor	Account Number	Current Balance	Payments	Name On Card
1.				
2.				
3.				
4.				
5.				
6.				
7.				
8.				

Other Pending Debts

	Creditor	Basis For Claim	When Debt Accrued	Date And Amount Due
1.				
2.				
3.				
4.				

Insurance

Life Insurance

	Insurer & Policy No.	Term/Whole Life	Owner	Beneficiary	Prem.	Death Benefit	Current Value
1.							
2.							
3.							

Home Or Renter's Insurance

	Insurer & Policy No.	Expiration Date	Premium	Named Insured	Agent
1.					
2.					

Automobile, Boat, Mobile Home, Motorcycles, Motor Home

	Insurer & Policy No.	Expiration Date	Premium	Named Insured	Vehicle	Agent
1.						
2.						
3.						
4.						
5.						

Health And Medical, Disability

	Insurer & Policy No.	Expiration Date	Premium	Person's Covered	Agent
1.					
2.					
3.					
4.					
5.					
6.					

Other Insurance

	Company & Policy No.	Expiration Date	Premium	Type Of Insurance	Beneficiary	Agent
1.						
2.						
3.						
4.						

_____
Petitioner

SS# _____

DOB _____

and

_____
Petitioner

SS# _____

DOB _____

HUSBAND _____ Occupation _____ Phone No _____

Current Residence Address: Current Mailing Address: (if different)
_____   _____

Employer/Complete Address _____

WIFE _____ Occupation _____ Phone No _____
Current Residence Address: Current Mailing Address: (if different)
_____   _____

Employer/Complete Address _____

Date And Place Of Marriage _____

CHILDREN: 1: _____   DOB_____
               2: _____   DOB_____
               3: _____   DOB_____
               4: _____   DOB_____

Medical Insurance coverage for the minor children is available to / or maintained by:
(Husband or Wife or Both or Neither) _____

INCOME

HUSBAND		**WIFE**
Receives [] 12 [] 24 [] 26		Receives [] 12 [] 24 [] 26
[] 52 paychecks per year		[] 52 paychecks per year
Specify Amounts Per Pay Period		Specify Amounts Per Pay Period
$ _____	Gross regular income from work	$ _____
$ _____	**Deductions:** (a) Income Tax & Social Security	$ _____
$ _____	(b) Retirement	$ _____
$ _____	(c) Loan Payments	$ _____
$ _____	(d) Savings	$ _____
$ _____	(e) Other	$ _____
$ _____	TOTAL withholding per pay period	$ _____
$ _____	NET REGULAR INCOME (employment)	$ _____
$ _____	Unemployment Compensation	$ _____
$ _____	Workers' Compensation (Claim#_____)	$ _____
$ _____	Other Income: _____	$ _____
$ _____	**TOTAL INCOME**	$ _____

III.   **MONTHLY INSTALLMENT PAYMENTS (Do not list expenses previously listed)**

To Whom Paid	Purpose	Balance Due	Monthly Payment
_____	_____	_____	_____
_____	_____	_____	_____
_____	_____	_____	_____
_____	_____	_____	_____

Total Installment Payments .... $_____

TOTAL MONTHLY EXPENSES (Sum I, II, & III) ....$ _____

FINANCIAL DISCLOSURE

List all funds on deposit in any and all accounts in any Bansk, Savings & Loan, Credit Union, Regulated Investment Company, Mutual Fund or Other Financial Institution. Accounts may include one or more of the following: checking, certificate of deposit (CD), investment, savings, individual retirement account (IRA), stock option, etc. USE REVERSE SIDE IF NEEDED.

Name Of Financial Institution	Address Of Financial Institution	Account No.	Names on Account	Balance as of this Date
_____	_____	_____	_____	_____
	_____			
_____	_____	_____	_____	_____
	_____			
_____	_____	_____	_____	_____
	_____			
_____	_____	_____	_____	_____
	_____			
_____	_____	_____	_____	_____
	_____			
_____	_____	_____	_____	_____
	_____			

OTHER INCOME   (Including but not limited to pension, annuity, allowance, sick pay, disability pay, or other benefit, commissions, trusts, bonus, profit sharing payments or distribution lottery winnings and lump sum payments).

Type	Source	Address Of Source	Amount		Date Received
_____	_____	_____	_____ per _____		_____
		_____			
_____	_____	_____	_____ per _____		_____
		_____			
_____	_____	_____	_____ per _____		_____
		_____			
_____	_____	_____	_____ per _____		_____

MONTHLY LIVING EXPENSES

Expenses listed are for _____ self only, _____ self and the minor child(ren).
Are any other persons included in this budget? Yes _____ No _____. How Many? _____.
What is the total amount of income (per month) attributable to those persons? $ _____.

I. **Housing**

    1. Rent or Mortgage Payment
    (including taxes & insurance) ....$ _____
    2. Utilities
        a. Gas & Electric ....$ _____
        b. Water & Sewer ....$ _____
        c. Telephone (excluding long distance) ....$ _____
        d. Trash Collection ....$ _____
        e. Water Softener ....$ _____
        f. Cable ....$ _____
    3. Housing Repairs ....$ _____
    4. Homeowners or Renters Insurance (if paid separately) ....$ _____
    5. Other: (specify) _____ ....$ _____
        TOTAL HOUSING COSTS ....$ _____

II. **Other Expenses**

    1. Car Repairs & License ....$ _____
    2. Insurance
        a. Auto ....$ _____
        b. Life ....$ _____
        c. Medical ....$ _____
        d. Other: (specify) _____ ....$ _____
    3. Medical (not covered by insurance) ....$ _____
    4. Clothing ....$ _____
    5. Haircare ....$ _____
    6. Dry Cleaning ....$ _____
    7. Newspapers, Periodicals and Books ....$ _____
    8. Grocery Items
        (to include food, laundry and cleaning products) ....$ _____
    9. Toilet Acessories ....$ _____
    10. Child Care ....$ _____
    11. School Lunch Program ....$ _____
    12. Children's Allowance ....$ _____
    13. Activities - Minor Children (Music, Sports, etc.) ....$ _____
    14. Tuition (for Minor Children or Self) ....$ _____
    15. Entertainment ....$ _____
    16. Contributions ....$ _____
    17. Gas and Oil ....$ _____
    18. Tax (not deducted from wages) ....$ _____
    19. Alimony/Support Payment (previous court order) ....$ _____
    20. Membership (associations, clubs) ....$ _____
    21. Travel and Vacations ....$ _____
    22. Other (specify) _____ ....$ _____

        TOTAL OTHER EXPENSES ....$ _____

THE FORMS YOU WILL NEED TO FILE WITH THE COURT

| Form Title | If No Children And No Spousal Support |

☐ Petition And Waiver of Service .... Blank Forms Section
☐ Separation Agreement .... Blank Forms Section
☐ Waiver of Representation .... Blank Forms Section
☐ Waiver of Financial Disclosure Affidavit .... Blank Forms Section
☐ or Financial Disclosure, Income and Expenses .... Blank Forms Section
   (In some counties (Franklin) the Financial Disclosure Income and Expenses
   cannot be waived and is mandatory for each spouse whether there are
   child/ren of the marriage or not. This form is *always mandatory* when
   spousal support or child support is paid.)
☐ Social Questionnaire or other local county form .... Clerk of Domestic Relations Court
☐ Decree .... Blank Forms Section
☐ Waiver of Venue .... Blank Forms Section
   (Complete and file *only* if filing your paperwork in a county other than
   your county of residence.)

| Form Title | If There Are Child(ren) of The Marriage |

☐ Petition And Waiver of Service .... Blank Forms Section
☐ Separation Agreement .... Blank Forms Section
☐ Waiver of Representation .... Blank Forms Section
☐ Financial Disclosure Affidavit .... Blank Forms Section
☐ and/or Financial Disclosure, Income and Expenses .... Blank Forms Section
☐ Group Health Insurance Affidavit .... Blank Forms Section
☐ Health Care Verification Form .... Blank Forms Section
☐ Affivadit in Compliance with ORC 3109.27 .... Blank Forms Section
☐ Social Questionnaire or other local county form .... Clerk of Domestic Relations Court
☐ Decree .... Blank Forms Section

If the Parties are requesting Shared Parenting
☐ Shared Parenting Plan .... Blank Forms Section
☐ Shared Parenting Decree .... Blank Forms Section

| For the Payment of Child Support and Health Care |

☐ Appropriate Child Support Worksheet .... Blank Forms Section
   ■ Sole Residential Parent / Shared Parenting or
   ■ Split Parental Rights And Responsibilities
☐ Appropriate Child Support Deduction Order .... Blank Forms Section
   ■ Employer - Workers' Compensation - Financial Institution - Public Pension **or**
   ■ Unemployment Notice Order
☐ Appropriate Health Care Order ...... Blank Forms Section
   ■ Obligor (coverage will be maintained by the parent paying child support) **or**
   ■ Obligee (coverage will be maintained by the parent receiving child support) **or**
   ■ Obligor and Obligee (there will be dual coverage by both parents) **or**
   ■ Shared Liability (no insurance is available and health care will be a shared cost)

| For the Payment of Spousal Support |

☐ Financial Disclosure Affidavit .... Blank Forms Section
☐ Appropriate Spousal Support Deduction Order .... Blank Forms Section
   ■ Employer **or**
   ■ Unemployment Notice Order

> Forms are perforated for easy removal
> carefully fold and tear along the
> perforation to remove pages

Blank Court Forms

For Parties **Without** Minor Children Of The Marriage

ALL COURT FORMS MUST BE TYPED

- ❑ Petition And Waiver Of Service
- ❑ Separation Agreement
- ❑ Decree Of Dissolution Of Marriage
- ❑ Financial Disclosure Income & Expenses

Spousal Support Deduction Order

- ❑ Employer

Additional Court Forms

- ❑ Waiver Of Representation (husband and wife)
- ❑ Waiver Of Fourteen Day Objection Period
- ❑ Waiver Of Property
- ❑ Waiver Of Venue
- ❑ Waiver Of Financial Documentation

LawPak Software In Development

We are currently developing software which can be used to download the Ohio Dissolution of Marriage court forms and a reference manual from our web site at www.elawpak.com.

The forms can be downloaded onto your disk and then into your word processing system. Use the word processing system on the computer to complete the required information on the forms and print them on the computer's printer.

When using this method you will not have to remove the blank forms from this publication and then type the required information on the form in a typewriter.

There is a charge to download the forms from our Internet site which will require that you input valid credit card information before the download can take place. Please check our web site to determine if we have completed the development of this option.

COURT OF COMMON PLEAS
DIVISION OF DOMESTIC RELATIONS
_____COUNTY, OHIO

IN RE THE MARRIAGE OF:

Name: _____ :
Address: _____ :
_____ :   Case No. _____
SS #: _____ :
DOB: _____ :
Telephone #: _____ :
        Petitioner, :
  :   **PETITION FOR DISSOLUTION OF**
        -and- :   **OF MARRIAGE AND WAIVER OF**
  :   **SERVICE OF SUMMONS**
Name: _____ :
Address: _____ :
_____ :
SS #: _____ :
DOB: _____ :
Telephone #: _____ :
        Petitioner,

1. At least one of the Petitioners has been a resident of the State of Ohio for at least six (6) months or more immediately prior to filing this Petition.
2. Petitioners were married on the _____ day of _____ _____,
in _____, _____.
3. There are no minor children of this marriage.
4. A Separation Agreement, agreed to and signed by both Petitioners, which provides for a division of all property and spousal support, where applicable, is attached hereto and incorporated herein.
5. Both Petitioners acknowledge that they have voluntarily entered into the attached Separation Agreement appended to the Petition herein; that they are satisfied with its terms; and that they seek a Dissolution of the Marriage.
6. The wife is not pregnant.
        WHEREFORE, both Petitioners request the Court to grant a Dissolution of Marriage, incorporating the attached Separation Agreement.

_____   _____
Signature of Petitioner/Wife   Date   Signature of Petitioner/Husband   Date

WAIVER OF SERVICE OF SUMMONS
        Petitioners state that they are at least eighteen (18) years of age and not under disability, and waive service of summons herein, and consent to the Court herein granting a Decree of Dissolution of Marriage, incorporating the Separation Agreement herein.

_____   _____
Signature of Petitioner/Wife   Date   Signature of Petitioner/Husband   Date

STATE OF OHIO   )
) SS:
COUNTY OF _____)

Sworn to and subscribed in my presence this _____ day of _____, 20_____.

Petition Page One   Notary Public _____

Separation Agreement

This Separation Agreement voluntarily made and entered into by Petitioner/Wife _____ _____ hereinafter referred to as "wife", and Petitioner/Husband _____ _____ hereinafter referred to as "husband", represents that:

1. The date and place of the marriage of the Petitioners are:
   Date Of Marriage: _____ Place of Marriage: _____, _____

2. Differences have a risen between the Petitioners and we are now living separate and apart from each other.

3. The parties hereto desire to, and by this Agreement do, settle and determine and hereby provide for a division of all property belonging to the parties, and provide for spousal support, where applicable.

NOWTHEREFORE, in consideration of the foregoing and the mutual promises and agreements hereinafter set forth, the parties agree as follows:

ARTICLE ONE: SEPARATION
Each party shall hereinafter continue to live separate and apart from each other, and neither shall annoy, molest, interfere with or harass the other in any manner, either directly or indirectly.

ARTICLE TWO: DIVISION OF PROPERTY
All property, real and personal, and whatever situated which the parties own jointly or individually, or in common with each other, shall be divided as follows:

A. REAL PROPERTY
- ☐ We have no real property.
- ☐ The husband has real property which he owned prior to marriage and the wife is waiving her claims on his real property, now and in the future.
- ☐ The wife has real property which she owned prior to marriage and the husband is waiving all his claims on her real property, now and in the future.
- ☐ The parties jointly own real property and agree that it shall be divided as follows:

_____
_____
_____
_____
_____
_____
_____
_____
_____
_____
_____

B. SPOUSAL SUPPORT
- ☐ Neither the wife or the husband shall pay spousal support to the other party and state that all future rights to spousal support are being waived.
- ☐ _____ shall pay spousal support to the _____ in the amount of _____ per week, plus _____ % poundage, payable through the _____ County Bureau of Support/Support Enforcement Agency effective _____, 20 _____. Said spousal support shall terminate on _____ 20 ____ or upon the happening of the earliest of the following events: death of the spouse receiving or paying the spousal support, cohabitation with another person, or _____.

C. MOTOR VEHICLES
☐ There are no motor vehicles.
☐ Husband shall receive no motor vehicle.
☐ Husband shall receive, free and clear of any claims of the wife, all right, title and interest in the
_____ automobile/truck.
Husband shall hold wife harmless from any debts owing thereon.
☐ Husband shall also receive the following vehicles: _____.
☐ Wife shall receive no motor vehicle.
☐ Wife shall receive, free and clear of any claims of the husband, all right, title and interest in the
_____ automobile/truck.
Wife shall hold husband harmless from any debts owing thereon.
☐ Wife shall also receive the following vehicles: _____.

D. HOUSEHOLD GOODS
☐ We agree that our household goods and possessions are already divided and we are satisfied with the division there.
☐ Husband shall receive the following household goods: _____
_____.
☐ Wife shall receive the following household goods: _____
_____.
☐ See the attached list for the division of household goods.

E. PERSONAL PROPERTY
☐ We agree that our personal property is already divided.
☐ We agree that each party may have his/her own personal property.
☐ See attached list for the division of personal property.

F. SAVINGS ACCOUNTS
☐ We agree that our savings accounts are already divided and we are satisfied with the division,
☐ Husband shall receive the following savings account(s): _____.
☐ Wife shall receive the following savings account(s): _____.
☐ We have no savings account.

G. CHECKING ACCOUNTS
☐ We agree that our checking accounts are already divided.
☐ Husband shall have the following checking account(s): _____.
☐ Wife shall have the following checking account(s): _____.
☐ We have no checking accounts.

H. CREDIT UNION ACCOUNTS AND/OR STOCKS AND/OR BONDS
☐ We agree that the above listed assets are already divided and we are satisfied with the division.
☐ Husband shall receive the following credit union accounts/stocks/bonds: _____
_____.
☐ Wife shall receive the following credit union accounts/stocks/bonds: _____
_____.
☐ We do not have any credit union accounts and/or stocks and/or bonds.

I. PENSION/PROFIT SHARING AND/OR IRA'S
☐ We agree that the above listed assets are already divided and we are satisfied with the division.
☐ Husband shall receive the following pension/profit sharing and/or IRA account(s)_____
_____.
☐ Wife shall receive the following pension/profit sharing and/or IRA account(s): _____
_____.
☐ We do not have any pension/profit sharing and/or IRA accounts.

J. LIFE INSURANCE
- ❑ We agree that the cash value of our life insurance policies has already been divided.
- ❑ Husband shall receive the following life insurance policy, free and clear of any claims of the wife:_____.
- ❑ Wife shall receive the following life insurance policy, free and clear of any claim of the husband: _____.

The parties have no life insurance policies with a cash surrender value.

K. INCOME TAX REFUNDS AND/OR LIABILITIES
- ❑ We agree that our income tax refund(s) for the last year has been divided to our satisfaction.
- ❑ Husband shall receive the following amount from our joint refund: $ _____.
- ❑ Husband shall pay the following amount $ _____ to _____ for taxes.
- ❑ Wife shall receive the following amount from our joint refund: $ _____.
- ❑ Wife shall pay the following amount $ _____ to _____ for taxes.

L. DEBTS
- ❑ Husband shall pay any debts incurred by him personally from this day forward, including any debts or expenses incurred after the separation and prior to the granting of divorce or dissolution. Wife shall pay any debts incurred by her personally from this day forward, including any debts or expenses incurred after the separation and prior to the granting of divorce or dissolution.
- ❑ We have no debts.
- ❑ We agree to the payment of all debts we owe as follows:

Husband shall pay:

OBLIGATION	CREDITOR	BALANCE
1.		
2.		
3.		
4.		
5.		

Wife shall pay:

1.		
2.		
3.		
4.		
5.		

ARTICLE THREE: NON-USE OF OTHER'S CREDIT
The parties agree that neither shall hereinafter incur any debts or obligations upon the credit of the other, and each shall indemnify the other from any debts and obligation so charged or incurred.

ARTICLE FOUR: NAME CHANGE
- ❑ The wife's name is not changed.
- ❑ The wife's name is changed to: _____.

ARTICLE FIVE: COMPLETE DISCLOSURE
The parties agree that each has made a full and complete disclosure of his or her property, and that neither has knowledge of any personal property of any kind which the parties so agreeing have any beneficial interest. If it is later discovered that either party has possession or control of, or has disposed of by gift or conveyance, any undisclosed beneficial interest in any property, such party on demand, shall transfer and assign to the other party one-half interest therein, or shall pay to the other party a sum equal to one-half of the fair market value of said beneficial interest.

ARTICLE SIX: INCORPORATION INTO DECREE

This Agreement or any amendment thereto, shall be submitted to any court in which a Petition for Dissolution of Marriage or action between the parties for a divorce may be pending, and if found by the Court to be fair and equitable, and approved or validated by the Court, shall be incorporated in the Final Decree of said Court as the order of said Court. It is understood that the parties contemplate the possibility of filing a divorce or dissolution within four (4) months after the execution of this separation agreement.

ARTICLE SEVEN: COMPLETE AGREEMENT

This Agreement shall inure to the benefits of and be binding upon the parties and their respective heirs, executors, administrators, successors and assigns, and may not be modified or changed other than by further agreement of the parties in writing.

ARTICLE EIGHT: PERFORMANCE OF NECESSARY ACTS

Each party shall execute any and all deeds, bills of sale, or other documents, and perform any acts which may be required or necessary to carry out and effectuate any and all of the purposes and provisions herein set forth:

ARTICLE NINE: ADDITIONAL MATTERS

- ☐ There are no additional matters that we have agreed to or need to agree to.
- ☐ We agree to the following additional matters: _____
_____
_____.

ARTICLE TEN: EQUAL DIVISION

The parties acknowledge that each is entitled to an equal division of marital property in accordance with R.C. 3105.171, and further acknowledge that the division of marital property provided for in the Agreement is not precisely equal. Accordingly, both parties waive any right to an equal division of marital property.

ARTICLE ELEVEN: SEVERABILITY

If any provision or clause in this Agreement is held invalid, such invalidity shall not affect any other provision of this Agreement.

ARTICLE TWELVE: APPLICABLE LAW

All provisions of this Agreement shall be construed and enforced in accordance with the laws of the State of Ohio.

ARTICLE THIRTEEN: ATTORNEY WAIVER

The Petitioners are aware of their rights to have an attorney represent them in this matter, hereby with full knowledge of all assets and liabilities of the marriage and of both parties own wish; the Petitioners are waiving their right to an attorney herein and specifically request the Court to proceed with full knowledge of such waiver.

ARTICLE FOURTEEN: EFFECTIVE DATE

This Agreement shall be effective upon the date last signed by a party to the Agreement.

_____   _____
Signature of Petitioner/Wife   Date   Signature of Petitioner/Husband   Date

STATE OF OHIO   )
) SS:
COUNTY OF _____   )

Sworn to and subscribed in my presence this _____ day of _____ , 20_____ .

Separation Agreement Page Four   Notary Public _____

IN RE THE MATTER OF:

Name: _____   :   Date _____
SS #: _____   :
DOB: _____   :
      Petitioner,   :   Case No. _____
                                       :
               -and-   :   Judge _____
                                       :

Name: _____   :
SS #: _____   :   **WAIVER OF REPRESENTATION**
DOB: _____   :
      Petitioner,   :

_____ , does hereby acknowledge and represent that he

is not represented by counsel in this proceeding. He further acknowledges that the undersigned was given

full opportunity to evaluate his need for legal representation and was advised to obtain, if so desired,

his own counsel. The undersigned realizes that this document constitutes and acknowledges his waiver of

right to counsel in this proceeding.

                                                _____

                                                Petitioner/Husband

STATE OF OHIO   )
) SS:
COUNTY OF _____)

Sworn to and subscribed in my presence this _____ day of _____ , 20_____.

                                     Notary Public _____

COURT OF COMMON PLEAS
DIVISION OF DOMESTIC RELATIONS
_____COUNTY, OHIO

IN RE THE MATTER OF:

Name: _____ :   Date _____
SS #: _____ :
DOB: _____ :
      Petitioner,   :   Case No. _____
                                          :
                  -and-   :   Judge _____
                                          :
                                          :
Name: _____ :
SS #: _____ :   **WAIVER OF REPRESENTATION**
DOB: _____ :
      Petitioner,   :

_____ , does hereby acknowledge and represent that she

is not represented by counsel in this proceeding. she further acknowledges that the undersigned was given

full opportunity to evaluate her need for legal representation and was advised to obtain, if so desired,

her own counsel. The undersigned realizes that this document constitutes and acknowledges her waiver of

right to counsel in this proceeding.

                                             _____
                                             Petitioner/Wife

STATE OF OHIO   )
) SS:
COUNTY OF _____)

Sworn to and subscribed in my presence this _____ day of _____ , 20____.

                              Notary Public _____

COURT OF COMMON PLEAS
DIVISION OF DOMESTIC RELATIONS
_____COUNTY, OHIO

IN RE THE MATTER OF:

Name: _____   :   Date _____
SS #: _____   :
DOB: _____   :
     Petitioner,   :   Case No. _____
          :
          :   Judge _____
     -and-   :
          :
Name: _____   :
SS #: _____   :   **WAIVER OF PROPERTY**
DOB: _____   :
     Petitioner,   :

The parties hereto being fully advised, hereby waive appraisal and valuation of their separate and marital property, waive determination of the period included in "duration of marriage", and waive findings of fact, and agree that while the property division herein may not be exactly equal, that it is equitable.

_____
Petitioner/Wife   Date

_____
Petitioner/Husband   Date

STATE OF OHIO   )
) SS:
COUNTY OF _____)

Sworn to and subscribed in my presence this _____ day of _____ , 20_____.

Notary Public _____

COURT OF COMMON PLEAS
DIVISION OF DOMESTIC RELATIONS
_____COUNTY, OHIO

IN RE THE MATTER OF:

Name: _____   :   Date _____

SS #: _____   :

DOB: _____   :

       Petitioner,   :   Case No. _____

                                            :   Judge _____

                  -and-   :

                                          :

Name: _____   :

SS #: _____   :   **WAIVER OF FOURTEEN DAY**

DOB: _____   :   **OBJECTION PERIOD**

       Petitioner,   :

The parties, this day in open Court before the Referee having heard the recommendations by him/her made and being in agreement therewith or having no objections thereto, do hereby waive their right to file objections thereto under Rule 53 and consent to immediate Entry of said recommendation(s) as the order of the Court to take effect upon docketing. Each party acknowledges that this is a voluntary act and each party understands that they are under no legal duty to sign this waiver.

_____

Petitioner/Husband

_____

Petitioner/Wife

_____

Referee

COURT OF COMMON PLEAS
DIVISION OF DOMESTIC RELATIONS
_____COUNTY, OHIO

IN RE THE MARRIAGE OF:

Name: _____   :   Date _____
SS #: _____   :
DOB: _____   :
        Petitioner,   :   Case No. _____
            :
            :   Judge _____
        -and-   :
            :
            :   **WAIVER OF**
Name: _____   :   **FINANCIAL DISCLOSURE AFFIDAVIT**
SS #: _____   :   **NO CHILDREN OR SPOUSAL SUPPORT**
DOB: _____   :   **O.R.C. 3113.21(C)**
        Petitioner,

Now comes _____ and _____
                     Party   Party
and after being duly cautioned and sworn, says:

There is no issue of spousal support and no children involved in this matter and the Separation

Agreement being filed with the Court, and which the Court is asked to approved, contains no orders to the

same.

It is therefore represented to the Court that there is no need to file a Financial Disclosure Affidavit

in the above captioned matter and that same is hereby waived.

_____   _____
Affiant / Petitioner / Wife   Affiant / Petitioner / Husband

STATE OF OHIO   )
)   SS:
COUNTY OF _____)

Sworn to and subscribed in my presence this _____ day of _____ , 20_____.

Notary Public _____

COURT OF COMMON PLEAS
DIVISION OF DOMESTIC RELATIONS
_____COUNTY, OHIO

IN RE THE MARRIAGE OF:

Name: _____ :   DATE: _____

SS #: _____ :   CASE NO. A: _____

     Petitioner,   DOB   :   FILE NO. E: _____

            -and-   :   JUDGE _____

Name: _____ :

SS #: _____ :   **FINANCIAL DISCLOSURE**

     Petitioner,   DOB   :   **O.R.C. 3113.21 (C)**

Now comes _____ and, after being duly cautioned and sworn, says:
                                    Obligor

1. I ☐   am employed.

      ☐   am not employed.   My employer is _____

_____

Employer's Payroll Address   City   State   Zip Code

I receive   ☐ 12   ☐ 24   ☐ 26   ☐ 52   paychecks per year.

2. I ☐ am ☐ am not receiving Workers' Compensation under Claim No. _____.

      ☐ am ☐ am not receiving Unemployment Compensation under Claim No. _____.

3. I ☐ do

    ☐ do not have funds on deposit in Financial Institutions. (List all funds in all accounts in any Bank, Savings & Loan, Credit Union, Regulated Investment Company, Mutual or Other Financial Institutions. Account may include one or more of the following: checking, certificate of deposit ("CD"), investment, savings, individual retirement ("IRA"), stock options, etc. USE ADDITIONAL PAGES IF NEEDED).

Name of Financial Institution	Address of Financial Institution	Account No.	Name(s) on Account	Balance as of Date of the Affidavit
_____	_____	_____	_____	_____
	_____			
_____	_____	_____	_____	_____
	_____			
_____	_____	_____	_____	_____

4. I have the following additional sources of income. (List sources, address and amount including but not limited to pension (public and private) annuities, allowance, sick pay, disability pay or other benefit, commissions, trusts, bonuses, profit sharing payments or distributions, lottery winnings, lump sum payments, and private Workers' Compensation payments).

_____

5. I ☐ do

    ☐ do not have other assets from which child support/spousal support can be paid or secured. (If affirmative, list all such assets on a separate sheet of paper).

_____
Affiant - Obligor

STATE OF OHIO   )

) SS:

COUNTY OF _____   )

Sworn to and subscribed in my presence this _____ day of _____ , 20____.

                       Notary Public _____

I hereby acknowledge receipt of a copy of this affidavit _____ .
                                                      Obligee

COURT OF COMMON PLEAS
DIVISION OF DOMESTIC RELATIONS
_____COUNTY, OHIO

IN RE THE MARRIAGE OF:

Name: _____ :
SS #: _____ :
     Petitioner, :
        -and- :
Name: _____ :
SS #: _____ :
     Petitioner, :

Case No. _____

ASSETS AND LIABILITIES AS
OF _____

FINANCIAL DISCLOSURE
AFFIDAVIT

INSTRUCTIONS: YOU ARE TO DISCLOSE ALL SUCH INFORMATION THAT IS REQUESTED HEREIN AND BY THE _____ COUNTY COURT OF COMMON PLEAS, DIVISION OF DOMESTIC RELATIONS. BE SPECIFIC, LIST ALL ASSETS, LIABILITIES, INCOME SOURCES AND RETIREMENT ACCOUNTS SEPARATELY. ALSO LIST ACCOUNT NUMBERS, NAMES, LOCATIONS AND VALUES AND WHETHER JOINTLY OR INDIVIDUALLY HELD.

ASSETS:

Cash	_____
Government Bonds	_____
Checking Account	_____
Savings Account	_____
Accts/Notes Receivable	_____
Stocks, Bonds, Securities	_____
Life Ins. Cash Value	_____
Real Estate	_____
Automobiles	_____
Other Assets (Itemize)	_____

LIABILITIES:

Notes Payable	_____
Accounts Payable	_____
Loans on Life Ins.	_____
Taxes	_____
Mortgages	_____
Other Debts (Itemize)	_____

INCOME:

From Employment	_____
Other Income (Itemize)	_____

CONTINGENT LIABILITY:

Notes / Accounts Payable _____
Guarantor
Other Contingent
Liabilities (Itemize) _____

RETIREMENT ACCOUNTS:

Husband _____
_____ Vested?

Wife _____
_____ Vested?

This may be supplemented with additional information on attached sheets. If income is derived from a business attach a profit and loss statement or copy of income tax return for the past business year and any current profit and loss information statement.

_____
Petitioner / Husband

_____
Petitioner / Wife

STATE OF OHIO   )
) SS:
COUNTY OF _____)

Sworn to and subscribed in my presence this _____ day of _____ , 20_____.

Notary Public _____

COURT OF COMMON PLEAS
DIVISION OF DOMESTIC RELATIONS
_____COUNTY, OHIO

IN RE THE MARRIAGE OF:

Name: _____ :   Date _____

SS #: _____ :

DOB: _____ :

     Petitioner,   :   Case No. _____

                                :

                                :   Judge _____

            -and-   :

                                :

                                :   **WAIVER OF**

Name: _____ :

SS #: _____ :   **FINANCIAL DOCUMENTATION**

DOB: _____ :

     Petitioner,   :

     I hereby certify that I have reviewed our financial documentation, to the extent I deem necessary, any documentation in support of computations therein, and hereby waive any right which I may have to submit such documentation to the Court for independent review. I further certify that any documentation which the Court might independently require shall be made available to the Court promptly upon request.

                                    _____

                                    Obligee

WAIVER

     I hereby certify that I have reviewed our financial documentation, to the extent I deem necessary, any documentation in support of computations therein, and hereby waive any right which I may have to submit such documentation to the Court for independent review. I further certify that any documentation which the Court might independently require shall be made available to the Court promptly upon request.

                                    _____

                                    Obligor

STATE OF OHIO   )

)   SS:

COUNTY OF _____)

Sworn to and subscribed in my presence this _____ day of _____ , 20____ .

                     Notary Public _____

IN RE THE MATTER OF:

Name: _____   :
Address: _____   :
      _____   :   Case No. _____
SS #: _____   :
DOB: _____   :   Judge _____
      Petitioner,   :
                                     :
              -and-   :
                                       :

Name: _____   :   **DECREE OF DISSOLUTION**
Address: _____   :   **OF MARRIAGE**
      _____   :
SS #: _____   :
DOB: _____   :
      Petitioner,   :

1. This matter came on for hearing on the _____ day of _____, 20_____ on the Petition for Dissolution Of Marriage, filed by both Petitioners. Both parties appeared before the Court at the hearing.

2. The Court finds that both petitioners had been notified of the hearing, in accordance with the Rules of the Court and the Ohio Rules of Civil Procedure. The Court finds that both spouses were duly served as required by law and said service is hereby approved, and the Court finds that the Court has jurisdiction of the claim for relief of the parties herein.

3. The Court finds that at least one of the Petitioners had been a resident of the State of Ohio for at least six (6) months prior to the filing the Petition herein.

4. The Court finds that the Petitioners were married on _____ day of _____, _____, in _____ , _____ .

5. The Court further finds that both spouses appeared before the Court and both spouses acknowledge under oath that they voluntarily entered into the Separation Agreement appended to the Petition, that they are satisfied with its terms, and that they seek dissolution of marriage.

6. It is further ordered that:
    ❐   Neither the wife nor the husband shall pay spousal support to the other party and that all future rights to spousal support are being waived.
    ❐   The Payor, _____ , shall pay as spousal support for the _____ the sum of $ _____ per week, plus _____ % poundage, payable through the _____ County Bureau of Support/Support Enforcement Agency effective on the aforementioned hearing date. For administrative purposes only, the order shall be administered in the amount of $ _____ per month, plus _____ % poundage, for a total monthly payment of $ _____ . Said spousal support shall terminate on _____ 20 _____ , or the death of the spouse receiving or paying spousal

support, cohabitation with another person or _____.
All payment in satisfaction of said obligation which are not made through the Bureau of
Support/Support Enforcement Agency account shall be deemed as gifts.

7. Until such time as the Support Deduction Order and Additional Orders are implemented, Payor shall be responsible for making all payments to the Bureau of Support/Support Enforcement Agency.

8. It is further ordered that:
   ☐ the wife's name is not changed.
   ☐ the wife's name is changed to _____.

9. It is further ordered that the Petitioners shall pay the costs of these proceedings, and all further orders of the Court.

10. Upon review of the testimony of both spouses, the Court hereby approves the Separation Agreement and the Court grants a Decree of Dissolution of Marriage to the Petitioners, incorporating the Separation Agreement, and all Orders herein.

11. IT IS THEREFORE ORDERED, ADJUDGED AND DECREED THAT the marriage relationship, heretofore existing between the parties be, and the same is hereby, terminated and held for naught, and both parties are hereby released and discharged from all obligations thereof.

_____   _____
Referee   Judge
Court of Common Pleas   Court of Common Pleas
Division of Domestic Relations   Division of Domestic Relations
_____County, Ohio   _____ County, Ohio

_____   _____
Petitioner/ Wife's Signature   Petitioner/Husband's Signature

WAIVER

Now comes _____ , payor, and says that he/she is eighteen (18) or more years of age and under no disability, that he/she has received a copy of the spousal support order and O.R.C. 3113.21 Order and instructions and that he/she waives service of same.

_____   _____
Date   Payor

IN RE THE MATTER OF:

Name: _____   :   Date _____

SS #: _____   :

DOB: _____   :

     Petitioner,   :   Case No. _____

                      :

                      :   Judge _____

          -and-   :

                      :

Name: _____   :

SS #: _____   :   **WAIVER OF VENUE**

DOB: _____   :

     Petitioner,   :

Now comes _____ and _____,

who are at least eighteen (18) years of age and not under disability and waive venue in _____

_____ County, Ohio and consent to the Court herein, hearing said cause,

granting a Decree of Dissolution of Marriage, and the incorporating of the Separation Agreement herein.

_____   _____

Petitioner/ Wife   Petitioner/ Husband

_____   _____

Date   Date

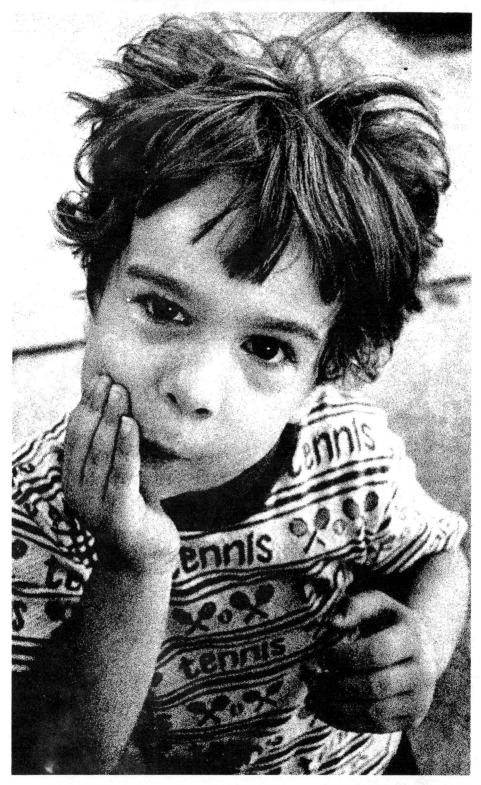

If There Are Minor Children
Of The Marriage, Use The
Following Court Forms:

You Have Minor Children Of The Marriage

BLANK COURT FORMS
FOR PARTIES *WITH* MINOR CHILDREN
(ALL COURT FORMS MUST BE TYPED)

☐ Petition And Waiver Of Service

☐ Separation Agreement

☐ Decree Of Dissolution Of Marriage

☐ Financial Disclosure Income And Expenses

CHILD SUPPORT COURT FORMS
Child Support Wooksheets (use only one type)

  ☐ Sole Residential Parent / Shared Parenting

  ☐ Split Parental Rights And Responsibilities

☐ Support Account Data Form

☐ Group Health Insurance Affidavit

☐ Health Insurance Verification

☐ Affidavit In Compliance With ORC 3109.27

Shared Parenting Forms

☐ Shared Parenting Plan

☐ Shared Parenting Decree

Child Support Deduction Order (use only one type)

  ☐ Employer Order

  ☐ Unemployment Order

Child Health Care Order (use only one type)

  ☐ Obligor

  ☐ Obligee

  ☐ Obligor And Obligee

  ☐ Shared Liability

Spousal Support Deduction Order

☐ Employer

Additional Court Forms

☐ Waiver Of Representation (husband and wife)

☐ Waiver Of Fourteen Day Objection Period

☐ Waiver Of Property

☐ Application For Child Support Services

☐ Waiver Of Venue

☐ Waiver Of Financial Documentation

IN RE THE MARRIAGE OF:

Name: _____ :
Address: _____ :
_____ : Case No. _____
SS #: _____ :
DOB: _____ :
Telephone #: _____ :
　　　　　Petitioner, :

-and- : **PETITION FOR DISSOLUTION OF**
: **OF MARRIAGE AND WAIVER OF**
: **SERVICE OF SUMMONS**

Name: _____ :
Address: _____ :
_____ :
SS #: _____ :
DOB: _____ :
Telephone #: _____ :
　　　　　Petitioner,

1. At least one of the Petitioners has been a resident of the State of Ohio for at least six (6) months or more immediately prior to filing this Petition.

2. Petitioners were married on the _____ day of _____ _____,
in _____, _____.

3. The names and dates of birth of all living minor child/ren, natural or adopted to the Petitioners are:

Name _____ Date of Birth _____
Name _____ Date of Birth _____
Name _____ Date of Birth _____

4. A Separation Agreement, agreed to and signed by both Petitioners, which provides for a division of all property and spousal support, child support, visitation rights, and provides for a residential parent and legal custodian of the minor child/ren, where applicable, is attached hereto and incorporated herein.

5. Both Petitioners acknowledge that they have voluntarily entered into the attached Separation Agreement appended to the Petition herein; that they are satisfied with its terms; and that they seek a Dissolution of the Marriage.

6. The wife is not pregnant.

　　　WHEREFORE, both Petitioners request the Court to grant a Dissolution of Marriage, incorporating the attached Separation Agreement.

_____　　　　　_____
Signature of Petitioner/Wife　　　　Date　　Signature of Petitioner/Husband　　　　Date

<h2>WAIVER OF SERVICE OF SUMMONS</h2>

　　　Petitioners state that they are at least eighteen (18) years of age and not under disability, and waive service of summons herein, and consent to the Court herein granting a Decree of Dissolution of Marriage, incorporating the Separation Agreement herein.

_____　　　　　_____
Signature of Petitioner/Wife　　　　Date　　Signature of Petitioner/Husband　　　　Date

STATE OF OHIO　　　　　　　　　　)
　　　　　　　　　　　　　　　　) SS:
COUNTY OF _____)

Sworn to and subscribed in my presence this _____ day of _____ , 20_____.

Petition Page One　　　　　　　　　　Notary Public _____

Separation Agreement

This Separation Agreement voluntarily made and entered into by Petitioner/Wife _____ _____ hereinafter referred to as "wife", and Petitioner/Husband _____ _____ hereinafter referred to as "husband", represents that:

1. The date and place of the marriage of the Petitioners are:
   Date Of Marriage: _____Place of Marriage: _____, _____

2. The names and date of birth of all living minor children, natural or adopted, common to the Petitioners are:

Name	Date of Birth
_____	_____
_____	_____
_____	_____
_____	_____

3. Differences have a risen between the Petitioners and we are now living separate and apart from each other.

4. The parties hereto desire to, and by this Agreement do, settle and determine and hereby provide for a division of all property belonging to the parties, spousal support, child support, visitation rights and provide for a residential parent and legal custodian of the minor children, where applicable.

NOWTHEREFORE, in consideration of the foregoing and the mutual promises and agreements hereinafter set forth, the parties agree as follows:

ARTICLE ONE: SEPARATION
Each party shall hereinafter continue to live separate and apart from the other, and neither shall annoy, molest, interfere with or harass the other in any manner, either directly or indirectly.

ARTICLE TWO: DIVISION OF PROPERTY
All property, real and personal, and whatever situated which the parties own jointly or individually, or in common with each other, shall be divided as follows:

A. REAL PROPERTY
- ❑ We have no real property.
- ❑ The husband has real property which he owned prior to marriage and the wife is waiving her claims on his real property, now and in the future.
- ❑ The wife has real property which she owned prior to marriage and the husband is waiving all his claims on her real property, now and in the future.
- ❑ The parties jointly own real property and agree that it shall be divided as follows:

_____
_____
_____
_____
_____
_____
_____
_____
_____
_____
_____
_____.

B. SPOUSAL SUPPORT

❒ Neither the wife or the husband shall pay spousal support to the other party and state that all future rights to spousal support are being waived.

❒ _____ shall pay spousal support to the _____ in the amount of _____ per week, plus _____ % poundage, payable through the _____ County Bureau of Support/Support Enforcement Agency effective _____, 20 _____. Said spousal support shall terminate on _____ 20 ____ or upon the happening of the earliest of the following events: death of the spouse receiving or paying the spousal support, cohabitation with another person, or

_____.

C. MOTOR VEHICLES

❒ There are no motor vehicles.

❒ Husband shall receive no motor vehicle.

❒ Husband shall receive, free and clear of any claims of the wife, all right, title and interest in the _____ automobile/truck. Husband shall hold wife harmless from any debts owing thereon.

❒ Husband shall also receive the following vehicles: _____.

❒ Wife shall receive no motor vehicle.

❒ Wife shall receive, free and clear of any claims of the husband, all right, title and interest in the _____ automobile/truck. Wife shall hold husband harmless from any debts owing thereon.

❒ Wife shall also receive the following vehicles: _____.

D. HOUSEHOLD GOODS

❒ We agree that our household goods and possessions are already divided and we are satisfied with the division there.

❒ Husband shall receive the following household goods: _____
_____.

❒ Wife shall receive the following household goods: _____
_____.

❒ See the attached list for the division of household goods.

E. PERSONAL PROPERTY

❒ We agree that our personal property is already divided.

❒ We agree that each party may have his/her own personal property.

❒ See the attached list for the division of personal property.

F. SAVINGS ACCOUNTS

❒ We agree that our savings accounts are already divided and we are satisfied with the division,

❒ Husband shall receive the following savings account(s): _____.

❒ Wife shall receive the following savings account(s): _____.

❒ We have no savings account.

G. CHECKING ACCOUNTS

❒ We agree that our checking accounts are already divided.

❒ Husband shall have the following checking account(s): _____.

❒ Wife shall have the following checking account(s): _____.

❒ We have no checking accounts.

H. CREDIT UNION ACCOUNTS AND/OR STOCKS AND/OR BONDS

☐ We agree that the above listed assets are already divided and we are satisfied with the division.

☐ Husband shall receive the following credit union accounts/stocks/bonds: _____
_____.

☐ Wife shall receive the following credit union accounts/stocks/bonds: _____
_____.

☐ We do not have any credit union accounts and/or stocks and/or bonds.

I. PENSION/PROFIT SHARING AND/OR IRA'S

☐ We agree that the above listed assets are already divided and we are satisfied with the division.

☐ Husband shall receive the following pension/profit sharing and/or IRA account(s)_____
_____.

☐ Wife shall receive the following pension/profit sharing and/or IRA account(s): _____
_____.

☐ We do not have any pension/profit sharing and/or IRA accounts.

J. LIFE INSURANCE

☐ We agree that the cash value of our life insurance policies has already been divided.

☐ Husband shall receive the following life insurance policy, free and clear of any claims of the wife:_____.

☐ Wife shall receive the following life insurance policy, free and clear of any claim of the husband:
_____.

The parties have no life insurance policies with a cash surrender value.

K. INCOME TAX REFUNDS AND/OR LIABILITIES

☐ We agree that our income tax refund(s) for the last year has been divided to our satisfaction.

☐ Husband shall receive the following amount from our joint refund: $ _____.

☐ Husband shall pay the following amount $ _____ to _____ for taxes.

☐ Wife shall receive the following amount from our joint refund: $ _____.

☐ Wife shall pay the following amount $ _____ to _____ for taxes.

L. DEBTS

☐ Husband shall pay any debts incurred by him personally from this day forward, including any debts or expenses incurred after the separation and prior to the granting of divorce or dissolution. Wife shall pay any debts incurred by her personally from this day forward, including any debts or expenses incurred after the separation and prior to the granting of divorce or dissolution.

☐ We have no debts.

☐ We agree to the payment of all debts we owe as follows:
Husband shall pay:

OBLIGATION	CREDITOR	BALANCE
1.		
2.		
3.		
4.		
5.		

Wife shall pay:
1.
2.
3.
4.
5.

ARTICLE THREE: NON-USE OF OTHER'S CREDIT

The parties agree that neither shall hereinafter incur any debts or obligations upon the credit of the other, and each shall indemnify the other from any debts and obligation so charged or incurred.

ARTICLE FOUR: NAME CHANGE
- ❏ The wife's name is not changed.
- ❏ The wife's name is changed to: _____.

ARTICLE FIVE: RESIDENTIAL PARENT AND LEGAL CUSTODIAN
- ❏ The mother shall be the sole residential parent and legal custodian of the following child/ren:
  _____.
- ❏ The father shall be the sole residential parent and legal custodian of the following child/ren:
  _____.
- ❏ The parties shall have shared parenting of the minor child/ren, pursuant to the Shared Parenting Plan attached hereto and incorporated herein.

A. VISITATION TIMES
- ❏ The nonresidential parent is granted reasonable visitation with the minor children, including every other weekend, every other holiday, and at least two weeks during the summer. All other visitation is subject to agreement by the parties.
- ❏ The nonresidential parent is granted the following visitation: _____
  _____
  _____
  _____.
- ❏ The parties shall have visitation of the minor child/ren, pursuant to the Shared Parenting Plan attached hereto and incorporated herein.

B. CHILD(REN) SUPPORT
- ❏ The nonresidential parent shall pay to the residential parent as child support the amount of
  $ _____ per child per week. Said payments shall begin the date of the final hearing on a divorce or dissolution, and shall be payable every week thereafter, through _____
  _____ County Bureau of Support (CSEA), with appropriate poundage, which payments, with current poundage of _____ %, total $ _____, or $ _____
  per child per month, with _____ % poundage, for a total monthly payment of $ _____.
  Said child support shall continue until each said minor child has reached the age of majority (18) eighteen and attends on a full time basis any recognized and accredited high school, or otherwise is emancipated. All payments is satisfaction of said obligation which are not made through the
  _____ County Bureau of Support (CSEA) shall be deemed gifts.
- ❏ The _____ shall pay child support for the minor children, prusuant to the Shared Parenting Plan attached hereto and incorporated herein.

C. LIFE INSURANCE FOR THE MINOR CHILD/REN
- ❏ The parties will not maintain life insurance policies for the benefit of the minor child/ren.
- ❏ The father shall maintain the minor children of the parties as beneficiaries on his life insurance policy in the amount of $ _____ until said child/ren are emancipated.
- ❏ The mother shall maintain the minor children of the parties as beneficiaries on her life insurance policy in the amount of $ _____ until said child/ren are emancipated.
- ❏ Life insurance shall be maintained for the benefit of the minor child/ren, pursuant to the Shared Parenting Plan attached hereto and incorporated herein.

D. MEDICAL INSURANCE

Each parent shall have access to all the child/ren's health records.

☐ The father shall provide and maintain health insurance coverage for the benefit of the minor child/ren through his employer as specified in the attached Health Care Order for the minor child/ren of the parties. A copy of the health care insurance policy enforce for the minor children shall be continuously submitted as due to the _____ County Child Support Enforcement Agency. The designated health insurance carrier is _____ _____ , whose address is _____ _____ .

☐ The mother shall provide and maintain health insurance coverage for the benefit of the minor child/ren through her employer as specified in the attached Health Care Order for the minor child/ren of the parties. A copy of the health care insurance policy enforce for the minor children shall be continuously submitted as due to the _____ County Child Support Enforcement Agency. The designated health insurance carrier is _____ _____ , whose address is _____ _____ .

☐ Both the mother and father shall provide and maintain dual health insurance coverage for the benefit of the minor child/ren through their employers as specified in the attached Health Care Order for the minor child/ren of the parties. A copy of the health care insurance policy enforce for the minor children shall be continuously submitted as due to the _____ County Child Support Enforcement Agency. The designated health insurance carrier of the father is_____ ,whose address is _____ _____ .

The designated health insurance carrier of the mother is _____ , whose address is _____ _____ .

☐ Neither the father nor the mother have health insurance coverage available to them at a reasonable cost through a group health insurance plan offered by an employer or through any other health insurance care policy, contract, or plan for the benefit of the minor children. The father and mother will share liability for the cost of the medical and health care needs of the child/ren as specified in the attached Health Care Order.

☐ The _____ shall provide health insurance coverage for the benefit of the minor child/ren, pursuant to the Shared Parenting Plan attached hereto and incorporated herein.

E. UNCOVERED MEDICAL, DENTAL, DRUG, OPTICAL, ORTHODONTAL, PSYCHIATRIC, AND PSYSCHOLOGICAL CARE

☐ Any medical, dential, drug, optical, orthodontal, psychiatric and psyschological expenses not covered by health insurance for the benefit of the minor child/ren will be divided equally between the parties as specified in the attached Health Care Order.

☐ Any medical, dential, drug, optical, orthodontal, psychiatric and psyschological expenses not covered by health insurance for the benefit of the minor child/ren will be covered one-hundred (100%) by the father.

☐ Any medical, dential, drug, optical, orthodontal, psychiatric and psyschological expenses not covered by health insurance for the benefit of the minor child/ren will be covered one-hundred (100%) by the mother.

☐ Any medical, dential, drug, optical, orthodontal, psychiatric and psyschological expenses not covered by health insurance for the benefit of the minor child/ren will be covered pursuant to the Shared parenting Plan attached hereto and incorporated herein.

ARTICLE SIX: TAX EXEMPTIONS

☐ The mother shall have the tax exemption for the following child/ren of the parties:
_____.

☐ The father shall have the tax exemption for the following child/ren of the parties:
_____.

☐ The parties shall alternate the tax exemption for the minor child/ren of the parties. The mother shall have the tax exemption for the year _____ and the father shall have the tax exemption for the year following; the parties shall alternate the tax exemption for the child/ren from that date forward.

☐ The parties shall allocate tax exemption(s) for the minor child/ren, pursuant to the Shared Parenting plan attached hereto and incorporated herein.

ARTICLE SEVEN: RECORDS

The parties agree that it is in the best interest of the minor child/ren that the nonresidential parent shall be entitled to access to all records pertaining to the child/ren as provided in R.C. 3109.05 (H), (I) and (N). The parties further agree that it is in the best interest of the minor child/ren that the nonresidential parent have equal access to any student activity of the minor child/ren as provided in R.C. 3109.051 (J).

ARTICLE EIGHT: RELOCATION

In the event that the residential parent intends to relocate their residence outside _____
County, Ohio the residential parent agrees to notify the nonresidential parent of their intent to do so in accordance with R.C. 3109.05 (G).

ARTICLE NINE: COMPLETE DISCLOSURE

The parties agree that each has made a full and complete disclosure of his or her property, and that neither has knowledge of any personal property of any kind which the parties so agreeing have any beneficial interest. If it is later discovered that either party has possession or control of, or has disposed of by gift or conveyance, any undisclosed beneficial interest in any property, such party on demand, shall transfer and assign to the other party one-half interest therein, or shall pay to the other party a sum equal to one-half of the fair market value of said beneficial interest.

ARTICLE TEN: INCORPORATION INTO DECREE

This Agreement or any amendment thereto, shall be submitted to any court in which a Petition for Dissolution of Marriage or action between the parties for a divorce may be pending, and if found by the Court to be fair and equitable, and approved or validated by the Court, shall be incorporated in the Final Decree of said Court as the order of said Court. It is understood that the parties contemplate the possibility of filing a divorce or dissolution within four (4) months after the execution of this separation agreement.

ARTICLE ELEVEN: COMPLETE AGREEMENT

This Agreement shall inure to the benefits of and be binding upon the parties and their respective heirs, executors, administrators, successors and assigns, and may not be modified or changed other than by further agreement of the parties in writing.

ARTICLE TWELVE: PERFORMANCE OF NECESSARY ACTS

Each party shall execute any and all deeds, bills of sale, or other documents, and perform any acts which may be required or necessary to carry out and effectuate any and all of the purposes and provisions herein set forth:

ARTICLE THIRTEEN: ADDITIONAL MATTERS

☐ There are no additional matters that we have agreed to or need to agree to.

☐ We agree to the following additional matters: _____
_____
_____.

ARTICLE FOURTEEN: EQUAL DIVISION
The parties acknowledge that each is entitled to an equal division of marital property in accordance with R.C. 3105.171, and further acknowledge that the division of marital property provided for in the Agreement is not precisely equal. Accordingly, both parties waive any right to an equal division of marital property.

ARTICLE FIFTEEN: SEVERABILITY
If any provision or clause in this Agreement is held invalid, such invalidity shall not affect any other provision of this Agreement.

ARTICLE SIXTEEN: APPLICABLE LAW
All provisions of this Agreement shall be construed and enforced in accordance with the laws of the State of Ohio.

ARTICLE SEVENTEEN: ATTORNEY WAIVER
The Petitioners are aware of their rights to have an attorney represent them in this matter, hereby with full knowledge of all assets and liabilities of the marriage and of both parties own wish; the Petitioners are waiving their right to an attorney herein and specifically request the Court to proceed with full knowledge of such waiver.

ARTICLE EIGHTEEN: EFFECTIVE DATE
This Agreement shall be effective upon the date last signed by a party to the Agreement.

_____   _____   _____   _____
Signature of Petitioner/Wife   Date   Signature of Petitioner/Husband   Date

STATE OF OHIO   )
) SS:
COUNTY OF _____)

Sworn to and subscribed in my presence this _____ day of _____ , 20_____.

Notary Public _____

COURT OF COMMON PLEAS
DIVISION OF DOMESTIC RELATIONS
_____COUNTY, OHIO

IN RE THE MATTER OF:

Name: _____   :

Address: _____   :   Case No. _____

             _____   :

SS #:   _____   :

DOB: _____   :   Judge _____

             Petitioner,   :

                                           :

                                           :

             -and-   :

                                           :

                                           :

Name: _____   :

Address: _____   :   **DECREE OF DISSOLUTION**

             _____   :   **OF MARRIAGE**

SS #:   _____   :

DOB: _____   :

             Petitioner,   :

1. This matter came on for hearing on the _____ day of _____, 20_____ on the Petition for Dissolution Of Marriage, filed by both Petitioners. Both parties appeared before the Court at the hearing.

2. The Court finds that both petitioners had been notified of the hearing, in accordance with the Rules of the Court and the Ohio Rules of Civil Procedure. The Court finds that both spouses were duly served as required by law and said service is hereby approved, and the Court finds that the Court has jurisdiction of the claim for relief of the parties herein.

3. The Court finds that at least one of the Petitioners had been a resident of the State of Ohio for at least six (6) months prior to the filing the Petition herein.

4. The Court finds that the Petitioners were married on _____ day of _____, _____, in _____ , _____ .

5. The Court finds that there were _____ child(ren) born the issue of the parties, namely:

_____ born _____ day of _____, _____ ;

_____ born _____ day of _____, _____ ;

_____ born _____ day of _____, _____ ;

_____ born _____ day of _____, _____ .

6. The Court further finds that both spouses appeared before the Court and both spouses acknowledge under oath that they voluntarily entered into the Separation Agreement appended to the Petition, that they are satisfied with its terms, and that they seek dissolution of marriage.

Decree Page One

UPON REVIEW OF TESTIMONY OF BOTH PETITIONERS, THE COURT HEREBY ORDERS THAT:

7.

❏ The mother shall be the sole residential parent and legal custodian of the following child (ren):
_____.

❏ The father shall be the sole residential parent and legal custodian of the following child(ren):
_____.

❏ The parties shall have shared parenting of the minor child(ren). The Shared Parenting Plan is attached hereto and incorporated herein.

8. The Payor, _____ shall pay as and for support of the minor children of the parties the sum of $ _____ per child per week, plus _____% process fee for a total weekly payment of $ _____, until each minor child(ren) has reached the age of majority (18) and attends on a full time basis any recognized and accredited high school, or otherwise is emancipated.

For administrative purposes only, the order shall be administered in the amount of $ _____ per month per child, plus _____% process fee, for a total monthly payment of $ _____. Said order shall be effective on the aforementioned hearing date. All payment shall be made through the _____ _____ County Bureau of Support / Child Support Enforcement Agency, with the requisite process fee. All payments in satisfaction of said obligation which are not made through the Bureau of Support / Child Support Enforcement Agency shall be deemed as gifts. The arrearage in the Bureau of Support Account shall be reduced to zero as of the commencement date.

9. It is further ordered that a Support Deduction Order and Additional Orders shall issue:

❏ The Court finds that the Payor is **employed** at _____, whose address is _____, the Payor's social security number is _____ - _____ - _____, and the Payor's date of birth is _____, _____. Said order is attached hereto and incorporated herein for all purposes.

❏ The Court finds that the Payor is receiving **Workers' Compensation** and the child support shall be deducted from Workers' Compensation. Said order is attached hereto and incorporated herein for all purposes.

❏ The Court finds that the Payor is receiving **Public Systems Benefits** from _____ _____, whose address is _____ _____ and thr child support shall be deducted from these benefits. Said order is attached hereto and incorporated herein for all purposes.

❏ The Court finds that the Payor has an account at _____ **Financial Institution**, whose address is _____, and the account number is _____. The account is under the name _____, and the child support shall be deducted from this account. Said order is attached hereto and incorporated herein for all purposes.

❏ The Court finds that the Payot has posted a **bond** in the Clerk's Office in the amount of $ _____, for the payment of child support.

❏ The Court finds that the payor is **not employed,** not receiving Workers' Compensation, does not have funds on deposit in accounts, and does not have any assets from which child support can be paid or secured.

10. It is further ordered that:

☐ Neither the wife nor the husband shall pay spousal support to the other party and that all future rights to spousal support are being waived.

☐ The Payor, _____ , shall pay as spousal support for the _____ the sum of $ _____ per week, plus _____ % process fee, payable through the _____ County Bureau of Support/Support Enforcement Agency effective on the aforementioned hearing date. For administrative purposes only, the order shall be administered in the amount of $ _____ per month, plus _____ % process fee, for a total monthly payment of $ _____. Said spousal support shall terminate on_____ 20 _____, or upon the death of the spouse receiving or _____ paying spousal support, cohabitation with another person or_____

_____.

All payments in satisfaction of said obligation which are not made through the Bureau of Support /Support Enforcement Agency account shall be deemed as gifts. The arrearage in the Bureau of Support Account shall be reduced to zero as of the commencement date.

11. Regardles of the frequency or amount of child support payment to be made under this order, the Child Support Enforcement Agency that is required to administer the order shall administer it on a monthly basis. Payments under the order are to be made in the manner ordered by the Court and, if the payments are to be made other than on a monthly basis, the required monthly administration by the agency does not affect the frequency or the amount of the support payments to be made under the order.

12. All child support and spousal support ordered by this order shall be withheld or deducted from the wages or assets of the obligor under the order in accordance with ORC 3113.21 and shall be forwarded to the obligee under the order in accordance with ORC 3113.21 to 3113.24. The specific withholding or deduction requirements or other appropriate requirements to be used to collect the support shall be set forth in and determined by reference to the notices that are mailed by the Court or Child Support Enforcement Agency in accordance with ORC 3113.21 (A) (2) and (D) and 2301.371 or the court orders that are issued and mailed in accordance with ORC 3113.21 (D) (6), (D) (7), or (H), and shall be determined without the need for any amendment to the support order. Those notices and court orders, plus the notices provided by the court or agency that require the person who is required to pay the support to notify the Child Support Enforcement Agency of any change in his/her employment status or of any other change in the status of his/her assets, are final and are enforceable by the court.

13. EACH PARTY TO THIS SUPPORT ORDER MUST NOTIFY THE CHILD SUPPORT ENFORCEMENT AGENCY IN WRITING OF HIS OR HER CURRENT MAILING ADDRESS, CURRENT RESIDENCE ADDRESS, CURRENT RESIDENCE TELEPHONE NUMBER, CURRENT DRIVER'S LICENSE NUMBER, AND OF ANY CHANGES IN THAT INFORMATION. EACH PARTY MUST NOTIFY THE AGENCY OF ALL CHANGES UNTIL FURTHER NOTICE FROM THE COURT. IF YOU ARE THE OBLIGOR UNDER A CHILD SUPPORT ORDER AND YOU FAIL TO MAKE THE REQUIRED NOTIFICATION, YOU MAY BE FINED UP TP $50. FOR A FIRST OFFENSE, $100. FOR A SECOND OFFENSE, AND $500. FOR EACH SUBSEQUENT OFFENSE. IF YOU ARE AN OBLIGOR OR OBLIGEE UNDER ANY SUPPORT ORDER AND YOU WILLFULLY FAIL TO MAKE THE REQUIRED NOTIFICATIONS, YOU MAY BE FOUND IN CONTEMPT OF COURT AND BE SUBJECTED TO FINES UP TO $1,000. AND IMPRISONMENT FOR NOT MORE THAN 90 DAYS.

14. IF YOU ARE AN OBLIGOR AND YOU FAIL TO MAKE THE REQUIRED NOTIFICATIONS, YOU MAY NOT RECEIVE NOTICE OF THE FOLLOWING ENFORCEMENT ACTIONS AGAINST YOU: IMPOSITION OF LIENS AGAINST YOUR PROPERTY; LOSS OF YOUR PROFESSIONAL OR OCCUPATIONAL LICENSE, DRIVER'S LICENSE, OR RECREATIONAL LICENSE; WITHHOLDING FROM YOUR INCOME; ACCESS RESTRICTION AND DEDUCTION FROM YOUR ACCOUNTS IN FINANCIAL INSTITUTIONS; AND ANY OTHER ACTION PERMITTED BY LAW TO OBTAIN MONEY FROM YOU TO SATISFY YOUR SUPPORT OBLIGATION.

15. Any notices required by the above provisions should be sent to _____, County Child Support Enforcement Agency. The following Notices are hereby incorporated into this Decree by agreement of the parties, and made an ORDER of the Court:

    A. RECORDS ACCESS NOTICE: Pursuant to ORC 3109.05 (H) and 3319.321 (b) (5) (a), the parties are notified as follows: Except as specifically modified or otherwise limited by court order, and subject to ORC 2301.35 (G) (2) and 3319.321 (F) both parties are entitled to equal access to any record that is related to the child/ren, including school and medical records. Any keeper of a record, public or private, who knowingly fails to comply with this order, is in contempt of Court.

    B. SCHOOL ACTIVITIES NOTICE: Pursuant to ORC 3109.051 (J) the parties are notified as follows: Except as specifically modified or otherwise limited by the court, and subject to ORC 3119.321, both parties are entitled to equal access to any student activity that is related to the child/ren.

    C. DAY CARE CENTER ACCESS NOTICE: Pursuant to ORC 3109.051 (I), the parties hereto are hereby notified as follows: Except as specifically modified or otherwise limited by court order, and in accordance with ORC 5104.011, both parties are entitled to equal access to any day care center that is or will be attended by the child/ren with whom visitation or parenting is granted.

    D. RELOCATION NOTICE: Pursuant to ORC 3109.051 (G), the parties are notified as follows: If either parent intends to move with the child/ren to a residence other than the last residence of court record, s/he shall file a notice of intent to relocate with this Court. Except as provided in ORC 3109.051 (G) (2), (3) and (4), a copy of such notice shall be mailed by the Court to the other parent. On receipt of the notice, the Court, on its own motion or on the motion of the other parent, may schedule a hearing with notice to both parties to determine whether it is in the best interest of the child/ren to revise the visitation or parenting schedule for the child/ren.

16. It is further ordered that:
    ❏ the wife's name is not changed.
    ❏ the wife's name is changed to _____.

17. It is further ordered that the Petitioners shall pay the costs of these proceedings, and all further orders of the Court.

18. Upon review of the testimony of both spouses, the Court hereby approves the Separation Agreement and the Court grants a Decree of Dissolution of Marriage to the Petitioners, incorporating the Separation Agreement, and all Orders herein.

19. IT IS THEREFORE ORDERED, ADJUDGED AND DECREED THAT the marriage relationship, heretofore existing between the parties be, and the same is hereby terminated and held for naught, and both parties are hereby released and discharged from all obligations thereof.

_____   _____
Referee   Judge
Court of Common Pleas   Court of Common Pleas
_____County, Ohio   _____ County, Ohio

_____   _____
Petitioner/ Wife's Signature   Petitioner/Husband's Signature

WAIVER

Now comes _____ , payor, and says that s/he is eighteen (18) or more years of age and under no disability, that s/he has received a copy of the child / spousal support order and O.R.C. 3113.21 order and instructions and that s/he waives service of same.

_____   _____
Date   Payor

COURT OF COMMON PLEAS
DIVISION OF DOMESTIC RELATIONS
_____COUNTY, OHIO

IN RE THE MARRIAGE OF:

Name: _____   :

SS #: _____   :

        Petitioner,   DOB   :

             -and-   :

Name: _____   :

SS #: _____   :

        Petitioner,   DOB   :

DATE: _____

CASE NO. A: _____

FILE NO. E: _____

JUDGE _____

FINANCIAL DISCLOSURE

O.R.C. 3113.21 (C)

Now comes _____ and, after being duly cautioned and sworn, says:
                                 Obligor

1. I ☐   am employed.

     ☐   am not employed.   My employer is _____

_____

Employer's Payroll Address   City   State   Zip Code

I receive   ☐ 12   ☐ 24   ☐ 26   ☐ 52   paychecks per year.

2. I ☐ am ☐ am not receiving Workers' Compensation under Claim No. _____.

    ☐ am ☐ am not receiving Unemployment Compensation under Claim No. _____.

3. I ☐ do

    ☐ do not have funds on deposit in Financial Institutions. (List all funds in all accounts in any Bank, Savings & Loan, Credit Union, Regulated Investment Company, Mutual or Other Financial Institutions. Account may include one or more of the following: checking, certificate of deposit ("CD"), investment, savings, individual retirement ("IRA"), stock options, etc. USE ADDITIONAL PAGES IF NEEDED).

Name of Financial Institution	Address of Financial Institution	Account No.	Name(s) on Account	Balance as of Date of the Affidavit
_____	_____	_____	_____	_____
	_____			
_____	_____	_____	_____	_____
	_____			
_____	_____	_____	_____	_____

4. I have the following additional sources of income. (List sources, address and amount including but not limited to pension (public and private) annuities, allowance, sick pay, disability pay or other benefit, commissions, trusts, bonuses, profit sharing payments or distributions, lottery winnings, lump sum payments, and private Workers' Compensation payments).

_____

5. I ☐ do

    ☐ do not have other assets from which child support/spousal support can be paid or secured. (If affirmative, list all such assets on a separate sheet of paper).

_____

Affiant - Obligor

STATE OF OHIO   )

) SS:

COUNTY OF _____)

Sworn to and subscribed in my presence this _____ day of _____ , 20_____ .

Notary Public _____

I hereby acknowledge receipt of a copy of this affidavit _____ .
                                            Obligee

WORKSHEET
_____ COUNTY DOMESTIC RELATIONS COURT
CHILD SUPPORT COMPUTATION
SOLE RESIDENTIAL PARENT OR SHARED PARENTING ORDER

Name of Parties _____ Case No. A _____

Number of minor children _____ . The following parent was designated as the residential parent and legal custodian (disregard if shared parenting order): _____ Mother _____ Father. Father has _____ pay periods annually; mother has _____ pay periods annually.

		Column I Father	Column II Mother	Column III Combined
1a.	Annual gross income from employment OR, when determined appropriate by the court or agency, average annual gross income from employment over a resonable period of years (exclude overtime and bonuses)	$ _____	$ _____	

1b. Amount of overtime and bonuses:

FATHER:	YR. 3 $ _____	MOTHER:	YR. 3 $ _____
	YR. 2 $ _____		YR. 2 $ _____
	YR. 1 $ _____		YR. 1 $ _____
AVERAGE	$ _____	AVERAGE	$ _____

(Include in Column I and/or Column II the average of the three years or the year 1 amount, whichever is less, IF THERE EXISTS A RESONABLE EXPECTATION THAT THE TOTAL EARNINGS FROM OVERTIME AND/OR BONUSES DURING THE CURRENT CALENDAR YEAR WILL MEET OR EXCEED THE AMOUNT THAT IS THE LOWER OF THE AVERAGE OF THE THREE YEARS OR THE YEAR 1 AMOUNT. IF, HOWEVER, THERE EXISTS A REASONABLE EXPECTATION THAT THE TOTAL EARNINGS FROM OVERTIME/BONUSES DURING THE CURRENT CALENDAR YEAR WILL BE LESS THAN THE LOWER OF THE AVERAGE OF THE THREE YEARS OR THE YEAR 1 AMOUNT, INCLUDE ONLY THE AMOUNT REASONABLY EXPECTED TO BE EARNED THIS YEAR.) ....

		Column I Father	Column II Mother	Column III Combined
2.	Annual income from interest and dividends (whether or not taxable)	_____	_____	
3.	Annual income from unemployment compensation	_____	_____	
4.	Annual income from workers' compensation or disability insurance benefits	_____	_____	
5.	Other annual income (identify)	_____	_____	
6.	Total annual gross income (add lines 1-5)	_____	_____	
7.	Annual court-ordered support paid for other children	_____	_____	
8.	Adjustment for minor children born to either parent and another parent, which children are living with this parent (number of children times federal income tax exemption less child support received for the year, not to exceed the federal tax exemption)	_____	_____	
9.	Annual court-ordered spousal support paid to a former spouse	_____	_____	
10.	Amount of local income taxes actually paid or estimated to be paid	_____	_____	
11.	For self-employed individuals, deduct 5.6% of adjusted gross income or the actual marginal difference between the actual rate paid by the self-employed individual and the F.I.C.A. rate	_____	_____	
12.	For self-employed individuals, deduct ordinary and necessary business expenses	_____	_____	
13.	Total gross income adjustments (add lines 7-12)	_____	_____	
14.	Adjusted annual gross income (subtract line 13 from 6)	_____	_____	
15.	Combined annual income that is basis for child support order (add line 14, Col. I and Col. II)			$ _____
16.	Percentage of parent's income to total income:			
	a. Father (divide line 14, Col. I by line 15, Col. III)	_____ %		
	b. Mother (divide line 14, Col. II by line 15, Col. III)		_____ % = 100%	

- 1 -

17. Basic combined child support obligation (Refer to basic child support schedule in division (D) of section 3113.215 of the Revised Code; in the first column of the schedule, locate the sum that is nearest to the combined annual income listed in line 15, Col. III of this worksheet, then refer to the column of the schedule that corresponds to the number of children in this family. If the income of the parents is more than one sum and less than another sum in the first column of the schedule, you may calculate the basic combined child support obligation based upon the obligation for those two sums.) .... _____

18. Annual child care expenses that are work, employment training, or education related, as approved by the court or agency (deduct the tax credit from annual cost, whether or not claimed) .... _____ _____

19. Marginal, out-of-pocket costs, necessary to provide for health insurance for the children who are the subject of this order .... _____ _____

20. Total child care and medical expenses (Add lines 18 and 19, Col. I and II) .... _____ _____

21. Combined annual child support obligation for this family (Add lines 17 and 20, Col. I and II) .... _____

22. Annual support obligation/parent:
    a. Father (multiply line 21, Col. III, by line 16a) .... _____
    b. Mother (multiply line 21, Col. III, by line 16b) .... _____

23. Adjustment for actual expenses paid for annual child care expenses and marginal, out-of-pocket costs, necessary to provide for health insurance (enter number from line 18 or 19 if applicable) .... _____ _____

24. Actual annual obligation (Subtract line 23 from Line 22a or 22b) .... _____ _____

25. Gross household income per party after exchange of child support (add lines 14 and 24, Col. I or II for residential parent or, in the case of shared parenting order, the parent to whom child support will be paid; subtract line 24 Col. I or II from line 14 for parent who is not the residential parent or, in the case of shared parenting order, the parent who will pay child support) .... _____ _____

26. Comments, rebuttal, or adjustments to correct figures in lines 24, Col. I and 24, Col. II if they would be unjust or inappropriate and would not be in best interest of the child or children (specific facts to support adjustments must be included .... _____ _____

27. Final figure (this amount reflects final annual child support obligation) ...... : .... _____ FATHER/MOTHER/OBLIGOR

28. For Decree: child support per month (divide obligor's annual shares, line 27, by 12 and by number of children) _____

29. For deduction order: child support per pay period (calculate support per pay period from figure on line 28) plus appropriate poundage _____

Calculations have been reviewed.

Signatures: _____
           Father - (I do/do not consent)

   Sworn to before me and subscribed in my presence this _____ day of _____ , _____

           _____
           Notary Public

           _____
           Mother - (I do/do not consent)

   Sworn to before me and subscribed in my presence this _____ day of _____ , _____

           _____
           Notary Public

WORKSHEET
_____COUNTY DOMESTIC RELATIONS COURT
CHILD SUPPORT COMPUTATION
SPLIT PARENTAL RIGHTS AND RESPONSIBILITIES

Name of Parties_____   Case No. A-_____

Number of minor children_____. The following parent was designated as the residential parent and legal custodian (disregard if shared parenting order): _____Mother _____Father. Father has _____pay periods annually; mother has _____pay periods annually.

	COLUMN I FATHER	COLUMN II MOTHER	COLUMN III COMBINED
1a. Annual gross income from employment OR, when determined appropriate by the court or agency, average annual gross income from employment over a reasonable period of years (exclude overtime and bonuses)......................................	$ _____	$ _____	

1b. Amount of overtime and bonuses:

FATHER: YR 3: $_____   MOTHER: YR 3: $_____

YR 2: $_____   YR 2: $_____

YR 1: $_____   YR 1: $_____

AVERAGE _____   AVERAGE _____

(Include in Column I and/or Column II the average of the three years or the year 1 amount, whichever is less.(If there exists a reasonable expectation that the total earnings from overtime and/or bonuses during the current calendar year will meet or exceed the amount that is the lower of the average of the three years or the year 1 amount. If, however, there exists a reasonable expectation that the total earnings from overtime/bonuses during the current calendar year will be less than the lower of the average of the three years or the year 1 amount, include only the amount reasonably expected to be earned this year)

	COLUMN I FATHER	COLUMN II MOTHER	COLUMN III COMBINED
	_____	_____	
2. Annual income from interest and dividends (whether or not taxable)	_____	_____	
3. Annual income from unemployment compensation...........................	_____	_____	
4. Annual income from workers' compensation or disability insurance benefits..	_____	_____	
5. Other annual income (identify)...	_____	_____	
6. **TOTAL ANNUAL GROSS INCOME** (add lines 1-5)	_____	_____	
7. Annual court-ordered support paid for other children..........................	_____	_____	
8. Adjustment for minor children born to either parent and another parent, which children are living with this parent (number of children times federal income tax exemption less child support received for the year, not to exceed the federal tax exemption...	_____	_____	
9. Annual court-ordered spousal support paid to a former spouse	_____	_____	
10. Amount of local income taxes actually paid or estimated to be paid	_____	_____	
11. For self-employed individuals, deduct 5.6% of adjusted gross income or the actual marginal difference between the actual rate paid by the self-employed individual and the FICA rate	_____	_____	
12. For self-employed individuals, deduct ordinary and necessary business expenses...	_____	_____	
13. **TOTAL GROSS INCOME ADJUSTMENTS** (add lines 7-12)...	_____	_____	
14. **ADJUSTED ANNUAL GROSS INCOME** (Subtract line 13 from 6)...	_____	_____	
15. Combined annual income that is basis for child support order (add line 14, Col. I and Col. II)..			$_____
16. Percentage of parent's income to total income:			
a. Father (divide line 14, Col. I by line 15, Col. III)	_____ %		
b. Mother (divide line 14, Col. II by line 15, Col. III)		+ _____	= 100%

17. Basic combined child support obligation/household

a. For children for whom the father is the residential parent and legal custodian (Refer to basic child support schedule in division (D) of section 3113.215 of the Revised Code; in the first column of the schedule, locate the sum that is nearest to the combined annual income listed in line 15, Col. III of this worksheet, then refer to the column of the schedule that corresponds to the number of children for whom the father is the residential parent and legal custodian. If the income of the parents is more than one sum, and less than another sum, in the first column of the schedule you may calculate the basic combined child support obligation based upon the obligation for those two sums.)... _____

b. For children for whom the mother is the residential parent and legal custodian (Refer to basic child support schedule in division (D) of this section 3113.215 of the Revised code; in the first column of the schedule, locate the sum that is

	COLUMN I FATHER	COLUMN II MOTHER	COLUMN III COMBINED

nearest to the combined annual income listed in line 15, Col. III of this worksheet, then refer to the column of the schedule that corresponds to the number of children for whom the father is the residential parent and legal custodian. If the income of the parents is more than one sum and less than another sum in the first column of the schedule you may calculate the basic combined child support obligation based upon the obligation for those two sums.   _____

18. Annual child care expenses that are work, employment training, or education related, as approved by the court or agency (deduct the tax credit from annual cost, whether or not claimed):
   a. Child(ren) for whom Father is residential parent and legal custodian   _____
   b. Child(ren) for whom Mother is residential parent and legal custodian   _____

19. Marginal, out-of-pocket costs, necessary to provide for health insurance for the children who are the subject of this order:
   a. Children for whom Father is residential parent and legal custodian   _____
   b. Children for whom Mother is residential parent and legal custodian   _____

20. Total annual child care and medical expenses:
   a. Of father for child(ren) for whom Mother is residential parent and legal custodian (add lines 18b and 19b)   _____
   b. Of Mother for child(ren) for whom Father is residential parent and legal custodian (add lines 18a and 19a)   _____

21. Total annual child support obligation:
   a. Of Father for child(ren) whom Mother is residential parent and legal custodian (add lines 20a and 17b and multiply by line 16a)............   _____
   b. Of Mother for child(ren) for whom Father is the residential parent and legal custodian (add lines 20b and 17a and multiply by line 16b)   _____

22. Adjustment for actual expenses paid for annual child care expenses and marginal out-of-pocket costs, necessary to provide for health insurance:
   a. For Father for children for whom the father is the residential parent and legal custodian (enter number from line 20b)...................................   _____
   b. For Mother for children for whom the Mother is the residential parent and legal custodian (enter number from line 20a).......................   _____

23. Actual annual obligation (subtract line 22a from 21a) and insert in Column I; subtract line 22b from line 21b and insert in Column II   _____   _____

24. Net annual support obligation (greater amount on line 23, Col. I or 23, Col. II, minus less amount on line 23 Col. I or line 23 Col. II)   _____   _____

25. Gross household income per party after exchange of child support (add lines 14 and 24, for the parent receiving a child support payment; subtract line 24 from line 14 for the parent making a child support payment)   _____   _____

26. Comments, rebuttal, or adjustments to correct figures in line 24, Col. I and 24, Col. II if they would be unjust or inappropriate and would not be in best interest of the child or children (specific facts to support adjustments must be included)   _____   _____

(Addendum sheet may be attached)

27. Final figure (this amount reflects final annual child support obligation   _____ FATHER/MOTHER/OBLIGOR

28. For Decree: child support per month (divide obligor's annual share, line 27, by 12 and by number of children)   _____

29. For deduction order: child support per pay period (calculate support per pay period from figure on line 28) and **add** appropriate poundage   _____

CALCULATIONS HAVE BEEN REVIEWED:

Signatures: _____
              Father - (I do/do not consent)
   Sworn to before me and subscribed in my presence this _____day of _____, _____

                     _____
                     Notary Public

              _____
              Mother - (I do/do not consent)
   Sworn to before me and subscribed in my presence this _____day of _____, _____

                     _____
                     Notary Public

SUPPORT ACCOUNT DATA FORM

A# _____

Court File # _____

Judge _____ Referee _____

Hearing Date _____

CSE # AA _____

CSEA 92 _____

☐ NEW ACCT
☐ NO CHG
☐ CHANGE
☐ COMPUTER UPDATE
☐ BY COURT EMPLOYEE

DATE _____

Plaintiff/Defendant/Petitioner _____ ☐ Obligor/AP ☐ Obligee/CP

MAILING ADDRESS

Name Last _____ First _____ MI _____
SSN _____ D.O.B. _____ Sex _____ Race _____
C/O _____
Street _____
City _____ State _____ Zip Code _____
Phone ( ) - _____ Driver License # _____ Eyes _____ Hair _____
Height _____ Weight _____

RESIDENTIAL ADDRESS

C/O _____
Street _____
City _____ State _____ Zip Code _____
Phone ( ) - _____ FIPS Code _____ Marital Status _____

EMPLOYEE WORK ADDRESS

Company Name _____ Phone ( ) - _____
C/O _____
Street _____
City _____ State _____ Zip Code _____

EMPLOYER HEADQUARTERS MAILING ADDRESS

C/O _____
Street _____
City _____ State _____ Zip Code _____
Emp. Beg. Date _____ Phone ( ) - _____

HEALTH CARE INFORMATION

Health Care Name: _____
Policy Number: _____ Eff. Date: _____

Plaintiff/Defendant/Petitioner _____ ☐ Obligor/AP ☐ Obligee/CP

MAILING ADDRESS

Name Last _____ First _____ MI _____
SSN _____ D.O.B. _____ Sex _____ Race _____
C/O _____
Street _____
City _____ State _____ Zip Code _____
Phone ( ) - _____ Driver License # _____ Eyes _____ Hair _____
Height _____ Weight _____

RESIDENTIAL ADDRESS

C/O _____
Street _____
City _____ State _____ Zip Code _____
Phone ( ) - _____ FIPS Code _____ Marital Status _____

EMPLOYEE WORK ADDRESS

Company Name _____ Phone ( ) - _____
C/O _____
Street _____
City _____ State _____ Zip Code _____

EMPLOYER HEADQUARTERS MAILING ADDRESS

C/O _____
Street _____
City _____ State _____ Zip Code _____
Emp. Beg. Date _____ Phone ( ) - _____

HEALTH CARE INFORMATION

Health Care Name: _____
Policy Number: _____ Eff. Date: _____

CHILDREN INFORMATION

Last Name	First	MI	Sex	SSN	DOB	Emancipation Date	Code	Relationship to Obligee	Pat Estab.	Pat. Est. Dt.	JCT Doc#	Out Of Wedlock
1)												
2)												
3)												
4)												

Category:

AFDC _____   AFDC-FC _____   AFDC ARR. Only _____
Non AFDC _____   Non IV-D _____
URESA INTT _____   RESP _____

Payee Other Than Client Name _____ Street _____ City, State, Zip _____
Ledger Type _____
Acct. # _____

HCDHS 4905 (Rev. 5/93)

COURT ORDER WORK SHEET

New Acct _____
Chg Info _____
No Chg _____
Chg Custody _____

Court File # _____

A # _____ Ref. Source: CDR ___ JCT ___ PAT ___ OTH ___ CSEA File _____

CSE Act.# _____ Date: _____ Prepared By _____ Updated in Computer By _____

1.___ This is Spousal Support ONLY.

2.___ Medication entry to be arranged before 75 (m) is mailed.

3.___ There is NO child/spousal support to be considered.

4.___ Adjustments in support are involved. SEND COPIES to CSEA.

_____

_____

5.___ Issue a deduction Order (3113.21):
   a. ___ Already Prepared, process it.
   b. ___ Ohio Bureau of Employment Services
   c. ___ Entry Terminating Deduction
   d. ___ Bond Order: Amount: _____
   e. ___ Work Comp.
   f. ___ Deduction Order to be sent to other than employer:

Name: _____

Addr: _____

City: _____ State: ___ ZIP: _____

Acct. # _____ Type _____

6.___ Issue Health Care Order:
   a. ___ Already Prepared, process it.
   b. ___ Obligor.
   c. ___ Obligee.
   d. ___ Both Parties,
   e. ___ Shared Liability.   Terms:

_____

_____

Designated to receive reimbursements:
      ___ Obligor   ___ Obligee

ORDER SECTION

Entry Date _____ / _____ / _____

75M Order ____   Interim Ord. ____   Decree ____
New Order ____   Order Mod. ____

Payment Frequency **MONTHLY**

CURRENT Order   Child Support Amount
Effective Date:

_____ / _____ / _____ Child (1) Amount: $ _____.____
_____ / _____ / _____ Child (2) Amount: $ _____.____
_____ / _____ / _____ Child (3) Amount: $ _____.____
_____ / _____ / _____ Child (4) Amount: $ _____.____
_____ / _____ / _____ Spousal Amount: $ _____.____
                     Subtotal Current Amount: $ _____.____
                     Current Poundage Amount: $ _____.____

ARREARAGE Order Effective Date: _____ / _____ / _____

Arrearage Set as of _____ / _____ / _____

($ _____.____) Arrearage Set

            Arrearage Payment Amount: $ _____.____
            Arrearage Poundage Amount: $ _____.____
($ _____.____) Interest Set
            Interest Pmt. Amt.: $ _____.____
($ _____.____) Medical Set
            Medical Pmt. Amt.: $ _____.____
($ _____.____) Birth Cost Set
            Birth Pmt Amt.: $ _____.____
($ _____.____) Genetic Set
            Genetic Amt.: $ _____.____

TOTAL MONTHLY ORDER AMOUNT: $ _____.____

PAY CYCLE _____ **WAGE (LEIN) AMOUNT:** $ _____.____

COMMENTS:

COURT OF COMMON PLEAS
DIVISION OF DOMESTIC RELATIONS
_____ COUNTY, OHIO

Name: _____   :   Date: _____
SS #: _____   :
DOB: _____   :
    Petitioner,   :   Case No. A _____
        -and-   :   File No. E _____
Name: _____   :
SS #: _____   :   **GROUP HEALTH INSURANCE**
DOB: _____   :   **AFFIDAVIT**
    Petitioner,   :

═══

HUSBAND / PETITIONER   ### WIFE / PETITIONER

Available through
____ yes ____ no .... employment .... ____ yes ____ no

____ yes ____ no .... Other group plan .... ____ yes ____ no

_____   Insurer's Name   _____
_____   Address   _____
_____   _____
_____   POLICY NO.   _____
$ _____   Monthly premium of Individual Plan (employee share) $ _____
$ _____   Monthly premium of Family Plan (employee share) $ _____
(Indicate "0" if available at no cost to party)

Coverages
Summarize health care benefits, ie., major medical only, deductible, co-payments, health maintence
organization, etc. Attach separate sheet where necessary.

_____   _____
_____   _____
_____   _____
_____   _____

☐ yes ☐ no   Is coverage presently in effect?   ☐ yes ☐ no
☐ self ☐ above named spouse   Who is covered?   ☐ self ☐ above named spouse
☐ dependent children of the marriage   ☐ dependent children of the marriage
☐ yes ☐ no   Is a participant card available?   ☐ yes ☐ no
☐ yes ☐ no   Is a prescription card available?   ☐ yes ☐ no
_____   Employer's Ins. Coordinator's   _____
_____   Name and Telephone Number   _____
$ _____   The cost to purchase COBRA coverage will be $ _____

_____   _____
Husband / Petitioner Signature   Wife / Petitioner Signature
STATE OF OHIO   )
) SS:
COUNTY OF _____   )

Sworn to and subscribed in my presence this _____ day of _____ , 20____ .

Notary Public _____

PURSUANT TO YOUR HEALTH CARE ORDER YOU MUST PROVIDE VERIFICATION TO THE CHILD SUPPORT ENFORCEMENT AGENCY. FAILURE TO DO SO MAY RESULT IN A FINDING OF CONTEMPT. FAILURE TO COMPLY WITH THE HEALTH CARE ORDER MAY RESULT IN ADDITIONAL PENALTIES AS WELL. RETURN THIS FORM TO:

_____**CHILD SUPPORT ENFORCEMENT AGENCY**
       ADDRESS: _____

_____
OR
ATTACH TO YOUR DECREE OR AGREED ENTRY

_____   Date _____
Plaintiff / Petitioner

_____   Case No. A _____
SS#   DOB
☐ Obligor   ☐ Obligee   File No . E _____
                                  Judge _____
          -vs / and-

                                      HEALTH CARE VERIFICATION
                                          (C.S.E.A.)
                                  ☐ Obligor   ☐ Obligee

_____
Defendant / Petitioner

_____   Insurance Policy No. _____
SS#   DOB
☐ Obligor   ☐ Obligee   Insurer _____

      Whereas, _____ is ordered to obtain/maintain health
                               Obligor or Obligee
coverage for the minor child(ren) and whereas O.R.C. 3163.217 imposes verification requirements upon the above named person, _____ hereby swears under penality of contempt
                                 Obligor or Obligee
as follows.

1. I have obtained / am maintaining health insurance coverage as ordered. Said coverage is in full force and effect.

2. I have sent, or will send contemporaneous with this affidavit, a copy of the health care order to the insurer.

3. (Obligor only) I have supplied Obligee with (a) insurance forms necessary to receive payment, reimbursement or other benefits, (b) necessary insurance cards, and (c) information regarding the benefits, limitations, and exclusions of the health insurance coverage.

                                 _____
                                   Affiant / Signature

STATE OF OHIO   )
)   SS:
COUNTY OF _____)

Sworn to and subscribed in my presence this _____ day of _____ , 20_____.

                  Notary Public _____

COURT OF COMMON PLEAS
DIVISION OF DOMESTIC RELATIONS
_____COUNTY, OHIO

IN RE THE MATTER OF:

Name: _____   :   Date _____

SS #: _____   :

DOB: _____   :   File No. _____

       Petitioner,   :   Case No. _____

             -and-   :   Judge _____

Name: _____   :

SS #: _____   :   **AFFIDAVIT IN COMPLIANCE WITH**

DOB: _____   :   **3109.27 OF THE OHIO REVISED CODE**

       Petitioner,

STATE OF OHIO   )

)   SS:

COUNTY OF _____)

Upon being duly sworn, _____ does hereby state the following:

                                         (name)

1. The child/ren involved is/are _____
_____ .

2. The child/ren's present address is/are _____
_____ .

3. The places where the child/ren has/have lived the last five years are _____
_____ .

4. The names and present address of the persons with whom the child/ren has/have lived during that period is/are _____
_____ .

5. I have not participated as a party, witness, or in any other capacity or any other litigation concerning the allocation of parental rights and responsibilities of the same child/ren or that otherwise concerned the custody in this or any other state.

6. I have no information of any parenting proceeding concerning the child/ren pending in a court of this or any other state.

7. I know of no person not a party to the proceeding who has physical custody of the child/ren or claims to be a parent of the child/ren who is designated the residential parent and legal custodian of the child/ren or to have visitation rights with respect to the child/ren.

8. I HAVE NOT been convicted of or pleaded guilty to any criminal offense involving any act that resulted in a child being an abused or neglected child nor have I been the perpetrator of the abusive or neglectful act that was the basis of an adjudication that a child is an abused or neglected child.

If you or your spouse have ever been a party to any civil or criminal case or investigation concerning child abuse, child neglect or domestic violence, state the name(s), case numbers, date(s) and nature of the case(s)
_____
_____ .

                                 _____

                                 Affiant / Father

STATE OF OHIO   )

)   SS:

COUNTY OF _____)

Sworn to and subscribed in my presence this _____ day of _____ , 20_____ .

                     Notary Public _____

COURT OF COMMON PLEAS
DIVISION OF DOMESTIC RELATIONS
_____COUNTY, OHIO

IN RE THE MATTER OF:

Name: _____ :   Date _____

SS #: _____ :

DOB: _____ :   File No. _____

       Petitioner, :   Case No. _____

      -and- :   Judge _____

Name: _____ :

SS #: _____ :   **AFFIDAVIT IN COMPLIANCE WITH**

DOB: _____ :   **3109.27 OF THE OHIO REVISED CODE**

       Petitioner,

STATE OF OHIO   )

) SS:

COUNTY OF _____)

Upon being duly sworn, _____ does hereby state the following:
                                       (name)

1. The child/ren involved is/are _____
   _____.

2. The child/ren's present address is/are _____
   _____.

3. The places where the child/ren has/have lived the last five years are _____
   _____.

4. The names and present address of the persons with whom the child/ren has/have lived during that period
   is/are _____
   _____.

5. I have not participated as a party, witness, or in any other capacity or any other litigation concerning the allocation of parental rights and responsibilities of the same child/ren or that otherwise concerned the custody in this or any other state.

6. I have no information of any parenting proceeding concerning the child/ren pending in a court of this or any other state.

7. I know of no person not a party to the proceeding who has physical custody of the child/ren or claims to be a parent of the child/ren who is designated the residential parent and legal custodian of the child/ren or to have visitation rights with respect to the child/ren.

8. I HAVE NOT been convicted of or pleaded guilty to any criminal offense involving any act that resulted in a child being an abused or neglected child nor have I been the perpetrator of the abusive or neglectful act that was the basis of an adjudication that a child is an abused or neglected child.

If you or your spouse have ever been a party to any civil or criminal case or investigation concerning child abuse, child neglect or domestic violence, state the name(s), case numbers, date(s) and nature of the case(s)

_____
_____.

_____
               Affiant / Mother

STATE OF OHIO   )

) SS:

COUNTY OF _____)

Sworn to and subscribed in my presence this _____ day of _____, 20____.
                                Notary Public _____

COURT OF COMMON PLEAS
DIVISION OF DOMESTIC RELATIONS
_____COUNTY, OHIO

IN RE THE MATTER OF:

Name: _____   :   Date _____
SS #: _____   :
DOB: _____   :   File No. _____
      Petitioner,   :   Case No. _____
           -and-   :   Judge _____
Name: _____   :
SS #: _____   :
DOB: _____   :   **SHARED PARENTING PLAN**
      Petitioner,

The following is a Shared Parenting Plan for the minor child/ren of the parties, namely:

_____ born _____ day of _____ _____;

_____ born _____ day of _____ _____;

_____ born _____ day of _____ _____;

_____ born _____ day of _____ _____;

submitted by _____, hereinafter referred to as "mother"

and _____, hereinafter referred to as "father".

The parties agree that it is in the best interest of the minor child/ren for the parties to have shared parenting. Acknowledging that each is a caring and appropriate parent with the ability to provide guidance, concern and a proper homelife for the minor child/ren, the parties agree as follows:

ARTICLE I   SHARED PARENTING TIME

The mother shall be the residential parent from _____
_____ to _____.

The father shall be the residential parent from _____
_____ to _____.
Each parent has separate sleeping quarters for the minor child/ren during the time he/she is the residential parent.

The nonresidential parent shall be allowed liberal phone contact with the minor child/ren. Should any major differences of opinion regarding the best interest if the child/ren arise, the matters will be resolved through mediation or counseling provided by professional therapists.

ARTICLE II   SCHOOL/DAY CARE

During the time the child/ren are of school age/day care age, the parties will mutually agree where the child/ren will attend school. Each parent is entitled to all school records and to attend all school functions.

ARTICLE III   DISCIPLINE

The child/ren will be disciplined by the parent who is the residential parent at that particular time. The parents shall consult on all discipline matters.

ARTICLE IV   TRANSPORTATION

The residential parent at the particular time said transportation is needed shall be responsible for transportation of the child/ren for school, recreation, and medical attention, inter alia.

ARTICLE V   HEALTH AND MEDICAL EXPENSES

Each parent shall have access to all health records of the minor child/ren. The parents will select a primary care physician for the minor child/ren and make decisions in collaboration with the physician. The _____ shall provide health insurance as specified in the attached Health Care Order for the minor child/ren of the parties. The health insurance carrier is _____ _____ whose address is _____ _____.
Any medical, dental, optical, orthodontical, psychiatric or psychological expenses not paid by health insurance shall be _____.

ARTICLE VI   TAX EXEMPTIONS

_____
_____.

ARTICLE VII   SUPPORT

The _____ shall pay child support in the amount of $ _____ per child per month. Said payment shall begin the date of the final hearing on a divorce or dissolution, and shall be payable every month thereafter, through the _____ County Bureau of Support (Child Support Enforcement Agency), with appropriate poundage, which payments with current poundage of _____ %, total $ _____, or $ _____ per child per week, with _____ % poundage, for a total weekly payment of $ _____. Said child support shall continue until each minor child has reached the age of eighteen (18) and attends on a full time basis any recognized and accredited high school, or otherwise is emancipated. All payments not made through the Bureau of Support (Child Support Enforcement Agency) shall be deemed gifts.

ARTICLE VIII   RELIGIOUS TRAINING

The minor child/ren shall be raised in the _____ _____.

ARTICLE IX   LIFE INSURANCE FOR THE MINOR CHILD/REN

The _____ shall maintain the minor child/ren of the parties as beneficiaries on his/her life insurance policy in the amount of $ _____ until said child/ren are emancipated.

ARTICLE X   RECORDS

Both parties shall have access to school/medical and all other records pertaining to the minor child/ren and access to all school activities and/or child care facilities.

ARTICLE XI   RELOCATION

The mother's present address is _____
City _____ State _____ Zip Code _____.

The father's present address is _____
City _____ State _____ Zip Code _____.

If either parent intends to move to a residence other than specified above, that parent must file a notice of intent to relocate with the Court.

ARTICLE XII   MISCELLANEOUS

Neither parent has been convicted of or pleaded guilty to a violation of the Ohio Revised Code 2919.25 involving a family member, or any other offense which resulted in physical harm to a family member, or has been determined to be the perpetrator of an abusive act that is the basis of an adjudication that a child is an abused child or has acted or contributed in any manner resulting in a child being a neglected child.

Findings of fact and conclusions of law pursuant to the Ohio Revised Code 3109.04, 3109.051 and 3109.052 are hereby waived.

The plan is submitted to the Court pursuant to the Ohio Revised Code 3109.04 (D) (1) (a) (ii).

ARTICLE XIII   MODIFICATIONS

The parties agree that this Shared Parenting Plan can be modified in the future without the mutual agreement of the parties; i.e., the Plan can be modified upon the motion of one party, with either the agreement of the other party, or with Court approval.

_____   _____
Signature of the Mother   Signature of the Father

_____   _____
Date   Date

STATE OF OHIO   )
) SS:
COUNTY OF _____   )

Sworn to and subscribed in my presence this _____ day of _____ , 20_____.

Page Three of Three   Notary Public _____

COURT OF COMMON PLEAS
DIVISION OF DOMESTIC RELATIONS
_____COUNTY, OHIO

IN RE THE MATTER OF:

Name: _____   :   Date _____

SS #: _____   :

DOB: _____   :   File No. _____

        Petitioner,   :   Case No. _____

              -and-   :   Judge _____

Name: _____   :

SS #: _____   :   **FINAL DECREE OF**

DOB: _____   :   **SHARED PARENTING**

        Petitioner,   :

This cause came before the Court on this _____ day of _____ 20 _____, upon the joint application of the parties for an order granting them shared parental rights and responsibilities for the care of the minor child/ren, namely:

_____ born _____ day of _____ _____;

_____ born _____ day of _____ _____;

_____ born _____ day of _____ _____;

_____ born _____ day of _____ _____;

and the shared parenting plan submitted by the parties.

Wherefore, upon review of the plan, the court approves said plan and grants a Final Decree of Shared Parenting to the parties in accordance with the plan attached hereto and incorporated herein.

The court further finds that the findings of fact/conclusions of law not required, are hereby waived by the parties, or have been addressed elsewhere by the Court. This plan is submitted in accordance with the Ohio Revised Code 3109.04 (D) (1) (i) and is not modifiable absent the express agreement of the parties.

The Final Decree of Shared Parenting is effective this _____ day of _____ 20 ___.

_____   _____
Referee   Judge
Court of Common Pleas   Court of Common Pleas
_____County, Ohio   _____ County, Ohio

_____   _____
Signature of the Mother   Signature of the Father

COURT OF COMMON PLEAS
DIVISION OF DOMESTIC RELATIONS
_____COUNTY, OHIO

Enter _____

_____
Plaintiff / Petitioner   ☐ Obligor ☐ Obligee

Date _____

_____
SS#   DOB
              -vs / and-

Case No. A _____

_____
Defendant / Petitioner   ☐ Obligor ☐ Obligee

File No. E _____

_____
SS#   DOB

Judge _____

TO:

☐ Employer (D)(1)/Employer Paying Workers' Compensation (D)(2)
☐ Bureau of Workers' Compensation (D)(2)
☐ Financial Institution (D)(5)
☐ Public Pension System (D)(3)
☐ Other (D)(4) _____

☐ SUPPORT DEDUCTION ORDER
☐ ORDER FOR MODIFICATION OF
   SUPPORT DEDUCTION ORDER
   O.R.C. 3113.21 (D)

☐ You are hereby ordered to comply in the following manner:

☐ You are hereby ordered to MODIFY the prior Order of this Court in the following manner:

     PURSUANT to Civil Rule 75(B)(3), as the employer/income withholder of _____,
(hereinafter referred to as the Obligor) Account/Claim No. _____ you are hereby joined as a party to this action and are
ordered to withhold from the personal earnings, benefits or funds of the Obligor in the sum of $_____ which includes poundage every _____
for support until further order. To defray expenses in complying with this order, an employer, including an employer paying Workers' Compensation benefits,
may deduct an additional sum not to exceed 1% of the amount withheld from personal earnings of the Obligor or $2.00 whichever is greater. A Financial
Institution my deduct a fee of $5.00 or a fee not to exceed the lowest rate, if any, charged for a similar debit transaction, whichever is less. Any Deducting
Organization under O.R.C. 3113.21 D (3) and (4) may deduct a fee of $2.00 or 1% of the deduction, whichever is less.
     THE DEDUCTING ORGANIZATION IS ORDERED to begin withholding NO LATER THAN ONE WEEK FROM RECEIPT OF THIS ORDER
or on _____ but you do not have to alter your pay cycle.
     THE DEDUCTING ORGANIZATION IS ORDERED to forward the payment IMMEDIATELY UPON WITHHOLDING to the _____
COUNTY Child Support Enforcement Agency (BUREAU OF SUPPORT), _____ COUNTY COURTHOUSE, _____
OHIO _____. The employee's name and file number shall accompany the check.
     To the extent possible, the Deducting Organization shall deduct the above amount notwithstanding the limitations of Sections 2329.66, 2329.70,
2716.02, 2716.05, 2716.13 and 4123.67 of the Ohio Revised Code. However, in no case shall the amount withheld including fees, exceed the maximum amount
permitted under Section 303(b) of the "Consumer Credit Protection Act", 15 U.S.C. 1673(b).
     IT IS ORDERED that the Obligor is personally responsible to make payments as indicated above by cash, certified check or money order to the Child
Support Enforcement Agency (Bureau of Support) until such time is as said amount is withheld from Obligor's funds.
     IT IS FURTHER ORDERED that said Deducting Organization shall notify the Child Support Enforcement Agency in writing within ten (10) days of
the occurrence of any of the events listed on the reverse side of said Deduction Organization's copy of this order;
     THE DEDUCTING ORGANIZATION IS FURTHER ORDERED to notify the Child Support Enforcement Agency immediately of any lump sum
payments of $500.00 or more to be paid to the Obligor, hold the lump sum payment for thirty (30) days after the date that it is due before making payment, and
upon Order of the Court pay any specified amount of the lump sum payment to the _____ COUNTY CHILD SUPPORT ENFORCEMENT
AGENCY (BUREAU OF SUPPORT). Notice shall be given to the Child Support Enforcement Agency no later than 45 days before payment is due unless the
determination is made in less than 45 days, then immediately.
     Failure to send any notification required by the Court is a Contempt of Court. In addition to all powers this Court has to punish contempt the
employer/Other deducting organization may also be subject to a fine of not more than $200.00.
     A Deducting Organization's failure to withhold in compliance with this order could subject the employer to liability for the amount that was not
witheld pursuant to O.R.C. 3113.213.
     The law provides penalties for an employer who discharges, refuses to hire or disciplines any employee based upon an order to withhold personal
earnings. THIS ORDER APPLIES TO ALL SUBSEQUENT EMPLOYERS AND/OR OTHER SOURCES OF INCOME OF THE OBLIGOR, as determined by
the Child Support Enforcement Agency. Upon the commencement of employment the Court may cancel any prior 3113.21 order and issue a Deduction Order to
Obligor's employer.
     IT IS FURTHER ORDERED that each party to this action shall notify the Child Support Enforcement Agency, in writing, of their respective current
mailing address and current residence address, and each party shall notify the court IMMEDIATELY IN WRITING of any change in either of these addresses.
This duty to notify the Court of any change in address shall continue until further notice from this Court. You are notified that service of future notices shall be
deemed complete upon the posting of ordinary mail to your last known address on record with the CHILD SUPPORT ENFORCEMENT AGENCY.
     IT IS FURTHER ORDERED that the obligor and obligee shall immediately notify the Child Support Enforcement Agency in writing of any of the
events on the reverse side of their copy of this order.

INSTRUCTIONS TO THE CLERK

YOU ARE DIRECTED TO MAIL A COPY OF THIS ORDER TO THE DEDUCTING ORGANIZATION AND TO THE OBLIGOR AND OBLIGEE BY
ORDINARY MAIL, WITH PROOF OF MAILING, UNLESS THEY HAVE ACKNOWLEDGED RECEIPT BY SIGNATURE BELOW.

☐ Deducting Organization   ☐ Obligor   ☐ Obligee

_____   _____   _____

_____   _____   _____

_____   _____   _____

Current order of support is $ _____ wk/mo. plus $ _____ wk/mo. past due support.

OBLIGOR NOTIFICATION

THE OBLIGOR IS ORDERED to notify the Child Suppor Enforcement Agency of any change in employment (including self-employment). The Obligor (employee) shall include in the notification a description of the nature of employment and the name, business address and telephone number of any new employer. DIRECT PAYMENTS ARE A GIFT. All payments are to the CHILD SUPPORT ENFORCEMENT AGENCY.

The Obligor is ordered to IMMEDIATELY notify the Child Support Enforcement Agency of any events specified in the list of instructions below.

The Obligor's failure to comply with the foregoing order of notification may result in a finding of contempt. Attorney fees and Court costs may then be assessed against the Obligor held in contempt.

INSTRUCTIONS

Please check the appropriate boxes below and fill in the needed information when any of these events occur and mail document to:

_____ COUNTY CHILD SUPPORT ENFORCEMENT AGENCY (BUREAU OF SUPPORT)

_____ , Ohio _____

A. EMPLOYMENT FINANCIAL CHANGES:

☐ I have been terminated effective _____ , 20 ____ .

☐ I will be laid off effective _____ , 20 _____ , for weeks _____ indefinitely.

☐ I will be employed at (Name of New Employer and Payroll Address) _____

My new rate of pay will be $ _____ gross per _____ ; I am scheduled to receive ☐ 12 ☐ 24 ☐ 26 ☐ 52 paychecks per year; I will receive my first pay on _____ , 20 ____ .

☐ I will become self-employed effective _____ , 20 ____ .
This business will operate under the name _____
Said business shall have its business accounts at (Finanacial Institution) _____

(Address) _____ (City, State, Zip Code) _____
_____ in the name of _____

☐ I am drawing ☐ sick leave ☐ disability benefits in the amount of $ _____ per _____ starting on _____
from (Institution) _____
_____ (Address) _____
(City, State, Zip Code) _____

☐ My Workers' Compensation (Claim No. _____) will ☐ commence _____
☐ terminate on _____ , 20 ____ . Benefit amount is $ _____ gross per _____ .

☐ My Unemployment Compensation (Claim No. _____) will ☐ commence _____
☐ terminate on _____ , 20 ____ . Benefit amount is $ _____ gross per _____ .

☐ I am retiring effective _____ , 20 ____ and will receive retirement benefits paid ☐ 12 ☐ 24 ☐ 26 ☐ 52 times per year. (Source) _____
(Address) _____

☐ I have opened a new Financial Institution account in the name of: _____
_____ , Account No. _____
at _____ , Address _____
_____ .

☐ I have acquired or expect to receive one or more of the following:
Lump sum payment in excess of $500. as a result of: _____
from _____ (Address) _____ .

☐ Real property located at _____ .

☐ Other property with a value in excess of $1000. described as follows: _____ .
Other income or assets not otherwise included on this form such as lottery proceeds, inheritance, insurance settlements, tax refunds, etc.,described as follows: _____
_____ .

☐ Other changes in employment or financial condition _____ .

B. CHILD SUPPORT / SPOUSAL (ALIMONY) OBLIGATION CHANGES:

☐ Effective _____ , 20 ____ , child support for _____
born _____ , _____ , should terminate because this child ☐ graduated from high school ☐ no longer resides with Obligee ☐ married ☐ enlisted in Armed Forces ☐ was adopted by Decree of Adoption. (Attach documentation. Example: copy of high school diploma, certificate of marriage, miltary ID card, etc.)

☐ Child support should ☐ increase ☐ decrease pursuant to specific terms of the Final Decree filed in this action.

☐ Effective _____ , 20 ____ , Spousal support (alimony) should terminate ☐ remarriage ☐ full-time employment
☐ ordered time has expired ☐ any other reason please describe _____ (Attach documentation)

☐ Spousal support (alimony) should ☐ increase ☐ decrease pursuant to specific terms of the Final Decree filed in this action.

_____
Obligor's Signature

Date: _____

Case No. A _____

File No. E. _____

Address: _____

_____

☐ Check if New Address
Telephone Number: _____

OBLIGEE NOTIFICATION

IT IS FURTHER ORDERED that where there are minor children the RESIDENTIAL PARENT shall notify the Child Support Enforcement Agency IMMEDIATELY IN WRITING of any reason for which the support order shall terminate, including but not limited to death, marriage emancipation, incarceration, enlistment in the Armed Services, deportation, or change of legal or physical custody of the child. In the case of joint custody or shared parenting, both parties are ordered to notify the Court as set forth above. FAILURE TO NOTIFY THIS COURT of any of these events could constitute contempt and could be punishable by this Court as contempt.

INSTRUCTIONS

You, as the residential parent/obligee must complete this form and notify the Court immediately on this document if any of the events below occur. You must mail this document to:

_____ COUNTY CHILD SUPPORT ENFORCEMENT AGENCY
(BUREAU OF SUPPORT)

_____

_____, Ohio _____

☐ Child support should terminate for _____

      born _____, _____ because this child:

      ☐ graduated from high school on _____, _____.
      (Attach copy of high school diploma)

      ☐ no longer resides with me as of _____, _____.

      ☐ married on _____, _____. (Attach copy of Certificate of Marriage)

      ☐ enlisted in the Armed Services on _____, _____.
      (Attach copy of military I.D. card)

      ☐ was adopted by Decree of Adoption on _____, _____ in the court.

      located at (Street Address) _____

      _____
      City   State   Zip Code

      under Case No. _____.

☐ Any other reason child support should not be paid. Please describe _____

_____

  as of _____, _____.

☐ Child Support should ☐ decrease purusant to the specific terms of the Final Decree filed in this action.

☐ Spousal support (alimony) should terminate as provided in the Final Decree on _____.
                                                               date

  due to ☐ Remarriage (attach copy of Certificate of Marriage)   ☐ Full-time employment   ☐ Ordered time has expired

☐ Please describe any other reason that spousal support (alimony) should not be paid:

_____

☐ Spousal support (alimony) should ☐ increase   ☐ decrease purusant to the specific terms of the Final Decree filed in this action.

_____
Obligee's Signature

Date: _____

Case No. A _____

File No. E. _____

Address: _____

_____

☐ Check if New Address
Telephone Number: _____

-2-

_____   :   Enter _____

Plaintiff/Petitioner   ☐ Obligor ☐ Obligee

_____   :   Date _____

SS#   -vs / and-   DOB

Case No. A _____

_____   :

Defendant/Petitioner   ☐ Obligor ☐ Obligee   File No. E _____

_____   :

SS#   DOB   Judge _____

☐ UNEMPLOYMENT/NOTICE ORDER
O.R.C. §3113.21(D)(7)

****

WHEREAS, Obligor has been ordered by this court to pay support and;

WHEREAS, Obligor has no employment income, Workers' Compensation, Unemployment Compensation, or other income, financial institution accounts or other assets from which support payments can be paid or secured or from which a bond can be posted.

NOW, THEREFORE, IT IS ORDERED that Obligor shall, unless medically unable, seek employment and IMMEDIATELY notify the Child Support Enforcement Agency, in writing, upon obtaining employment, or upon the occurrence of any of the events listed on the reverse side of his/her copy of this order.

IT IS FURTHER ORDERED that a Deduction/Bond Order shall be imposed at such time as Obligor becomes employed or acquires other income or assets.

IT IS FURTHER ORDERED that each party to this action shall notify the Child Support Enforcement Agency, in writing, of their respective current mailing address AND current residence address, and each party shall notify the Agency IMMEDIATELY IN WRITING of any change in either of their addresses. This duty to notify the Court of any change in either address shall continue until further notice from the Court.

IT IS FURTHER ORDERED that the residential parent (Obligee) shall notify the Court IMMEDIATELY IN WRITING, of any reason for which the support order shall terminate, including but not limited to death, marriage, emancipation, incarceration, enlistment in the Armed Services, deportation, or change of legal or physical custody of the child. The Obligor may notify the Child Support Enforcement Agency as well.

TAKE NOTICE THAT A WILLFUL FAILURE TO NOTIFY THE COURT AS REQUIRED ABOVE IS CONTEMPT OF COURT AND WILL BE PUNISHED BY LAW.

This order shall remain in full force and effect until further order of this court.

INSTRUCTIONS TO THE CLERK:
YOU ARE DIRECTED TO MAIL BY ORDINARY FIRST CLASS MAIL, WITH PROOF OF MAILING, A COPY OF THIS ORDER TO ANYONE BELOW WHO HAS NOT OTHERWISE ACKNOWLEDGED RECEIPT OF IT BY SIGNATURE.

☐ Obligor: ☐ Obligee:

_____   _____

_____   _____

Street Address   Street Address

_____   _____

City   State   Zip Code   City   State   Zip Code

COURT OF COMMON PLEAS
DIVISION OF DOMESTIC RELATIONS
_____ **COUNTY, OHIO**

Plaintiff/Petitioner _____   ☐Obligor ☐Obligee

SS# _____   DOB

-vs- / -and-

Defendant/Petitioner _____   ☐Obligor ☐Obligee

SS# _____   DOB

Enter _____

Date _____

Case No. A _____

File No. E. _____

Judge _____

DEPENDENT HEALTH CARE ORDER
(Obligor)
O.R.C. 3113.217

DESIGNATED INSURER _____

WHEREAS, the Court finds that health insurance coverage for the named child(ren) is available to the Obligor at a reasonable cost and that the Obligor has been ordered to secure/maintain health insurance coverage for the child(ren),

IT IS THEREFORE ORDERED THAT:

1. The following group health insurance and health care policies, contracts and plans are available at a reasonable cost to the Obligor or Obligee (Include name of insurer that issues each policy, contract or plan):

_____

2. Obligor shall designate (list full names and birth dates of children) _____

_____

_____ as dependents eligible for health insurance coverage in the group health insurance policy offered (i) by Obligor's Employer or (ii) through a group health care policy, contract, or plan available to Obligor and as indicated above within thirty (30) days from the date of this order.

3. Obligor shall provide the insurance company with a copy of this order. Obligor shall within thirty (30) days of the issuance of this order furnish written proof to the Child Support Enforcement Agency that the coverage has been obtained, that the insurer has been provided with a copy of this order, and that Obligee has been provided with all documents/information as set forth in paragraph 4 below.

4. Obligor shall supply Obligee with (i) insurance forms necessary to receive payment, reimbursement or other benefits, (ii) necessary insurance cards, and (iii) information regarding the benefits, limitations, and exclusions of the health insurance coverage.

5. (a) Obligee shall be responsible for the first $200.00 per calendar year per child to a maximum amount of $600.00 per calendar year (for three or more children) for all uninsured medical, dental, hospital, prescription, optical, psychological, psychiatric and orthodontic expenses including co-payments and deductibles (designated "ordinary"), or (other agreement or order)

_____

(b) Costs of remaining uninsured (designated "extraordinary") expenses, including additional co-payments and/or deductibles under the health insurance plan for the child(ren), shall be shared by Obligor and Obligee in the following amounts: Obligor 50% and Obligee 50% or (other agreement or order)

_____

6. Obligor shall be entitled to secure a second opinion at his/her own expense for all psychological, psychiatric and orthodontic treatment of a non-emergency nature.

7. The insurer of Obligor shall reimburse directly to ☐Obligor ☐Obligee the amount of out of pocket medical, optical, hospital, dental, prescription or other reimbursable expenses covered under the policy and paid for by the named person on behalf of the insured child(ren) upon filing of the necessary insurance claims forms. The insurer may continue to make payment for medical, optical, hospital, dental or prescription services directly to any health care provider in accordance with the applicable health insurance or health care policy, contract or plan.

8. Pursuant to O.R.C. 3113.217 (E), this order is binding upon the Obligor and Obligee, their employers, and any insurer that provides health insurance for them or their child(ren).

9. If the Obligor fails to provide health insurance coverage for the child(ren) within 30 days as ordered or to comply within 30 days with any of the foregoing orders, the Child Support Enforcement Agency shall notify the Court in writing of the failure to comply. Upon receipt of the notice from the agency, the Court shall issue an order to the employer. The employer, upon written order of the Court, is required to take whatever action is necessary to make application to enroll the Obligor in any available group health insurance policy or health care policy with coverage for the child(ren) who are the subject of the child support order, to submit a copy of this order for health insurance coverage to the insurer at the time that the employer makes application to enroll the child(ren) in the health insurance or health care policy contract or plan, and, if the Obligor's application is accepted, to deduct any additional amount from the Obligor's earnings necessary to pay the additional cost for that health insurance coverage.

10. During the time that this order is in effect, and after the employer has received a copy of this order, the employer of the Obligor who is the subject of the order shall comply with the order and, upon written request from the Obligee or agency, shall release to the Obligee and the Child Support Enforcement Agency all information about the Obligor's health insurance coverage that is necessary to ensure compliance with this section or any order issued under this section, including, but not limited to, the name and address of the insurer and any policy, plan, or contract number. Any information provided by an employer pursuant to this division shall be used only for the purpose of the enforcement of an order issued pursuant to O.R.C. 3113.217.

11. Any employer who receives a copy of an order issued under O.R.C. 3113.217 shall notify the Child Support Enforcement Agency of any change in or the termination of the Obligor's health insurance coverage that is maintained pursuant to an order issued under this section.

12. Any insurer who receives a copy of an order issued under O.R.C. 3113.217 shall comply with that section, and any order issued under that section, regardless of the residence of the child(ren).

INSTRUCTIONS TO THE CLERK
YOU ARE DIRECTED TO MAIL A COPY OF THIS ORDER TO THE EMPLOYER AND TO THE OBLIGOR AND OBLIGEE BY ORDINARY MAIL, WITH PROOF OF MAILING, UNLESS THEY HAVE ACKNOWLEDGED RECEIPT BY SIGNATURE BELOW.

☐Employer of Obligor   ☐Obligor   ☐Obligee

_____   _____   _____

_____   _____   _____

Telephone No. _____   Telephone No. _____

NOTIFICATION
(Obligor)

TO THE OBLIGOR:

Pursuant to O.R.C. Sec. 3113.217, you have been ordered to maintain health care coverage for the minor child(ren) through a group health insurance or health care policy, contract or plan offered by your employer or through any other available source.

Complete this document as appropriate immediately after the occurrence of any of the events listed and mail the original of this document to the office and address listed below.

TO: Hamilton County Child Support Enforcement Agency
800 Broadway
Cincinnati, Ohio 45202-1399

_____ 1. My health care insurer has changed or,

My employer (or new employer) now offers health care coverage for the minor child(ren) effective _____ , _____ .

Employer's name and address is _____

_____

Insurer's name, address, policy number, employee cost to cover child(ren) is _____

_____

_____

_____ 2. I now have health care coverage available to the child(ren) from another source. State source, address, insurer, insurer's address, policy number and cost to cover child(ren).

_____

_____

_____

_____

_____

Date: _____

Case No. A _____

File No. E _____

Obligor's Signature

Address

☐ Check here if new address

Daytime Telephone number _____

COURT OF COMMON PLEAS
DIVISION OF DOMESTIC RELATIONS
_____COUNTY, OHIO

Plaintiff/Petitioner _____ ☐Obligor ☐Obligee

Enter _____

SS# _____ DOB

Date _____

-vs- / -and-

Case No. A _____

File No. E _____

Defendant/Petitioner _____ ☐Obligor ☐Obligee

Judge _____

SS# _____ DOB

DEPENDENT HEALTH CARE ORDER
(Obligee)
O.R.C. 3113.217

DESIGNATED INSURER _____

WHEREAS, the Court finds that health insurance coverage for the named child(ren) is available at a more reasonable cost to Obligee than to Obligor and that the above named Obligee has been ordered to secure/maintain health insurance coverage for the child(ren),

IT IS THEREFORE ORDERED THAT:

1. The following group health insurance and health care policies, contracts and plans are available at a reasonable cost to the Obligee (Include name of insurer that issues each policy, contract or plan):

_____

2. Obligee shall designate (list full names and birth dates of children) _____

_____ as dependents eligible for health insurance coverage in the group health insurance policy offered (i) by Obligee's Employer or (ii) through the group health care policy, contract, or plan available to Obligee and as indicated above within thirty (30) days from the date of this order.

3. Obligee shall provide the insurer with a copy of this order. Obligee shall within thirty (30) days of the issuance of this order furnish written proof to the Child Support Enforcement Agency that the coverage has been obtained and that the insurer has been provided with a copy of this order.

4. (a) Obligee shall be responsible for the first $200.00 per calendar year per child to maximum amount of $600.00 per calendar year (for three or more children) for all uninsured medical, dental, hospital, prescription, optical, psychological, psychiatric and orthodontic expenses including co-payments and deductibles (designated "ordinary"), or (other agreement or order)

_____

(b) Costs of remaining uninsured (designated "extraordinary") expenses, including additional co-payments and/or deductibles under the health insurance plan for the child(ren), shall be shared by Obligor and Obligee in the following amounts: Obligor 50% and Obligee 50% or (other agreement or order)

_____

5. Obligor shall be entitled to secure a second opinion at his/her own expense for all psychological, psychiatric and orthodontic treatment of a non-emergency nature.

6. The insurer of Obligee shall reimburse directly to ☐OBLIGOR ☐OBLIGEE the amount of out of pocket medical, optical, hospital, dental, prescription or other reimbursible expenses covered under the policy and paid for by the named person on behalf of the insured child(ren) upon filing of the necessary insurance claims forms. The insurer may continue to make payment for medical, optical, hospital, dental or prescription services directly to any health care provider in accordance with the applicable health insurance or health care policy, contract or plan.

7. Pursuant to O.R.C. 3113.217 (E), this order is binding upon the Obligor and Obligee, their employers, and any insurer that provides health insurance coverage for either of them or their children.

8. If the Obligee fails to provide health insurance coverage for the child(ren) within 30 days as ordered or to comply within 30 days with any of the foregoing orders, the Child Support Enforcement Agency shall notify the Court in writing of the failure to comply.

9. During the time that this order is in effect, and after the employer has received a copy of this order, the employer of the Obligee who is the subject of the order shall comply with the order and, upon written request from the Child Support Enforcement Agency, shall release to the Agency all information about the Obligee's health insurance coverage that is necessary to ensure compliance with this section or any order issued under this section, including, but not limited to, the name and address of the insurer and any policy, plan, or contract number. Any information provided by an employer pursuant to this division shall be used only for the purpose of the enforcement of an order issued pursuant to O.R.C. 3113.217.

10. Any employer who receives a copy of an order issued under O.R.C. 3113.217 shall notify the Child Support Enforcement Agency of any change in or the termination of the Obligee's health insurance coverage that is maintained pursuant to an order issued under this section.

Any insurer who receives a copy of an order issued under O.R.C. 3113.217 shall comply with that section, and any order issued under that section, regardless of the residence of the child(ren).

INSTRUCTIONS TO THE CLERK
YOU ARE DIRECTED TO MAIL A COPY OF THIS ORDER TO THE EMPLOYER AND TO THE OBLIGOR AND OBLIGEE BY ORDINARY MAIL, WITH PROOF OF MAILING, UNLESS THEY HAVE ACKNOWLEDGED RECEIPT BY SIGNATURE BELOW.

☐Employer of Obligee   ☐Obligor   ☐Obligee

_____   _____   _____

_____   _____   _____

_____   _____   _____

Telephone No. _____   Telephone No. _____

NOTIFICATION
(Obligee)

TO THE OBLIGEE:

Pursuant to O.R.C. Sec. 3113.217, Obligor is required to maintain health care coverage for the minor child(ren) at a reasonable cost through a group health insurance or health care policy, contract or plan offered by his/her employer or through any other available source. It is important for the well-being of your child(ren) that the best (and reasonable) health care coverage be maintained.

Complete this document as appropriate immediately after the occurrence of any of the events listed and mail the original of this document to the office and address listed below.

TO: Hamilton County Child Support Enforcement Agency
       800 Broadway
       Cincinnati, Ohio 45202-1399

_____ 1. My employer (or new employer) now offers health care coverage for the minor child(ren) effective _____ , _____ .

Employer's name and address is _____

_____

Insurer's name, address, policy number, employee cost to cover child(ren) is _____

_____

_____

_____ 2. I now have health care coverage available to the child(ren) from another source. State source, address, insurer, insurer's address, policy number and cost to cover child(ren).

_____

_____

_____

_____

_____

Date: _____

Case No. A _____

File No. E _____

_____
Obligee's Signature

_____
Address

☐ Check here if new address

Daytime Telephone number _____

COURT OF COMMON PLEAS
DIVISION OF DOMESTIC RELATIONS
_____ COUNTY, OHIO

_____
Plaintiff/Petitioner   ☐Obligor ☐Obligee

_____
SS#   DOB
                    -vs- / -and-

_____
Defendant/Petitioner   ☐Obligor ☐Obligee

_____
SS#   DOB

Enter _____

Date _____

Case No. A _____

File No. E _____

Judge _____

DEPENDENT HEALTH CARE ORDER
(Obligor and Obligee)
O.R.C. 3113.217

DESIGNATED INSURER _____(Obligor)
DESIGNATED INSURER _____(Obligee)

WHEREAS, the Court finds that health insurance coverage is available at a reasonable cost to both the Obligor and Obligee and that dual coverage by both parents would provide for coordination of medical benefits without unnecessary duplication of coverage and that the above-named OBLIGOR and OBLIGEE have been ordered to secure/maintain health insurance coverage for the child(ren), subject of a child support order ("children").

IT IS THEREFORE ORDERED THAT:

1. The following group health insurance and health care policies, contracts and plans are available at a reasonable cost to the Obligor or Obligee (Include name of insurer that issues each policy, contract or plan):

2. Obligor and Obligee shall designate (list full names and birth dates of children)

as dependents eligible for health insurance coverage in the group health insurance policy offered (i) by Obligor and/or Obligee's Employer(s) and/or (ii) through a group health care policy, contract, or plan available to Obligor and/or Obligee and as indicated above within thirty (30) days from the date of this order.

3. Obligor and Obligee shall provide the insurer with a copy of this order. Obligor and Obligee shall within thirty (30) days of the issuance of this order furnish written proof to the Child Support Enforcement Agency that the coverage has been obtained, that the insurer has been provided with a copy of this order, and that Obligor has provided Obligee with all documents/information as set forth in paragraph 4 below.

4. Obligor shall supply Obligee with (i) insurance forms necessary to receive payment, reimbursement or other benefits, (ii) necessary insurance cards, and (iii) information regarding the benefits, limitations, and exclusions of the health insurance coverage.

5. (a) Obligee shall be responsible for the first $200.00 per calendar year per child to a maximum amount of $600.00 per calendar year (for three or more children) for all uninsured medical, dental, hospital, prescription, optical, psychological, psychiatric and orthodontic expenses including co-payments and deductibles (designated "ordinary"), or (other agreement or order)

(b) Costs of remaining uninsured (designated "extraordinary") expenses, including additional co-payments and/or deductibles under the health insurance plan for the child(ren) shall be shared by Obligor and Obligee in the following amounts: Obligor 50% and Obligee 50% or (other agreement or order)

6. Obligor shall be entitled to secure a second opinion at his/her own expense for all psychological, psychiatric and orthodontic treatment of a non-emergency nature.

7. The insurers of Obligor and Obligee shall reimburse directly to ☐ Obligor ☐ Obligee the amount of out of pocket medical, optical, hospital, dental, prescription or other reimbursable expenses covered under the policy and paid for by the named person on behalf of the insured children upon filing of the necessary insurance or claims forms. The insurer may continue to make payment for medical, optical, hospital, dental or prescription services directly to any health care provider in accordance with the applicable health insurance or health care policy, contract or plan.

8. Pursuant to O.R.C. 3113.217 (E), this order is binding upon the Obligor and Obligee, their employers, and any insurer that provides health insurance for them or their child(ren).

9. If the Obligor or Obligee fails to provide health insurance coverage for the child(ren) within 30 days as ordered or to comply within 30 days with any of the foregoing orders, the Child Support Enforcement Agency shall notify the Court in writing of the failure to comply. Upon Obligor's default and upon receipt of the notice from the Agency, the Court shall issue an order to Obligor's employer. The employer, upon written order of the Court, is required to take whatever action is necessary to make application to enroll the Obligor in any available group health insurance policy or health care policy with coverage for the children who are the subject of the child support order, to submit a copy of this order for health insurance coverage to the insurer at the time that the employer makes application to enroll the children in the health insurance or health care policy contract or plan, and, if the Obligor's application is accepted, to deduct any additional amount from the Obligor's earnings necessary to pay the additional cost for that health insurance coverage.

10. During the time that this order is in effect, and after the employer(s) have received a copy of this order, the employer of the Obligor and Obligee who are the subjects of the order shall comply with the order, and, upon written request from the Obligee or Agency, shall release to the Obligee and the Child Support Enforcement Agency all information about the Obligor's or Obligee's health insurance coverage that is necessary to insure compliance with this section or any order issued under this section, including, but not limited to, the name and address of the insurer and any policy, plan, or contract number. Any information provided by an employer pursuant to this division shall be used only for the purpose of the enforcement of an order issued pursuant to O.R.C. 3113.217.

11. Any employer who receives a copy of an order issued under O.R.C. 3113.217 shall notify the Child Support Enforcement Agency of any change in or the termination of the Obligor's or Obligee's health insurance coverage that is maintained pursuant to an order issued under this section.

12. Any insurer that receives a copy of an order issued under O.R.C. 3113.217 shall comply with that section, and any order issued under that section, regardless of the residence of the child(ren).

INSTRUCTIONS TO THE CLERK
YOU ARE DIRECTED TO MAIL A COPY OF THIS ORDER TO THE EMPLOYERS AND TO THE OBLIGOR AND OBLIGEE BY ORDINARY MAIL, WITH PROOF OF MAILING, UNLESS THEY HAVE ACKNOWLEDGED RECEIPT BY SIGNATURE BELOW.

☐Employer [Obligor]   ☐Obligor   ☐Obligee

_____   _____   _____

_____   _____   _____

_____   _____   _____

☐ Employer [Obligee]   Telephone No. _____   Telephone No. _____

_____

_____

_____

COURT OF COMMON PLEAS
DIVISION OF DOMESTIC RELATIONS
_____ COUNTY, OHIO

_____
Plaintiff/Petitioner   ☐ Obligor ☐ Obligee

ENTER: _____

Date: _____

_____
SS#   DOB

-vs/and-

Case No. A _____

File No. E _____

_____
Defendant/Petitioner   ☐ Obligor ☐ Obligee

Judge _____

ORDER

_____
SS#   DOB

**SHARED LIABILITY
FOR MEDICAL AND HEALTHCARE NEEDS**
(No Insurance Available)
O.R.C. 3113.217 (C) (9)

The Court finds that neither the Obligor nor Obligee has health insurance for the child(ren) available to them at a reasonable cost either through a group health insurance plan offered by an employer or through any other group health insurance or health care policy, contract, or plan.

IT IS THEREFORE ORDERED, ADJUDGED AND DECREED that the Obligor and Obligee share liability for the cost of the medical and health care needs of the child(ren) according to the following formula:

(a) Obligee shall be responsible for the first $200 per calendar year per child to a maximum amount of $600 per calendar year (if three or more children) for all (uninsured) medical, dental, hospital, prescription, optical, psychological, psychiatric and orthodontic

expenses (designated "ordinary"), or (other agreement or order) _____

_____

_____

(b) Costs of remaining (uninsured) (designated "extraordinary") expenses, for the child(ren), shall be shared by Obligor and Obligee in the following amounts:

Obligor 50% and Obligee 50% or (other agreement or order) _____

_____

_____

(c) Obligor shall be entitled to secure a second opinion at his/her own expense for all psychological, psychiatric and orthodontic treatment of a non-emergency nature.

IT IS FURTHER ORDERED, ADJUDGED AND DECREED that Obligor and Obligee immediately inform the Court through the _____ County Child Support Enforcement Agency if health insurance coverage for the child(ren) becomes available at a reasonable cost through a group health insurance plan offered by the Obligor's or Obligee's employer or through any other group health insurance or health care policy, contract or plan available to the Obligor or Obligee.

IT IS SO ORDERED.

INSTRUCTIONS TO THE CLERK:
YOU ARE DIRECTED TO MAIL BY ORDINARY FIRST CLASS MAIL A COPY OF THIS ORDER WITH PROOF OF MAILING TO ANYONE BELOW WHO HAS NOT OTHERWISE ACKNOWLEDGED RECEIPT OF IT BY SIGNATURE.

☐ Obligor: ☐ Obligee

_____   _____

_____   _____
Street Address   Street Address

_____   _____
City   State   Zip Code   City   State   Zip Code

COURT OF COMMON PLEAS
DIVISION OF DOMESTIC RELATIONS
_____COUNTY, OHIO

_____

Plaintiff / Petitioner   ☐ Obligor ☐ Obligee

Enter _____

_____

SS#   DOB

-vs / and-

Date _____

Case No. A _____

File No. E _____

_____

Defendant / Petitioner   ☐ Obligor ☐ Obligee

_____

SS#   DOB

Judge _____

TO:

     ☐ Employer (D)(1)/Employer Paying Workers' Compensation (D)(2)

     ☐ Bureau of Workers' Compensation (D)(2)

     ☐ Financial Institution (D)(5)

     ☐ Public Pension System (D)(3)

     ☐ Other (D)(4) _____

☐ SUPPORT DEDUCTION ORDER

☐ ORDER FOR MODIFICATION OF

     SUPPORT DEDUCTION ORDER

     O.R.C. 3113.21 (D)

☐ You are hereby ordered to comply in the following manner:

☐ You are hereby ordered to MODIFY the prior Order of this Court in the following manner:

     PURSUANT to Civil Rule 75(B)(3), as the employer/income withholder of _____, (hereinafter referred to as the Obligor) Account/Claim No. _____ you are hereby joined as a party to this action and are ordered to withhold from the personal earnings, benefits or funds of the Obligor in the sum of $_____ which includes poundage every _____ for support until further order. To defray expenses in complying with this order, an employer, including an employer paying Workers' Compensation benefits, may deduct an additional sum not to exceed 1% of the amount withheld from personal earnings of the Obligor or $2.00 whichever is greater. A Financial Institution my deduct a fee of $5.00 or a fee not to exceed the lowest rate, if any, charged for a similar debit transaction, whichever is less. Any Deducting Organization under O.R.C. 3113.21 D (3) and (4) may deduct a fee of $2.00 or 1% of the deduction, whichever is less.

     THE DEDUCTING ORGANIZATION IS ORDERED to begin withholding NO LATER THAN ONE WEEK FROM RECEIPT OF THIS ORDER or on _____ but you do not have to alter your pay cycle.

     THE DEDUCTING ORGANIZATION IS ORDERED to forward the payment IMMEDIATELY UPON WITHHOLDING to the _____ COUNTY Child Support Enforcement Agency (BUREAU OF SUPPORT), _____ COUNTY COURTHOUSE, _____ OHIO _____. The employee's name and file number shall accompany the check.

     To the extent possible, the Deducting Organization shall deduct the above amount notwithstanding the limitations of Sections 2329.66, 2329.70, 2716.02, 2716.05, 2716.13 and 4123.67 of the Ohio Revised Code. However, in no case shall the amount withheld including fees, exceed the maximum amount permitted under Section 303(b) of the "Consumer Credit Protection Act", 15 U.S.C. 1673(b).

     IT IS ORDERED that the Obligor is personally responsible to make payments as indicated above by cash, certified check or money order to the Child Support Enforcement Agency (Bureau of Support) until such time is as said amount is withheld from Obligor's funds.

     IT IS FURTHER ORDERED that said Deducting Organization shall notify the Child Support Enforcement Agency in writing within ten (10) days of the occurrence of any of the events listed on the reverse side of said Deduction Organization's copy of this order;

     THE DEDUCTING ORGANIZATION IS FURTHER ORDERED to notify the Child Support Enforcement Agency immediately of any lump sum payments of $500.00 or more to be paid to the Obligor, hold the lump sum payment for thirty (30) days after the date that it is due before making payment, and upon Order of the Court pay any specified amount of the lump sum payment to the _____ COUNTY CHILD SUPPORT ENFORCEMENT AGENCY (BUREAU OF SUPPORT). Notice shall be given to the Child Support Enforcement Agency no later than 45 days before payment is due unless the determination is made in less than 45 days, then immediately.

     Failure to send any notification required by the Court is a Contempt of Court. In addition to all powers this Court has to punish contempt the employer/Other deducting organization may also be subject to a fine of not more than $200.00.

     A Deducting Organization's failure to withhold in compliance with this order could subject the employer to liability for the amount that was not witheld pursuant to O.R.C. 3113.213.

     The law provides penalties for an employer who discharges, refuses to hire or disciplines any employee based upon an order to withhold personal earnings. THIS ORDER APPLIES TO ALL SUBSEQUENT EMPLOYERS AND/OR OTHER SOURCES OF INCOME OF THE OBLIGOR, as determined by the Child Support Enforcement Agency. Upon the commencement of employment the Court may cancel any prior 3113.21 order and issue a Deduction Order to Obligor's employer.

     IT IS FURTHER ORDERED that each party to this action shall notify the Child Support Enforcement Agency, in writing, of their respective current mailing address and current residence address, and each party shall notify the court IMMEDIATELY IN WRITING of any change in either of these addresses. This duty to notify the Court of any change in address shall continue until further notice from this Court. You are notified that service of future notices shall be deemed complete upon the posting of ordinary mail to your last known address on record with the CHILD SUPPORT ENFORCEMENT AGENCY.

     IT IS FURTHER ORDERED that the obligor and obligee shall immediately notify the Child Support Enforcement Agency in writing of any of the events on the reverse side of their copy of this order.

INSTRUCTIONS TO THE CLERK

YOU ARE DIRECTED TO MAIL A COPY OF THIS ORDER TO THE DEDUCTING ORGANIZATION AND TO THE OBLIGOR AND OBLIGEE BY ORDINARY MAIL, WITH PROOF OF MAILING, UNLESS THEY HAVE ACKNOWLEDGED RECEIPT BY SIGNATURE BELOW.

☐ Deducting Organization   ☐ Obligor   ☐ Obligee

_____ _____ _____

_____ _____ _____

_____

Current order of support is $_____ wk/mo. plus $_____ wk/mo. past due support.

COURT OF COMMON PLEAS
DIVISION OF DOMESTIC RELATIONS
_____COUNTY, OHIO

IN RE THE MATTER OF:

Name: _____ : Date _____
SS #: _____ :
DOB: _____   :
        Petitioner,   : Case No. _____
                               :
                               : Judge _____
        -and-   :
                               :
                               :
Name: _____ :
SS #: _____ : **WAIVER OF REPRESENTATION**
DOB: _____   :
        Petitioner,   :

_____ , does hereby acknowledge and represent that he

is not represented by counsel in this proceeding. He further acknowledges that the undersigned was given

full opportunity to evaluate his need for legal representation and was advised to obtain, if so desired,

his own counsel. The undersigned realizes that this document constitutes and acknowledges his waiver of

right to counsel in this proceeding.

                              _____
                              Petitioner/Husband

STATE OF OHIO   )
) SS:
COUNTY OF _____)

Sworn to and subscribed in my presence this _____ day of _____ , 20____.

                    Notary Public _____

Waiver of Counsel Husband Page One

COURT OF COMMON PLEAS
DIVISION OF DOMESTIC RELATIONS
_____COUNTY, OHIO

IN RE THE MATTER OF:

Name: _____   :   Date _____
SS #: _____   :
DOB: _____   :
    Petitioner,   :   Case No. _____
        :
        :   Judge _____
    -and-   :
        :
        :
Name: _____   :
SS #: _____   :   **WAIVER OF REPRESENTATION**
DOB: _____   :
    Petitioner,   :

_____ , does hereby acknowledge and represent that she

is not represented by counsel in this proceeding. she further acknowledges that the undersigned was given

full opportunity to evaluate her need for legal representation and was advised to obtain, if so desired,

her own counsel. The undersigned realizes that this document constitutes and acknowledges her waiver of

right to counsel in this proceeding.

_____
            Petitioner/Wife

STATE OF OHIO   )
)   SS:
COUNTY OF _____)

Sworn to and subscribed in my presence this _____ day of _____ , 20_____.

             Notary Public _____

Waiver of Counsel Wife Page One

COURT OF COMMON PLEAS
DIVISION OF DOMESTIC RELATIONS
_____COUNTY, OHIO

IN RE THE MATTER OF:

Name: _____   :   Date _____
SS #: _____   :
DOB: _____   :
      Petitioner,   :   Case No. _____
                                   :
              -and-   :   Judge _____
                                   :
                                   :
Name: _____   :
SS #: _____   :   **WAIVER OF FOURTEEN DAY**
DOB: _____   :   **OBJECTION PERIOD**
      Petitioner,   :

The parties, this day in open Court before the Referee having heard the recommendations by him/her made

and being in agreement therewith or having no objections thereto, do hereby waive their right to file

objections thereto under Rule 53 and consent to immediate Entry of said recommendation(s) as the order of

the Court to take effect upon docketing. Each party acknowledges that this is a voluntary act and each party

understands that they are under no legal duty to sign this waiver.

                         _____
                         Petitioner/Husband

                         _____
                         Petitioner/Wife

                         _____
                         Referee

COURT OF COMMON PLEAS
DIVISION OF DOMESTIC RELATIONS
_____COUNTY, OHIO

IN RE THE MATTER OF:

Name: _____ : Date _____

SS #: _____ :

DOB: _____ :

       Petitioner, : Case No. _____

                                  : Judge _____

          -and- :

                                  :

Name: _____ :

SS #: _____ : **WAIVER OF PROPERTY**

DOB: _____ :

       Petitioner, :

The parties hereto being fully advised, hereby waive appraisal and valuation of their separate and marital property, waive determination of the period included in "duration of marriage", and waive findings of fact, and agree that while the property division herein may not be exactly equal, that it is equitable.

_____
Petitioner/Wife   Date

_____
Petitioner/Husband   Date

STATE OF OHIO   )

) SS:

COUNTY OF _____)

Sworn to and subscribed in my presence this _____ day of _____ , 20____.

Notary Public _____

APPLICATION FOR CHILD SUPPORT SERVICES
NON-PUBLIC ASSISTANCE APPLICANT

ODHS 7076 (Rev. 11/92)

IMPORTANT: If you are receiving ADC or Medicaid, do **not** complete this application, because you became eligible for child support services when you became eligible to receive ADC or Medicaid.

I the undersigned, _____ , request Child Support Services from the _____ County Child Support Enforcement Agency. I understand and agree to the following conditions:

A. I am a resident of the County in which services are requested.

B. Recipients of child support services shall cooperate to the best of their ability with the CSEA. *(See attached rights and responsibility information).*

The Child Support Enforcement Agency can assist you in providing the following services:

1. **Location of Absent Parents.**

    The agency can assist in finding where an absent parent is currently living, in what city, town or state. The applicant can request "Location Services Only", if the sole need is to find the whereabouts of the absent parent.

2. **Establishment or Modification of Child Support and Medical Support.**

    The CSEA can assist you to obtain an order for support if you are separated, have been deserted or need to establish paternity *(fatherhood)*. The CSEA can also assist you in changing the amount of support orders *(modification)*, and to establish a medical support order.

3. **Enforcement of Existing Orders.**

    The CSEA can help you collect current and back child support.

4. **Federal and State Income Tax Refund Offset Submittals for the Collection of Child Support Arrearages.**

    The agency can assist in collecting back support *(arrearages)* by intercepting a non-payor's federal and state income tax refunds on some cases.

5. **Withholding of Wages and Unearned Income for the Payment of Court Ordered Support.**

    The agency can help you get payroll deductions for current and back child support and can intercept unemployment compensation to collect child support.

6. **Establishment of Paternity.**

    The agency can obtain an order for the establishment of paternity *(fatherhood)*, if you were not married to the father of the child.
    An absent parent may request paternity services.

7. **Collection and Disbursement of Payments.**

    The CSEA can collect the child support for you, and send you a check for the amount of the payments received. Back support collected will be paid to you until all of the back support you are owed is paid.

    If you received ADC in the past and support was assigned to the state, back support collected will be paid to the state after you receive back support owed to you.

8. **Interstate Collection of Child Support.**

    The agency can assist you in collecting support if the payor is living in another state or in some foreign countries.

C. The only fee you can be charged for services is a one dollar application fee. Some counties pay this fee for the applicants.

D. In providing IV-D services, the CSEA and any of its contracted agents (e.g., prosecutors, attorneys, hearing officers, etc.) represent the best interest of the children of the state of Ohio and do not represent any IV-D recipient or the IV-D recipient's personal interest.

APPLICANT INFORMATION *(INFORMATION ABOUT YOU)*	
Name	Date of Birth
Social Security Number (SSN)	Current Marital Status *(Check One)* ☐ Single ☐ Married ☐ Divorced ☐ Separated ☐ Deserted ☐ Widowed

Type(s) of Service(s) Requested: All services listed _____ Location of absent parent only _____
Other *(please explain)* _____

I understand that the Child Support Agency - within 20 days of receiving this application will contact me by a written notice to inform me if my case has been accepted for child support services (IV-D Services).

Signature of Applicant	Date

Applicants Name (Last, First, Middle)	Telephone Number (Home)
Address (Street/Route, P.O. Box)	(Work)
City, State, and Zip Code	

INFORMATION ON CHILDREN

	Child 1	Child 2	Child 3	Child 4
a. Name				
b. Sex				
c. SSN				
d. Date of Birth (DOB)				
e. Name(s) of Absent Parent				
f. Has Paternity (Fatherhood) Been Established?				
g. Is There An Order For Support (Yes or No)				

ABSENT PARENT INFORMATION OR PARENT ORDERED TO PAY CHILD SUPPORT

	Absent Parent #1	Absent Parent #2	Absent Parent #3
Name			
Address City, State, Zip Code			
SSN			
Date of Birth (DOB)			
Name of Employer			
Address of Employer (City, State, Zip Code)			
Amount of Support Ordered (Wk, Bi-Wk, Mo)			
Case Number on Support Order			
Date of Support Order			
Location Where Order Was Issued (City, County, State)			
Military Service Give Date and Branch Entered			
Arrest Record: Give Date and Place of Arrest			
If the absent parent has been on Public Assistance: Give Date and Place			
Give Name and Address of Current Spouse of Absent Parent			

- Have you ever been on public assistance? ☐ Yes ☐ No

When _____ Where _____ _____
　　　　　Date　　　　　　　　　　　　　City and State　　　　　　　　　　　County

(Do Not Write In This Space) FOR AGENCY USE ONLY		
Case Name	Date Requested	Date Mailed or Provided
Case Number	Date Returned or File Date	

COURT OF COMMON PLEAS
DIVISION OF DOMESTIC RELATIONS
_____COUNTY, OHIO

IN RE THE MATTER OF:

Name: _____   :   Date _____
SS #: _____   :
DOB: _____   :
     Petitioner,   :   Case No. _____

                      -and-   :   Judge _____
                               :

Name: _____   :
SS #: _____   :
DOB: _____   :   **WAIVER OF VENUE**
     Petitioner,   :

Now comes _____ and _____,

who are at least eighteen (18) years of age and not under disability and waive venue in _____

_____ County, Ohio and consent to the Court herein, hearing said cause,

granting a Decree of Dissolution of Marriage, and the incorporating of the Separation Agreement herein.

_____
Petitioner/ Wife

_____
Date

_____
Petitioner/ Husband

_____
Date

COURT OF COMMON PLEAS
DIVISION OF DOMESTIC RELATIONS
_____COUNTY, OHIO

IN RE THE MARRIAGE OF:

Name: _____ :   Date _____

SS #: _____ :

DOB: _____ :

    Petitioner, :   Case No. _____

                   :

                   :   Judge _____

          -and- :

                   :

                   :   **WAIVER OF**

Name: _____ :

SS #: _____ :   **FINANCIAL DOCUMENTATION**

DOB: _____ :

    Petitioner, :

I hereby certify that I have reviewed our financial documentation, to the extent I deem necessary, any documentation in support of computations therein, and hereby waive any right which I may have to submit such documentation to the Court for independent review. I further certify that any documentation which the Court might independently require shall be made available to the Court promptly upon request.

_____
           Obligee

WAIVER

I hereby certify that I have reviewed our financial documentation, to the extent I deem necessary, any documentation in support of computations therein, and hereby waive any right which I may have to submit such documentation to the Court for independent review. I further certify that any documentation which the Court might independently require shall be made available to the Court promptly upon request.

_____
           Obligor

STATE OF OHIO   )

) SS:

COUNTY OF _____)

Sworn to and subscribed in my presence this _____ day of _____, 20_____.

Notary Public _____

COURT OF COMMON PLEAS
DIVISION OF DOMESTIC RELATIONS
_____COUNTY, OHIO

IN RE THE MARRIAGE OF:

Name: _____ :   Case No. _____

SS #: _____ :

    Petitioner,   :   **ASSETS AND LIABILITIES AS**

        -and-   :   **OF _____**

Name: _____ :

SS #: _____ :   **FINANCIAL DISCLOSURE**

    Petitioner,   :   **AFFIDAVIT**

INSTRUCTIONS: YOU ARE TO DISCLOSE ALL SUCH INFORMATION THAT IS REQUESTED HEREIN AND BY THE _____ COUNTY COURT OF COMMON PLEAS, DIVISION OF DOMESTIC RELATIONS. BE SPECIFIC, LIST ALL ASSETS, LIABILITIES, INCOME SOURCES AND RETIREMENT ACCOUNTS SEPARATELY. ALSO LIST ACCOUNT NUMBERS, NAMES, LOCATIONS AND VALUES AND WHETHER JOINTLY OR INDIVIDUALLY HELD.

ASSETS:		**LIABILITIES:**	
Cash	_____	Notes Payable	_____
Government Bonds	_____	Accounts Payable	_____
Checking Account	_____		
Savings Account	_____	Loans on Life Ins.	_____
Accts/Notes Receivable	_____	Taxes	_____
Stocks, Bonds, Securities	_____	Mortgages	_____
Life Ins. Cash Value	_____	Other Debts (Itemize)	_____
Real Estate	_____		_____
Automobiles	_____		_____
Other Assets (Itemize)	_____		_____

INCOME:

From Employment	_____	_____	_____
Other Income (Itemize)	_____	_____	_____

CONTINGENT LIABILITY:		**RETIREMENT ACCOUNTS:**	
Notes / Accounts Payable	_____	Husband	_____
Guarantor	_____	_____	Vested?
Other Contingent			
Liabilities (Itemize)	_____	Wife	_____
	_____	_____	Vested?

This may be supplemented with additional information on attached sheets. If income is derived from a business attach a profit and loss statement or copy of income tax return for the past business year and any current profit and loss information statement.

_____
Petitioner / Husband

_____
Petitioner / Wife

STATE OF OHIO   )

)   SS:

COUNTY OF _____)

Sworn to and subscribed in my presence this _____ day of _____, 20____.

Notary Public _____

Glossary

Action The legal term for what is commonly called a lawsuit.

Adult An individual who has reached the legal age of majority. Age eighteen for most purposes in Ohio.

Adversary Proceeding A court action which has opposing sides

Affidavit A written statement of facts made under oath and signed before a notary public or other officer who has authority to administer oaths.

Alimony The payment of support by one spouse to another in satisfaction of marital obligations; also referred to as "maintenance" or "spousal support".

Annulment A legal proceeding in which a marriage is terminated. If a court terminates a marriage by annulment the court is declaring that the marriage never existed because something prevented a valid marriage.

Antenuptial Agreement A contract signed between two individuals before marriage that limits a spouse's rights to property, support, and inheritance in the event of a divorce; also referred to as a "prenuptial agreement".

Arbitration A proceeding where both sides submit their dispute to the binding decision of arbitrators rather than judges.

"Best interest of the child" The legal standard most often used by judges when making decisions regarding custody and support for the child.

Bigamy Having two or more husbands or wives at the same time.

Bureau of Support A bureau established in each court of common pleas for the collection of payment due under a support order, also known as the "Child Support Enforcement Agency".

Child Custody Upon the legal termination of a marriage (unless shared parenting is granted), the court will formally grant one individual legal control over the care of a minor child. In Ohio this person is called the "residential parent" and a child custody is called "the allocation of rights and responsibilities".

Child Support A sum of money that the court orders to be paid by a divorcing parent for the continued medical, educational and financial needs of the minor child or sometimes called "maintenance".

Child Support Guidelines A set of guidelines used by the court in determining the dollar amount of child support to be paid by the nonresidential parent.

Clerk of Courts An official of the court who determines whether court papers are properly filed and court procedures followed.

Cohabitants Persons residing together.

Cohabitation Agreement A contract signed between two individuals, typically lovers, that defines the rights, property and interests of the parties.

Community Property Assets and property acquired during a marriage and owned equally by the parties regardless of who holds title, with the exception of property acquired by inheritance or gift.

Common-law Marriage A marriage legally recognized in some states even though the parties did not participate in a formal civil ceremony.

Contested Case Any case where the court must decide one or more issues that are not agreed to by the parties.

Contempt Of Court A contempt of court is committed when an individual fails or refuses to do something ordered by the court.

Contract An enforceable agreement, either written, oral, or implied between two or more people and is legally binding.

Creditor The party to whom money is owed.

Custodial Parent The parent which has custody of the minor children. In Ohio the custodial parent is called the "residential parent".

Debtor The party who owes money.

Decree A decree is a judgment of a court.

Defendant The person or entity who is sued in a lawsuit.

Discretion Of The Court The area of choice available to a judge to make a legally acceptable decision on their interpretation of the evidence..

Dissolution Of Marriage A legal action by which a marriage is legally terminated by mutual agreement of the parties when the agreement is approved by the court.

Domestic Relations Court A division of the court of common pleas which considers divorce, dissolution, annulment proceedings, support and child visitation.

Divorce A legal action by which a marriage is legally terminated. Ohio provided eleven grounds for which a court a terminate a marriage.

Domicile The place where a person lives and to which, whenever absent, he or she has the intention of returning.

Duress Unlawful threats, pressure, or force that induce a person to act contrary to his or her intentions; if proved, allows a party to disavow a contract.

Emancipation The status whereby a child is no longer legally eligible to receive financial support from a parent.

Filing Fee Money paid to the court to start a lawsuit. In a dissolution action a filing fee is paid to the court to cover the costs associated with processing the necessary paperwork to obtain a dissolution.

Equitable Distribution Laws governing the distribution of property and assets upon divorce.

Family Court Generally any court that presides over matters pertaining to the family.

Final Decree A court order or directive of a permanent nature. The final ruling of the judge.

Financial Statement A document, usually prepared by an accountant, which reflects a business' or individual's assets, liabilities, and financial condition.

Flat Fee A sum of money paid to a lawyer as compensation for services.

Flat Fee Plus Time A form of payment where a lawyer receives one sum for services and then receives additional money calculated on an hourly basis.

Garnishment A legal proceeding used to gain access to the property or money of another to satisfy the payment of a money judgment. In Ohio an individual's paycheck may be garnished to satisfy the payment of child support.

Guardian A person given the legal power to take care of another.

Hourly Fee Money paid to a lawyer which is computed on an hourly basis.

Joint Custody/Shared Parenting An arrangement where both divorced parents must mutually agree on all major decisions affecting their children and create and file a Shared Parenting Plan with the court.

Legal Separation A cause of action for support while the spouses are living separate and apart. Actions for legal separations provide maintenance, child custody, and support, but generally do not provide for division of property. A decree of legal separation does not dissolve the marriage and does not allow the parties to remarry.

Maintenance The payment of support from one spouse to another in satisfaction of marital obligations; also referred to as alimony.

Marital Assets Property, assets, or income produced, developed and acquired by the spouses during the marriage that both spouses may claim and which are subject to equitable division by the court upon divorce.

Non custodial/Nonresidential Parent The parent with who the child does not reside.

No-Fault Divorce A marriage dissolution system whereby divorce is granted without the necessity of proving one of the parties guilty of marital misconduct.

Obligee A person who is to receive payment.

Obligor A person required to pay something.

Palimony The payment of money by one lover to another.

Petition A written application or complaint for divorce or dissolution of marriage.

Plaintiff The party who commences a lawsuit. Same as petitioner.

Prenuptial Agreement A contract signed between two individuals before marriage that limits one of the spouse's rights to property, support, and inheritance in the event of a divorce; also referred to as an "antenuptial agreement".

Residence The place where a person physically lives; also called "domicile".

Retainer A sum of money paid to a lawyer for services to be rendered.

Separate Property Assets or property typically produced prior to or after marriage and not subject to division upon divorce.

Separation Agreement A contract typically entered into between divorcing spouses that spells out their rights; provides for a division of property; spousal support; allocation of parental rights; responsibilities for the care of the minor children and the designation of a residential parent and legal custodian of the minor children.

Settlement The agreed resolution of disputed issues.

Settlement Agreement The settlement reduced to a written document.

Shared Parenting When both parents share the care, control, discipline and custody of the minor children. Shared parenting is also known as "joint custody".

Sole Custody/Sole Residential Parent The condition whereunder the child of divorcing parents resides with one parent who has the legal authority to make all decisions regarding the child.

Split Custody When each parent is awarded custody of at least one minor child of the marriage.

Visitation Rights The rights granted by the court to a nonresidential parent to visit with his/her children.

Will (Last Will And Testament) The instrument (legal document) which ultimately fixes the disposition of property at death.

County Clerk of Courts

Division Of Domestic Relations

The following is a listing of Ohio counties with the telephone number for the clerk of courts for domestic relations, the county seat (location of the courthouse to file your paperwork), and the filing fee (amount the court requires to process your paperwork). The clerk of court will accept cash only for the filing fee. In addition, many counties may have a different filing fee for parties with minor children or parties without minor children. A few counties require that both parties in a dissolution case with minor children take parental education classes before a dissolution will be granted. Also note that some counties require a notary signature on all your court forms (the parties must sign their forms in the presence of a notary public before filing them with the clerk of courts for domestic relations.

Court of Common Pleas
Clerk Of Courts / Division of Domestic Relations   Filing Fee as of 01/2000

County	Telephone	Clerks Office	Without Children / With Children
Adams	(937) 544-2344	West Union	$150.00 / $150.00
Allen	(419) 228-3700	Lima	$150.00 / $150.00
Ashland	(419) 289-0000	Ashland	$175.00 / $175.00
Ashtabula	(440) 576-3637	Jefferson	$132.00 / $142.00
Athens	(740) 592-3242	Athens	$157.00 / $157.00
Auglaize	(419) 738-4219	Wapakoneta	$157.00 / $207.00
Belmont	(740) 695-2121	St Clairsville	$145.00 / $145.00
Brown	(937) 378-3100	Georgetown	$175.00 / $200.00
Butler	(513) 887-3270	Hamilton	$137.00 / $232.00
Carroll	(303) 627-4886	Carrollton	$142.00 / $167.00
Champaign	(937) 653-4152	Urbana	$132.00 / $132.00
Clark	(937) 328-2458	Springfield	$132.00 / $132.00
Clermont	(513) 732-7327	Batavia	$150.00 / $150.00
Clinton	(937) 382-2316	Wilmington	$175.00 / $175.00
Columbiana	(330) 424-7777	Lisbon	$172.00 / $172.00
Cochocton	(740) 622-1456	Cochocton	$132.00 / $132.00
Crawford	(419) 562-2766	Bucyrus	$100.00 / $100.00
Cuyahoga	(216) 443-7950	Cleveland	$132.00 / $132.00
Darke	(937) 547-7335	Greenville	$160.00 / $160.00
Defiance	(419) 782-1936	Defiance	$223.00 / $273.00
Delaware	(740) 368-1850	Delaware	$155.00 / $180.00
Erie	(419) 627-7706	Sandusky	$232.00 / $232.00
Fairfield	(740) 687-7030	Lancaster	$160.00 / $160.00
Fayette	(740) 335-6371	Washington CH	$150.00 / $150.00
Franklin	(614) 462-4410	Columbus	$175.00 / $175.00
Fulton	(419) 337-9230	Wauseon	$223.00 / $273.00
Gallia	(740) 446-4612 ext 221	Gallipolis	$182.00 / $182.00
Geauga	(440) 285-2222 ext2380	Chardon	$132.00 / $132.00
Greene	(937) 376-5290	Xenia	$200.00 / $200.00
Guernsey	(740) 432-9230	Cambridge	$135.00 / $160.00
Hamilton	(513) 852-8000	Cincinnati	$250.00 / $250.00
Hancock	(419) 424-7818	Findlay	$205.00 / $255.00
Hardin	(419) 674-2278	Kenton	$125.00 / $185.00
Harrison	(740) 942-8863	Cadiz	$132.00 / $132.00
Henry	(419) 592-5886	Napoleon	$255.00 / $300.00
Highland	(937) 393-9957	Hillsboro	$150.00 / $175.00

County Clerk of Courts

County	Telephone	Clerks Office	Without Children / With Children
Hocking	(740) 385-2616	Logan	$110.00 / $110.00
Holmes	(330) 674-1876	Millersburg	$150.00 / $150.00
Huron	(419) 668-5113	Norwalk	$175.00 / $175.00
Jackson	(740) 286-2006	Jackson	$150.00 / $150.00
Jefferson	(740) 283-8583	Steubenville	$100.00 / $100.00
Knox	(740) 393-6788	Mt Vernon	$150.00 / $150.00
Lake	(440) 350-2556	Painesville	$205.00 / $205.00
Lawrence	(740) 533-4355	Ironton	$150.00 / $150.00
Licking	(740) 349-6215	Newark	$150.00 / $150.00
Logan	(937) 599-7275	Bellefontaine	$200.00 / $200.00
Lorain	(216) 329-5277	Elyria	$200.00 / $200.00
Lucas	(419) 249-6901	Toledo	$167.00 / $217.00
Madison	(740) 852-9776	London	$182.00 / $182.00
Mahoning	(330) 740-2104	Youngstown	$132.00 / $132.00
Marion	(740) 387-8128	Marion	$182.00 / $182.00
Medina	(330) 764-8299	Medina	$182.00 / $182.00
Meigs	(740) 992-5290	Pomeroy	$150.00 / $150.00
Mercer	(419) 586-6461	Celina	$150.00 / $150.00
Miami	(937) 332-6855	Troy	$152.00 / $152.00
Monroe	(740) 472-0761	Woodsfield	$200.00 / $200.00
Montgomery	(937) 225-4562	Dayton	$200.00 / $200.00
Morgan	(740) 962-4752	McConnelsville	$157.00 / $157.00
Morrow	(419) 947-2085	Mt Gilead	$110.00 / $125.00
Muskingum	(740) 455-7898	Zanesville	$125.00 / $125.00
Noble	(740) 732-4408	Caldwell	$112.00 / $112.00
Ottawa	(419) 734-6755	Port Clinton	$300.00 / $300.00
Paulding	(419) 399-8210	Paulding	$175.00 / $200.00
Perry	(740) 342-1022	New Lexington	$120.00 / $120.00
Pickaway	(740) 474-5231	Circleville	$150.00 / $150.00
Pike	(740) 947-2715	Waverly	$150.00 / $150.00
Portage	(330) 297-4266	Ravenna	$170.00 / $195.00
Preble	(937) 456-8160	Eaton	$130.00 / $190.00
Putnam	(419) 523-3110	Ottawa	$150.00 / $200.00
Richland	(419) 774-5544 or 5573	Mansfield	$212.00 / $212.00
Ross	(740) 773-2330	Chillicothe	$150.00 / $150.00
Sandusky	(419) 334-6161	Fremont	$175.00 / $175.00
Scioto	(740) 355-8226	Portsmouth	$145.00 / $145.00
Seneca	(419) 447-0671	Tiffin	$200.00 / $200.00
Shelby	(937) 498-7221	Sidney	$150.00 / $150.00
Stark	(330) 438-0792	Canton	$152.00 / $152.00
Summit	(330) 643-8476	Akron	$152.00 / $182.00
Trumbull	(216) 675-2625	Warren	$140.00 / $140.00
Tuscarawas	(330) 364-8811ext 243	New Philadelphia	$125.00 / $140.00
Union	(937) 645-3006	Marysville	$165.00 / $165.00
Van Wert	(419) 238-1022	Van Wert	$200.00 / $200.00
Vinton	(740) 596-3001	McArthur	$150.00 / $150.00
Warren	(513) 420-4120	Lebanon	$250.00 / $250.00
Washington	(740) 373-6623ext 365	Marietta	$142.00 / $182.00
Wayne	(330) 287-5590	Wooster	$132.00 / $132.00
Williams	(419) 636-1551	Bryan	$225.00 / $225.00
Wood	(419) 354-9280	Bowling Green	$212.00 / $212.00
Wyandot	(419) 294-1432	Upper Sandusky	$182.00 / $182.00

Thank You for Purchasing LawPak

It is our goal to design and develop the best in self-help legal publications. We hope that we have been successful in assisting you to better understanding your legal situation and offered a more affordable solution.

To assist us in the development of future publications, please remove this page from the publication, complete the information below, fold and mail to LawPak. We will then be able to inform you of changes in the law within the next ninety days as these changes may affect the LawPak you purchased. This service is part of our continued commitment to you, the customer. All customer information that we receive is kept in strict confidentially. We do not sell customer information or address listings to anyone. We hold your privacy in the highest regard.

In addition, if you encountered any new or additional information, forms, or processing procedures (not included in this edition) that you think would be helpful to others and should be incorporated into future LawPak editions, please take a few moments to send us the form and/or explain the procedure. We welcome your comments and suggestions.

name _____

address _____

city_____ state _____ zip _____

county _____ date of purchase _____

title of LawPak _____

place of purchase _____

Did you find the information in this publication helpful? _____

Was it helpful and easy to use this book to accomplish your goals? (circle one of each)

(very helpful)   1   2   3   4   5   6   (not at all)

(very easy)   1   2   3   4   5   6   (very difficult)

Comments and suggestions: _____

_____

_____

_____

_____

_____.

(Fold)

_____
_____
_____

LawPak, Inc.
P.O. Box 221
Terrace Park, Ohio 45174

(Fold)

Other LawPak Affordable Legal Solutions

☐ Bankruptcy Chapter 7

This LawPak will assist the user in deciding if bankruptcy may be a legal solution to financial problems. Covers the topics of debts, property, and legal procedures, and includes the forms which are filed with the court to obtain a personal bankruptcy. Appropriate for single individuals or married couples.

$27.95 --

☐ Landlord/Tenant

This LawPak presents the legal obligations and rights of both the landlord and the tenant of residential property. Topics covered include security deposits, lease agreements, evictions, and liability for repairs or injury. Forms include a nine-page lease agreement, legal notices for evictions, and rental application.

$16.95 --

☐ Last Will and Testament

One of life's most neglected necessities is the Last Will and Testament. It allows *you* – not the state – to specify how you want your estate distributed upon your death, who you want to manage and oversee the distribution, and to whom you want to entrust the guardianship of your minor children. This LawPak covers provisions for determining beneficiaries, making specific bequests, appointing guardians for minor children, and naming executors for the estate. It is appropriate for anyone age 18 or older, regardless of marital status, whether or not they have minor children.

$16.25 --

☐ Living Will & Child's Medical Authorization

You can draft a Living Will to express in writing your preferences regarding the continuation or cessation of life-support efforts in the event you should become terminally ill — sparing loved ones the difficulty of making such decisions on your behalf. This LawPak also includes a Child's Medical Authorization form that parents can use to appoint other adults to make emergency health care decisions for their child when they, the parents, are not available.

$15.75 --

☐ Name Change

This LawPak allows the user to legally change an adult's or minor's name in the event of divorce, remarriage, adoption, errors in the birth certificate. It can also be used to select a name which is more appropriate to the user's personal preference. The publication includes the legal forms which are filed with the court to get the new name formally recognized by government agencies.

$15.95 --

☐ Ohio Dissolution of Marriage

There is a way to avoid the expense and time of using an attorney for a no-fault divorce. Thousands of couples have used this LawPak to obtain an Ohio Dissolution of Marriage. Among the topics it covers are: property, custody of minors, visitation rights, support, debts, and legal procedures. This publication contains the forms which are filed with the court to obtain a legal Ohio Dissolution.

$29.95 --

☐ Power of Attorney

By drafting this type of document, you can legally appoint another individual to act on your behalf. The authority you grant through this document may be broad (management of all financial affairs) or limited (sale of a home). This LawPak also contains a Durable Power of Attorney to appoint others to act on your behalf should you become incapacitated, thus avoiding guardianship/conservatorship court proceedings.

$14.95 --

☐ Real Estate Contracts (Buy & Sell)

Buying and selling a home may be the single most important financial transaction most consumer will ever make. LawPak's forms meet the requirements that make your real estate transactions legal and enforceable. A wide range of related topics and forms are included in this publication: real estate purchase contracts and contingencies, easement, land contracts, disclosure statements, option to purchase agreements, deeds and more.

$17.75 --

Three Ways to Order LawPak Publications

Mail order form with payment (check or money order) to:
LawPak, Inc., PO Box 221, Terrace Park OH 45174

Fax Credit Card Number with order form to:
1-513-831-1620

Call toll-free with credit card number to:
1-800-552-9725

- -

ORDER FORM

Ship to:

name _____

address _____

city _____ state _____ zip _____

telephone (_____) _____

TITLE	PRICE

* Shipping & handling
first-class shipping = $5.25
third-class shipping = $3.85
Add $15.00 to shipping cost for rush orders requiring overnight delivery.

subtotal $ _____

Ohio Sales Tax (6%) $ _____

shipping & handling* $ _____

TOTAL $ _____

Check one:

☐ Check or money order *(payable to LawPak)* enclosed.

☐ Charge to: ☐ MasterCard ☐ Visa

MAIL ORDER TO:
**LawPak, Inc.
PO Box 221
Terrace Park OH 45174**

card expiration date: ___ ___ / ___ ___ account # _____

signature _____

Bill Of Rights

What the amendments say:

I   Congress shall make no law respecting an establishment of religion, or prohibiting the free exercise thereof; or abridging the freedom of speech, or of the press; or the right of the people peaceably to assemble, and to petition the Government for redress of grievances.

II   A well regulated Militia, being necessary to the security of a free State, the right of the people to keep and bear Arms, shall not be infringed.

III   No soldier shall, in time of peace be quartered in any house, without the consent of the owner, nor in time of war, but in a manner to be prescribed by law.

IV   The right of the people to be secure in their persons, houses, papers, and effects, against unreasonable searched and seizures, shall not be violated, and no warrants, shall issue, but upon probable cause, supported by oath or affirmation, and particularly describing the place to be searched, and the persons or things to be seized.

V   No person shall be held to answer for a capital, or otherwise infamous crime, unless on a presentment or indictment of a Grand Jury, except in cases arising in the land or naval forces, or in the Militia, when actual service in time of War or public danger; nor shall any person be subject for the same offense to be twice put in jeopardy of life or limb; nor shall be compelled in any criminal case to be a witness against himself, nor be deprived of life, liberty, or property, without due process of law, nor shall private property be taken for public use, without just compensation.

VI   In all criminal prosecutions, the accused shall enjoy the right to a speedy and public trial, by an impartial jury of the State and district wherein the crime shall have been committed, which district shall have been previously ascertained by law, and to be informed of the nature and cause of the accusation; to be confronted with the witnesses against him; to have compulsory process for obtaining Witnesses in his favor, and to have the Assistance of Counsel for his defense.

VII   In Suits of common law, where the value in controversy shall exceed twenty dollars, the right of trial by jury shall be preserved, and no fact tried by a jury, shall otherwise re-examined in any Court of the United States, than according to the rules of the common law.

VIII   Excessive bail shall not be required, nor excessive fines imposed, nor cruel and unusual punishments inflicted.

IX   The enumeration in the Constitution, of certain rights, shall not be construed to deny or disparage others retained by the people.

X   The powers not delegated to the United States by the Constitution, nor prohibited by it to the States, are reserved to the States respectively, or to the people.

WE THE PEOPLE ...

Over two hundred years ago the founding fathers of our nation recognized that while a form of government was necessary, the People would need protection against the awesome power of an unrestrained government. It is our responsibility as citizens to protect, defend and understand our rights and freedoms given to us by our forefathers who in some cases gave their lives in order for us to live in a country where freedom is truly practiced. The first ten Amendments to the Constitution of the United States were adopted to provide this protection. These ten Amendments have become known as the "Bill of Rights".

What does the Bill of Rights mean to us today?

- It protects your right to read this book and our right to produce, publish and distribute it.
- It protects your right to practice the religion of your choice, or if you choose, no religion at all.
- It protects you from unreasonable searches, seizures and governmental interference.
- It protects you against cruel and unusual punishment and against unfair arrests and trials.
- It limits the power of the government to those given to the government by the Constitution.
- It protects you from testifying against yourself.
- It guards your individual liberty, guarantees your enumerated rights, and recognizes the need to protect other fundamental rights, although not specifically stated in the Constitution.

The First Amendment
The First Amendment guarantees freedom of speech, freedom of the press, freedom of assembly, freedom of religion, and separation between church and state.

This Amendment guarantees your right to speak up and speak out. Benjamin Franklin realized the importance of the fundamental right to freedom of speech when he said, "Whoever would overthrow the liberty of a nation must begin by subduing the freedom of speech."

The freedom of speech and the freedom of the press are closely related. Just as you can print and speak your mind in all forms, the government may not interfere with the press or censor the news. The government cannot tell the press what it may or may not print.

The freedom of assembly and the right to petition the government are other First Amendment rights that are essential to your fundamental rights of free expression.

In addition, the Bill of Rights, protects your religious freedom by protecting you from being forced to practice any religion; by allowing you to practice the religion of your choice, or practice no religion at all; and by mandating the separation of church and state.

The Second Amendment
The Second Amendment prohibits the infringing of "the right of the people to keep and bear arms", in order to permit the existence of a "well regulated Militia", which recognizes as being "necessary to the security of a free State".

The Third Amendment
The Third Amendment guarantees that soldiers will not be housed in your home during peace time without your consent, or in time of war except under a specific law.

The Fourth Amendment
The Fourth Amendment protects you against unreasonable searches and seizures and guarantees your right to privacy.

This amendment requires that any search or arrest takes place only when a police officer has probable cause which means police officers may not arrest or search you without a direst link between you and the criminal activity. If there is not an emergency situation, they must first obtain search and arrest warrants. These warrants are only issued by a Judge or magistrate after he/she are convinced that there is probable cause for such warrants.

The Fifth Amendment

The Fifth Amendment prohibits denial of life, liberty, or property without due process of law. It guarantees that if you are arrested, your arrest and trial will be conducted according to established legal procedures. It also protects you against unreasonable police tactics by guaranteeing that you cannot be forced to testify against yourself. This is your right to silence. The government must create their case against you and you do not have to speak to them or assist them in this process.

In addition, this amendment protects you from being prosecuted by the same sovereign twice for the same crime. It also requires that under the Miranda Rule, that an arresting officer inform you that you have the right to remain silent, along with your right to an attorney, if she/he plans to question you following an arrest.

This amendment also protects your property from being taken by the government without just compensation.

The Sixth Amendment

The Sixth Amendment guarantees that you receive a fair trial. It guarantees a speedy, public trial by jury. You must also be informed of the charges being brought against you and you must be confronted with the witnesses against you. It guarantees your right to have a lawyer if you are facing a possible jail sentence, (if you choose to have a lawyer). If you cannot afford to hire a lawyer in a criminal case, this amendment guarantees your right to court appointed counsel.

The Seventh Amendment

The Seventh Amendment reinforces the power of the jury system by guaranteeing that the facts found by a Federal jury will not be re-examined. Once a jury has decided what occurred in a case (the actual facts of the case), another party may not ask for a re-examination of the facts, unless there is no basis in the law for the jury's finding of the facts. The losing party may appeal a ruling but only on points of law or legal technicalities.

The Eighth Amendment

The Eighth Amendment protects you from cruel and unusual punishment; protects you from having excessive fines imposed on you as punishment; and excessive bail as a guarantee of your appearance at trial.

The Ninth Amendment

The Ninth Amendment recognizes that the rights granted by the Constitution, including the Bill of Rights and other Amendments are not the only rights that we have as citizens. The Constitution lists many rights and freedoms, but it is not totally inclusive and it would be impossible to list every right. The Ninth Amendment guarantees that these other rights shall not be denied or lessened because they are not enumerated (stated) in the Constitution.

The Tenth Amendment

The Tenth Amendment prohibits the Federal Government from exercising powers not given to it by the Constitution. This amendment reserves any power not given to the Federal government, and not prohibited to the States, to the individual States, or to the People.